L.A. STORY

L.A. STORY

IMMIGRANT WORKERS AND THE FUTURE OF THE U.S. LABOR MOVEMENT

RUTH MILKMAN

RUSSELL SAGE FOUNDATION • NEW YORK

Library of Congress Cataloging-in-Publication Data

Milkman, Ruth, 1954–
  L.A. story : immigrant workers and the future of the U.S. Labor Movement /
  Ruth Milkman.
    p. cm.
  Includes bibliographical references and index.
  Contents: The "Wicked City": labor and Los Angeles exceptionalism — Turning the clock back: anti-union reaction, the return of the sweatshop, and the new immigration — Organizing the "Unorganizable": immigrant unionization and labor revitalization in the 1990s — "Si, Se Puede": union organizing strategies and immigrant workers.
  ISBN 10: 0-87154-635-3 (paperback)
  ISBN 13: 978-0-87154-635-7 (paperback)
    1. Alien labor—Labor unions—Organizing—California—Los Angeles. I. Title.

  HD6490.O72U652 2006
  331.8806'9120979494—dc22

                                                                    2006043947

Text design by Genna Patacsil.

RUSSELL SAGE FOUNDATION
112 East 64th Street, New York, New York 10021
10 9 8 7 6 5 4 3 2

CONTENTS

ABOUT THE AUTHORS

RUTH MILKMAN is professor of sociology and director of the Institute of Industrial Relations at the University of California, Los Angeles.

KENT WONG (coauthor of chapter 4) is director of the UCLA Center for Labor Research and Education, and previously worked as a labor attorney.

Preface and Acknowledgments

This book is a valentine to Los Angeles, the city so many love to hate. Almost all of the research for it was conducted in southern California, and my perspective on the material is the product of an extended engagement with the vibrant labor and intellectual communities of the region. But as I argue in the pages that follow, Los Angeles is of interest not only in its own right but as a window into a wider set of developments. The nation's second city has emerged in recent years as one of the few bright spots for the beleaguered U.S. labor movement and a unique proving ground for strategic organizing innovations. The successful experiments that took place there in the 1990s gave Los Angeles a special role in the ongoing process of national union revitalization.

My research began as an effort to document and analyze those experiments. Both on my own and with Kent Wong and other collaborators, I spent countless hours roaming greater L.A. to talk with the organizers who planned and carried out campaigns like those analyzed in chapter 4. We also interviewed union officials, rank-and-file workers, and labor attorneys, as well as managers, contractors, and the occasional government official. No sampling frame or other systematic methodology guided this research; we simply began by interviewing the readily identifiable leaders of key campaigns, and they helped us identify other informants. In a few cases, the individuals we approached did not make themselves available for interviews, even after repeated requests, but such refusals were surprisingly rare. Nearly all of the interviews were tape-recorded and transcribed. Some of our informants shared copies of documentary materials they had collected in the course of the campaigns; I also mined online databases for journalistic accounts of the campaigns and related developments.

At some point in this process it dawned on me that I should investigate the earlier labor history of Los Angeles—especially in relation to the four industries that are the book's focus—in order to better understand how the region came to be a nodal point of union revitalization in the late twentieth century. Surprised to find that this history had attracted relatively scant attention from scholars, I then extended my interviewing to include retired union officials and others with some firsthand knowledge of the past; simultaneously I set about collecting primary and secondary historical documents (including some extraordinary archival materials on the SEIU housed in the Wayne State University Labor Archives in Detroit). In reconstructing the contours of what I came to understand as the exceptional and largely unexplored labor history of Los Angeles, I found Carey McWilliams's prescient books and essays on the region, although written many decades ago, to be especially helpful. Another line of inquiry led me to examine U.S. census data to reconstruct the evolution of employment patterns and the impact of immigration on the four industries that are the book's focus (see appendix B for details).

I completed this manuscript during a period of intense debate and upheaval within the U.S. labor movement, culminating in mid-2005 with the disaffiliation of several major unions from the AFL-CIO and the formation of the Change to Win (CTW) Federation. Although the bulk of the research for this book was done before the debate that led up to that dramatic schism, these recent events highlight the importance of the L.A. case and my interpretation of it. Because the unions that now make up the CTW Federation have been disproportionately influential in southern California, my own thinking has been greatly influenced by the CTW perspective on organized labor's current dilemma—a perspective that both helped shape and was shaped by the successful organizing efforts in Los Angeles that are analyzed in detail in this book.

In the course of producing this book, I incurred many debts. I am especially grateful to Kent Wong, director of the UCLA Labor Center, who generously shared with me his virtually limitless access to key union organizers and officials in and around Los Angeles. During the mid- to late 1990s, we jointly conducted dozens of interviews with L.A. unionists and organizers that became a key source of data for this book, and particularly for chapter 4, which Kent and I coauthored.

I have two major institutional debts to acknowledge here as well. One is to the University of California's statewide Institute for Labor and Employment (ILE). The ILE was established in July 2000, building on the preexisting Institutes of Industrial Relations (IIR) at UCLA and UC Berkeley. I was privileged to be appointed director of the ILE soon after its establishment, a position I held until mid-2004. This extraordinary collaboration between the university and the California labor movement built on the foundation laid over the preceding decades by the UCLA Labor Center and its counterpart at UC Berkeley, and by the IIRs on those two campuses. Although my administrative duties inevitably delayed the book's completion, the myriad insights I gained from this experience can only have improved the final product.

My other crucial institutional debt is to the Russell Sage Foundation, where I was privileged to spend the 2004–2005 academic year as a visiting scholar. Under the wise and unfailingly generous leadership of Eric Wanner, RSF provided the ideal environment for completing this project. I owe special thanks to Suzanne Nichols, the foundation's intrepid publications director, who was enthusiastic about the book from the outset.

The research trajectory that culminated in this book had its inception over a decade ago when, along with several colleagues at UCLA—Chris Erickson, Dan Mitchell, Abel Valenzuela, Roger Waldinger, Kent Wong, and Maurice Zeitlin—I became intrigued by the L.A. "Justice for Janitors" organizing campaign, which had burst onto the scene just a few miles away from our campus. We decided to interview the unionists who had led that pioneering effort and then wrote an article about it in 1995 (later published as Waldinger et al. 1998). Aware of other immigrant organizing campaigns in the L.A. area, some of us went on to investigate those as well. Kent and Roger from the original janitors' group, along with economist Carol Zabin and myself, secured funding from the Rosenberg Foundation to explore this wider terrain. Carol accompanied Kent and me on many of the subsequent interviews, and Hector Delgado, then of UC Irvine, also joined me in some of the fieldwork on the port truckers' campaign. I learned from all these collaborations, and in myriad ways they have helped shape the ideas in this book. It could not have been completed without the funding so generously provided not only from Rosenberg but also from the George Meany Center for Labor Studies, UC Mexus, the UCLA Academic Senate, and the ILE.

I owe special thanks to Christine Schwartz, a talented UCLA graduate student who assisted me with the analysis of the U.S. census data discussed in chapter 2. I am also grateful to another extraordinary UCLA graduate student, Daisy Rooks, who worked closely with me on the ILE-sponsored California Union Census (see Milkman and Rooks 2003), which is only briefly mentioned in the text but nevertheless had a deep influence on my thinking about the L.A. labor movement. Finally, at Russell Sage, I was blessed with the cheerful and expert assistance of Sarah

Lowe, who helped me with all the figures in the book and countless other research-related tasks. Rebecca Frazier also assisted me with formatting and related tasks involved in preparing the manuscript.

Over the past several years I have presented portions of this research in a variety of venues that generated extremely valuable comments and suggestions. These included colloquia at the Massachusetts Institute of Technology, UC Berkeley, UC Davis, UC San Diego, the University of Southern California, Yale University, the University of Minnesota, the University of Manchester (U.K.), New York University, and the Cornell University School of Industrial and Labor Relations (both the Ithaca and New York City branches); as well as conference presentations at the University of Arizona, UC Irvine, the University of Québec at Montréal, Ben-Gurion University, the University of Havana, the International Labor Office (Geneva), the Radcliffe Institute, and the Industrial Relations Research Association. I also benefited from feedback from colleagues in the Workshop on Comparative Social Analysis and the Law School Faculty Colloquium, both at UCLA, and the visiting scholar seminar at the Russell Sage Foundation.

Many individual colleagues and friends were generous enough to read drafts of the manuscript at various stages over the past several years and to take the time to provide me with detailed and insightful comments. Although I did not always follow their advice, I offer heartfelt thanks to Michael Burawoy, Dan Clawson, Dorothy Sue Cobble, Janice Fine, Marshall Ganz, Nelson Lichtenstein, Carolina Bank Muñoz, Chris Tilly, and Roger Waldinger for their many helpful suggestions.

Loving thanks go to my son, Jonathan Laks, who grew into a young man during the years I spent working on this project and who is at least as glad as I am to see it completed. My steady companion and inspiration for the past thirteen years, he has always supported my work even though it so often diverted my attention from him.

Finally, there is the one person who influenced this book more profoundly than any other, although she never read a word of it. My mother, Beatrice Milkman (née Mozon), died midway through the project's gestation, just days before the end of the twentieth century. A first-generation American who came of age during the Depression in the long-vanished left-wing milieu of Brooklyn's Russian-Jewish immigrant community, she was the first to teach me what labor unions were and why they mattered. Even more important, I inherited her instinctive habits of critique, her surprisingly durable political worldview, and her lifelong passion for social justice. This book is dedicated to her memory.

Union Acronyms

Amalgamated Clothing and Textile Workers' Union (ACTWU)
Amalgamated Clothing Workers (ACW)
American Federation of Labor and Congress of Industrial Organizations (AFL-CIO)
Building Service Employees' International Union (BSEIU)
Committee on Industrial Organization (CIO)
Change to Win (CTW) Federation
Communication Workers of America (CWA)
Hotel Employees and Restaurant Employees (HERE)
International Association of Machinists (IAM)
International Brotherhood of Electrical Workers (IBEW)
International Brotherhood of Teamsters (IBT)
International Longshoremen's Association (ILA)
International Ladies' Garment Workers' Union (ILGWU)
International Longshoremen's and Warehousemen's Union (ILWU)
Southern California Council of Carpenters (SCCC)
Service Employees International Union (SEIU)
United Auto Workers (UAW)
United Food and Commercial Workers Union (UFCW)
United Farm Workers (UFW)
Union of Needletrades, Industrial, and Textile Employees (UNITE)

INTRODUCTION

Hardly anyone expected them to succeed. But in 1990, after a few years of intensive organizing, a group of immigrant janitors in Los Angeles went on strike, endured a brutal police beating, and then won union recognition. Previously all but invisible to the public, these workers cleaned up after hours for the well-paid lawyers and other professionals who inhabit the glitzy office towers of Century City, an upscale section of Los Angeles. Most were immigrants from Mexico and Central America, many of them undocumented. Like countless other foreign-born workers who populate the lower echelons of southern California's vast blue-collar labor market, they worked long hours for minimal pay, often under substandard (and sometimes illegal) conditions.

The Century City victory was a turning point for the national "Justice for Janitors" campaign of the Service Employees International Union (SEIU), which would go on to win a series of contracts guaranteeing improved wages and working conditions for an ever-growing number of southern California janitors, as well as janitors in several other cities around the nation. By the end of the century the local janitors' union not only had consolidated its position within the L.A. building services industry but also had become one of the most dynamic and politically influential labor unions in the city and a vocal advocate for its burgeoning population of low-wage Latino immigrant workers.

In numerical terms, the janitors' triumph was an insignificant development, involving only a few thousand workers in the nation's second-largest metropolis. Yet in the early 1990s, after decades of deunionization, and in an extremely unfavorable political climate, any forward movement on the part of the U.S. labor movement was a notable achievement. A union breakthrough in the once-legendary "company town" of Los Angeles was especially impressive. And one in which the protagonists included undocumented immigrants—long presumed by friend and foe alike to be "unorganizable"—seemed almost miraculous.

The L.A. janitors' campaign soon became an icon, a beacon of hope for the long-beleaguered U.S. labor movement.[1] It sparked a wave of immigrant organizing efforts in California and across the nation in the 1990s and was even the subject of a major motion picture (Ken Loach's *Bread and Roses*, released to critical acclaim in 2000). It also helped propel then-SEIU president John Sweeney to the helm of the nation's giant labor federation, the American Federation of Labor and Congress of Industrial Organizations (AFL-CIO), in a fiercely contested election in 1995. Sweeney urged all the federation's affiliates to make a commitment to renewed organizing of just the sort the janitors' campaign exemplified. Today the SEIU is the fastest-growing union in the United States, with many other recent organizing successes to its credit—not only under Sweeney's leadership but also under that of Andy Stern, who succeeded him in the SEIU presidency and went on to become the nation's most prominent twenty-first-century labor leader. Over the past quarter-century, while overall U.S. union density (the unionized proportion of the workforce) declined dramatically, SEIU membership nearly tripled.[2]

The janitors' organizing success in Los Angeles, then, was far more significant than the number of workers involved would suggest, in that it highlighted the potential for a broader, nationwide labor resurgence. To be sure, that scenario may seem improbable in the present climate, with a political regime that is overtly hostile to organized labor and with union density at its lowest level since the 1920s. Fewer than 13 percent of the nation's workers today are union members; in the private sector, the figure is only 8 percent—down from 24 percent as recently as 1973 (Hirsch and Macpherson 2005). Although organized labor's political clout has been more resilient (see Dark 2001), many legal and regulatory constraints on employer power won by unions in earlier years have been rolled back, and others that remain on the books are honored more in the breach than the observance.

For all these reasons, the labor movement's obituary appears regularly in the press and in journals of opinion. Yet recent developments in southern California—often a harbinger of national trends—suggest that reports of organized labor's demise may be exaggerated. In Los Angeles, where inequality by both class and nativity is so stark that the city is routinely compared to the Third World, the dynamics that generated the janitors' 1990 victory sparked a decade-long resurgence of union organizing and community-based economic justice campaigns—highlighting the possibility that labor might become an agent of social transformation once again.[3]

Whether or not that possibility is realized will have major implications for the wider society. Today, at both the local and national levels, the labor movement is the one organized entity that regularly and systematically challenges the rapidly growing inequality between rich and poor, as well as that between native- and foreign-born workers. The ebb and flow of unionism over the past century has been a key determinant of the life chances of working people in the United States, for immigrants and natives alike. The last great wave of labor organizing, led in the 1930s and 1940s by the industrial unions in the breakaway CIO (which in 1955 would reunite with its parent organization, the AFL, to form the AFL-CIO), did much to narrow inequalities between the haves and have-nots. In that era, unionism was a vehicle of social mobility that carried impoverished first- and second-generation working-class immigrants from southern and eastern Europe into the middle-class mainstream. But the rapid erosion of union density in recent decades has helped to widen economic inequalities once again, with disproportionate effects on recent immigrants from Latin America and Asia, many of whom work for poverty-level wages under conditions that harken back to the pre–New Deal era. Could these newcomers take the lead in rebuilding the nation's labor movement, as their European predecessors did so many years ago?

This book explores that prospect through an analysis of the factors that fostered labor's revitalization in southern California in the 1990s, highlighting the central role of immigrants in that revitalization. A historical perspective is central to my argument: in Los Angeles, which for the first few decades of the twentieth century had a legendary reputation as an open-shop city, unions did not gain a solid foothold until the late 1930s. And when they finally did so, it was not the CIO's industrial unionism that took root but instead the occupationally based unionism historically associated with the AFL. The CIO later developed a modest presence in southern California but was overshadowed consistently in the region by the AFL.

Although this unusual history led Los Angeles to be regarded as a labor movement backwater for many decades, AFL predominance ultimately laid the groundwork for the city's emergence as a crucible of labor movement revitalization in the 1990s. Los Angeles was home not only to the janitors' campaign but also to other innovative organizing initiatives that gave the city its maverick reputation as, in Mike Davis's (2000, 145) words, "the major R&D center for 21st century trade unionism."

The central role of the former AFL unions is relevant not only to understanding the recent revitalization of the L.A. labor movement but also to making sense of current efforts to transform and energize organized labor nationally. Consider the new Change to Win (CTW) Federation, which formed in 2005 after several key affiliates broke away from the AFL-CIO. The SEIU, the largest CTW union, led the debate that took place within the AFL-CIO, starting in 2003, and two years later sparked the largest split in U.S. labor since the 1930s. CTW also includes the garment and hotel workers' unions (which merged into UNITE HERE in 2004), as well as two of the nation's largest building trades unions, the Carpenters and Laborers. The giant Teamsters and the United Food and Commercial Workers (UFCW) are also CTW affiliates, along with the (relatively small) United Farm Workers (UFW) union.

The immigrant organizing of recent years has been centered in this group of unions, and they have been disproportionately engaged in the efforts to revitalize the U.S. labor movement since the 1980s. Yet they are not new organizations—far from it. With the exception of the farm workers, these are actually among the nation's oldest labor unions, with roots that go back to the beginning of the twentieth century, and in some cases even earlier. Former AFL affiliates, they have a history and structure that set them apart from the CIO unions, which were long regarded as the progressive wing of organized labor.[4] Disdained by many as staid, conservative bastions of "business unionism," hostile to the interests of women and racial minorities, and often plagued by corruption, these former AFL unions are the last organizations one would have expected to be leading labor movement renewal. So why have these unions, and not those originating in the CIO, dominated recent efforts to rebuild organized labor?

There are a number of reasons. First, as Dorothy Sue Cobble (1991b) has pointed out, the occupational focus that was long characteristic of AFL organizing is well suited to the "post-industrial" age as workplaces have become increasingly unstable entities. More generally, the former AFL affiliates are products of historical circumstances that are strikingly similar to those that unions face at present, in sharp contrast to the conditions under which the CIO emerged during the 1930s and 1940s. The AFL unions date from the years before mass production manufacturing became the central motor of U.S. economic growth; before the emergence of the New Deal political order, with its commitment to economic regulation and to narrowing inequalities between rich and poor; and before the 1935 National Labor Relations Act (NLRA) established the legal right of workers to organize collectively and helped propel union density to its peak level in the mid-1950s, when over one-third of the U.S. workforce was organized.

Precisely because they emerged under these antediluvian conditions, the strategic and tactical repertoire of the SEIU and the other former AFL affiliates that have led recent efforts to revitalize the labor movement includes a variety of organizing approaches with which the CIO unions have little or no experience but which are well suited to the contemporary era. For much of their history, for example, these AFL unions devoted a great deal of energy to developing strategies to take wages out of competition in unregulated, highly competitive labor markets.[5] They also have extensive historical experience in winning recognition from employers through mechanisms independent of the NLRA-based representation election system, since they were actively organizing for decades before that system existed.

As the L.A. janitors' campaign and other recent organizing successes illustrate, this traditional AFL repertoire is highly adaptable to contemporary economic conditions, which in many ways resemble those of the pre–New Deal era. By contrast, many of the CIO's strategies and tactics were tailored to the historical conditions of the 1930s and 1940s—conditions that have been largely swept aside over the past three decades by deindustrialization, deregulation, and deunionization. Like a movie running backwards, since the mid-1970s the mass production manufacturing economy has virtually collapsed, the New Deal regulatory order has been effectively dismantled, and the labor relations machinery established by the NLRA has devolved to the point where it no longer functions to protect workers. It makes sense that the unions best able to survive and grow today in the aftermath of these massive shifts are those that first took shape under the economic and political conditions that have now been restored.

This historical perspective—which is developed at length in chapter 1 —helps explain why Los Angeles emerged as a leading site of labor movement revitalization in the late twentieth century and lends larger significance to recent developments in that city. But the unanticipated comparative advantage that the AFL's historical predominance lent to the L.A. labor movement is not the only factor that makes the southern California region a useful prism through which to view workplace and labor movement transformation in the nation as a whole. Two additional dimensions are especially important here.

First, as elaborated in chapter 2, Los Angeles emerged as a key testing ground for employer-initiated deunionization efforts and related work-place restructuring strategies in the 1970s and 1980s—what have come to be called "low-road" managerial strategies—that would soon spread to workplaces nationwide. As unions were weakened or eliminated, wages fell, fringe benefits and job security guarantees evaporated, and illegal sweatshop-like labor practices became commonplace. This took place in the context of a booming economy and massive population growth. As Beverly Silver (2003, 5) notes, even as labor movements have been weakened in most of the global North, the opposite has occurred in "the favored new sites of investment." She has in mind "the cheap labor economic 'miracles' of the 1970s and 1980s" in the global South, like Brazil and South Africa, but her point also applies to Los Angeles, which enjoyed an economic boom in this same period that was equally predicated on the exploitation of cheap labor—much of it imported from south of the U.S. border.

Indeed, partly as a result of its pioneering role in employer-driven workforce casualization, and once again anticipating a national trend, greater Los Angeles attracted a massive influx of immigrants to its burgeoning low-wage labor market. Contrary to the conventional wisdom, the foreign-born workforce proved to be a key factor facilitating union renewal in the region, as chapter 3 explains and as a burst of immigrant organizing in the 1990s (not only in the SEIU's janitors' campaign but in other cases as well) would reveal. Thus, three basic conditions laid the groundwork for the unexpected emergence of Los Angeles as a center of labor movement resurgence: the historical predominance of the AFL, low-road employment restructuring strategies, and a massive immigrant influx.

THE TRANSFORMATION OF LOS ANGELES: WORK, IMMIGRATION, AND UNIONISM

The late twentieth century was not the first time janitors had organized in Los Angeles. In the late 1940s and early 1950s, as chapter 1 recounts, the AFL-affiliated Building Service Employees' International Union (BSEIU, which in 1968 would drop the "B" and become the SEIU) had recruited an earlier generation of the city's office cleaners into its ranks. In those days most L.A. janitors were native-born whites and African Americans. Unionization brought them middle-class wages, extensive fringe benefits, and decent working conditions for the first time. These gains were rolled back in the 1970s, however, when the city's building services industry was radically restructured, and "flexible" employment arrangements based on highly competitive subcontracting gradually replaced the old union-based regime.

As the SEIU's janitorial membership in the city fell, wages collapsed, fringe benefits disappeared, and working conditions deteriorated. Native-born workers began to abandon the increasingly undesirable janitorial jobs for more attractive fields, and employers turned to the burgeoning immigrant population to fill the resulting vacancies. Then in the late 1980s, against all odds, the city's newly recruited foreign-born janitors unionized once again, winning contracts guaranteeing improved wages and conditions. Those gains have been sustained and expanded in the years since 1990, when the SEIU's janitors' campaign achieved its initial breakthrough in Los Angeles (Erickson et al. 2002).

This sequence of events—deunionization and employment restructuring, followed by an exodus of native-born workers, an immigrant influx, and then renewed union organizing efforts—took place not only in building services but in many other fields of employment in southern California during the closing decades of the twentieth century. This book examines four specific cases: the janitors, whose history has already been outlined; the truck drivers who haul freight to and from the Los Angeles–Long Beach port, now the nation's largest; "drywallers" in the region's residential construction industry, who successfully unionized throughout southern California in 1992; and the garment workers of greater Los Angeles, which some years ago replaced New York as the city with the nation's largest concentration of apparel manufacturing.

All four of these occupations were extensively unionized in Los Angeles by the middle of the twentieth century—in each case by AFL affiliates. In all four fields, employment continued to grow during the 1970s and 1980s even as economic restructuring undermined unionism. By the early 1990s, low-wage, casualized employment had become entrenched, immigrants had replaced native-born workers, and renewed organizing efforts were under way in all four occupations, although those struggles led to lasting unionization only for the janitors and drywallers.

The late-twentieth-century transformation of work through deunionization and restructuring, as well as the influx of immigrants into low-wage employment, were national and global rather than local or regional developments. But as with so many other social trends, these changes emerged earlier and on a larger scale in southern California than elsewhere. The region's rapidly expanding economy was an early testing ground for the low-road managerial strategies that sprouted up all across the United States in the 1970s and 1980s. As social protections once provided by government and unionism alike withered away in industry after industry, employment relations became increasingly casualized. Wages, no longer taken out of competition, were driven ever downward as corporate managers moved to externalize market risk, subcontracting more and more work to smaller enterprises that fiercely vied with one another for business.

These developments not only led to dramatic deterioration in working-class living standards but also helped revive what initially appeared to be anachronistic labor practices of dubious legality: all-cash wage payments, lack of overtime compensation, substandard pay for "training periods," and the like. Defying the optimistic forecasts of many commentators in the 1980s who believed that working conditions would improve in the post-industrial age, the late twentieth century instead saw the widespread resurgence of sweatshop-like employment and the social problems historically associated with it.[6]

Los Angeles enjoys the dubious distinction of being on the leading edge of these emergent tendencies. There, as chapter 2 details, low-wage, casualized employment regimes came to prevail not only in manufacturing, where international competition spurred the "race to the bottom," but also in many nonmobile industries, suggesting that globalization and accelerating capital mobility may be less centrally implicated in the process of work restructuring than is often presumed.[7] Casualization was a product of employers' broader low-road competitive strategies in the 1970s and 1980s, and attacks on unionism were foundational to these strategies. In manufacturing the threat of capital flight was the key lever used to reduce labor costs, but employers advanced their agenda equally effectively in many place-bound industries. They used subcontracting and "double-breasting" (setting up parallel union and nonunion divisions in the same firm) to nurture "union-free" operations in sectors like residential construction and janitorial services. They also promoted deregulation, which was the main mechanism of deunionization and restructuring in trucking and other transportation industries—another type of employment that cannot be outsourced to other nations. And in the L.A. garment industry, employers reduced wages and eliminated unionism even as employment *expanded* in the 1970s and 1980s—a case of deunionization without deindustrialization.

Thanks in part to the region's explosive economic growth and the resulting demand for huge quantities of low-wage labor, southern California attracted an enormous supply of immigrant workers starting in the

1970s. Many—especially those from Mexico and Central America—arrived with few economic resources and little education. The newcomers often lacked legal documentation as well, making them especially vulnerable to the super-exploitative labor practices that flourished anew in this period. Contradicting the claims of some commentators that the influx of impoverished immigrants precipitated the deterioration of wages, benefits, and working conditions in blue-collar jobs (see, for example, Briggs 2001), the timing suggests that the causality runs in the opposite direction: immigrants were hired mainly *after* the jobs in question had been degraded by deunionization and restructuring, as chapter 2 demonstrates.

In southern California, where rapid economic expansion in the 1970s and 1980s provided an escape valve for the native-born incumbent workers adversely affected by these changes, organized labor at first offered little resistance to employers' restructuring initiatives. Not only were many unionists caught off guard by the shift in management strategies, but most of them also considered the foreign-born workers who were already pouring into the region's burgeoning low-wage labor market to be "unorganizable." Latino immigrants, in this view, posed a threat to established labor standards because they evaluated the jobs they found in "el Norte" using a yardstick imported from south of the border. They were therefore seen as "willing" to work for low wages and under substandard conditions and were considered unlikely to respond favorably to union recruitment efforts. Most labor leaders believed that the new immigrants, and especially the undocumented, simply would not take the risks involved in union organizing, given their vulnerability to deportation.

As the janitors' example suggests, however, these pessimistic assumptions proved groundless. Low-wage Latino immigrants, some of them veterans of intense collective political struggles at home and most of them far less individualistic in orientation than their native-born counterparts, turned out to be unusually receptive to unionism. This was another reason, indeed, that southern California in the late 1980s and 1990s became the proving ground for some of the most dynamic, if still embryonic and unstable, social movement responses to the labor market transformations that are under way nationwide. Now Los Angeles, previously seen as a remote backwater by the national leadership of organized labor, and with a lingering reputation from a century ago as an open-shop city, became a leading center of union innovation—and one where low-wage immigrants were on the front lines. More than anywhere else in the United States, in southern California the labor movement experimented with new strategies for rebuilding power in the 1990s; these strategies were especially tailored to the casualization of blue-collar employment that was already deeply entrenched in the region.

During this period labor also developed a formidable political presence, both in the L.A. region and in California as a whole. Organizing success and political influence were mutually reinforcing in a virtuous circle—at least until the 2003 recall election that propelled Arnold Schwarzenegger into the governor's office. In the years just before that political earthquake, California labor even managed, for a time, to reverse the decline in union density that had continued unrelentingly in most other states (Milkman and Rooks 2003). Nor is it an accident that most of organized labor's recent initiatives in support of immigrant rights—most importantly, the AFL-CIO's February 2000 call for amnesty for the undocumented and against employer sanctions—have emanated from the West.

Apart from the fact that it boasts the nation's largest single concentration of Latino immigrants and thus reaped disproportionate benefits from their unanticipated receptivity to union recruitment efforts, Los Angeles has other distinctive features that facilitated union revitalization and strategic innovation. Geography itself was one advantage: simply being distant from the national center of gravity of organized labor on the East Coast as well as the regional power hub in San Francisco provided a degree of freedom from scrutiny by the entrenched, risk-averse, old-guard labor leadership, especially before 1995 (when Sweeney won the AFL-CIO presidency). Their peripheral location, ironically, gave union organizers in southern California more political space to experiment than many of their counterparts elsewhere enjoyed.[8]

But the key advantage was the historical weakness of industrial unionism in the region, where the SEIU and other occupationally based unions originally affiliated with the AFL had long accounted for a disproportionate share of organized labor's ranks. As chapter 1 elaborates, the conventional historical narrative that constructs the former CIO unions as the most dynamic wing of the U.S. labor movement is not unproblematic. But whatever one makes of the historical record, what is critical for the future is that recently the former AFL unions generally, and the SEIU in particular, have proven especially adept at crafting new survival strategies for labor in the post-industrial economy. They have led the way forward, while most of the former CIO unions have found themselves deeply mired in defensive struggles, all but devastated by plant closings and outsourcing.

The L.A. labor movement, then, was transformed from a marginal backwater into a union powerhouse thanks to a combination of historical AFL predominance, an economic boom driven by employer-led work-force casualization, and a massive influx of Latino immigrants. But will the burst of low-wage immigrant worker organizing in southern Califor-nia that emerged in the 1990s turn out to be a transitory phenomenon, or is it part of an ongoing process of union revitalization? Organized labor has suffered serious setbacks in the new century, both regionally and na-tionally. Inequalities that had begun to narrow in the late 1990s boom years widened once again after 2000 with the economic downturn and a new wave of regressive tax policies. Anti-union employers and their allies have been newly emboldened by the sharp political right turn that fol-lowed the tragic events of September 11, 2001. Immigration reform, which had risen to the top of the national political agenda by mid-2001, thanks largely to labor movement lobbying, went into the deep freeze im-mediately after the September 11 attacks; since then, attacks on immi-grant rights have not only increased in number but gained broader legit-imacy. Moreover, union density, which had leveled off in the late 1990s and in California even briefly turned upward, has now resumed its long decline.

Whether these recent reversals will prove to be permanent, or merely interruptions in a long-term process of social change, is difficult to pre-dict. But whatever the future may bring, the vigorous labor movement responses to the rapid economic transformations that emerged in south-ern California in recent years are important insofar as they prefigure an alternative to the low-road path that a growing number of U.S. employ-ers have chosen to follow. The highly polarized, immigrant-rich L.A. la-bor market embodies—in a relatively "advanced" form—that dominant economic trajectory in which firms compete to minimize direct labor costs rather than seek a marketplace advantage on the basis of innova-tion, productivity, or quality. At the same time Los Angeles has emerged as a key incubator of challenges from below to the casualization of work and to the associated growth of economic inequality, with immigrant or-ganizing drives like the janitors' campaign and the others discussed in chapter 4.

Los Angeles's recent labor history, then, is of interest not just for its own sake, but also because it highlights some of the key ingredients that will be needed for the construction of an alternative, high-road national economic agenda and a social movement powerful enough to take wages out of competition nationwide once again. But in order to assess the prospects of the embryonic labor union renewal that has taken root in that unlikely venue becoming the spur for a wider national transformation, we must situate it in the context of the broader forces that have so profoundly weakened unionism not only in Los Angeles but throughout the United States during the past few decades.

DEUNIONIZATION AND NEOLIBERAL RESTRUCTURING

If consensus on the precise causes and consequences of the neoliberal turn that began in the 1970s remains elusive, virtually everyone agrees that the global political economy today is utterly different from that of the 1960s. Nor is there any doubt that this great transformation has had far-reaching effects on the organization of work and on the living standards of workers in the United States, especially for the non-college-educated population (the foreign-born share of which has grown significantly over this period). Economic inequalities increased dramatically during these years (Levy 1999), even as the casualization of employment undermined job security and rendered precarious the livelihoods of millions. In many respects these shifts involved a return to conditions that prevailed in the early twentieth century; indeed, from that perspective, it is not the recent era but rather the period between the 1930s and the 1970s—what Claudia Goldin and Robert Margo (1992; see also Krugman 2002) felicitously call "the Great Compression"—that is anomalous. The era of reduced immigration to the United States (from 1924 to 1965) nearly coincides with this critical period. And organized labor's influence reached its peak during these years as well, during the glory days of U.S. economic hegemony.

From the outset, indeed, declining unionization has been both a leading indicator and a major driver of the neoliberal transition. U.S. union density peaked in the 1950s, but the decline really took off in the 1970s, following some modest erosion in the intervening years (Goldfield 1987; Hirsch and Macpherson, various years). This sharp drop in union density contributed directly to the growth of inequality over the past three decades. Not only do unionized workers earn, on average, substantially higher wages than their nonunion counterparts, but nonunion employers have become less and less likely to match the level of union wages, as many had done in the 1950s and 1960s, as the threat (real or imagined) of unionization has receded. Deunionization has also undermined job security and facilitated the casualization of employment arrangements.

So what explains the free fall in union density over this period? Initially, it appeared to be a by-product of the deindustrialization process that riveted both public and scholarly attention in the 1980s. Hundreds of thousands of blue-collar workers, most of them unionized, lost their jobs as the huge manufacturing empires that had once been the linchpin of U.S. economic hegemony dismantled their domestic operations, outsourcing production to regions where wages were lower and unions weak or absent. As historian Jefferson Cowie (1999) points out, capital mobility in search of cheap and tractable labor has a long history, but its pace accelerated sharply in the 1970s and 1980s as transportation and communication costs plummeted and more and more U.S. firms faced the unaccustomed challenge of foreign competition (Bluestone and Harrison 1982).

Deindustrialization was indeed life-threatening for the industrial unions that had been built in the great CIO drives half a century earlier. Hammered by the continuing threat of factory closings, in the 1980s these once-formidable unions embraced the logic of concession bargaining, giving up decades' worth of hard-won improvements in pay, benefits, and shop-floor control in hopes of maintaining employment for their remaining members. This desperate gambit proved largely futile, however, and even in settings where jobs were preserved intact, union power and legitimacy rapidly crumbled. As they contemplated the apparent collaboration of union leaders in the chain of events that left them impoverished and powerless, many workers lost confidence in the labor movement, in effect blaming the victim (Lopez 2004).

But deindustrialization was only one of the factors shaping labor's decline in the 1970s and 1980s. Union density fell rapidly not only in the footloose manufacturing sector but also in industries, like construction and transportation, that were largely invulnerable to capital mobility and in which employment was stable or growing during this period. In such cases deunionization was driven by political and legal forces. Starting in the late 1960s, business interests mobilized to dismantle a wide array of governmental regulations that had been in place since the New Deal. The resulting deregulatory trend was at least as detrimental for workers and their unions in service-producing industries like communications and transportation as deindustrialization was in manufacturing. Business's political agenda also included privatization, which further eroded unionization, since density was far higher in the public sector than in the private sector.

Long-standing labor laws were eviscerated in this period as well, thanks to an employer-driven legal offensive that generated a steady succession of administrative and legal decisions unfavorable to labor. Employer violations of the laws that survived also increased sharply in the 1970s, quickly becoming an effective brake on the labor movement's ongoing efforts to organize new workers, which (contrary to popular belief) had continued at a steady pace during the postwar years (Voos 1984). Indeed, some contemporary commentators (for example, Freeman and Medoff 1984) directly linked the precipitous decline in union strength in the 1970s and 1980s to the rapid rise of management violations of the National Labor Relations Act, the legislation that has governed collective bargaining in the private sector since 1935.

Yet, in retrospect, the legal offensive was only one feature of the era's multipronged employer assault on unionism (Flanagan 2005). The NLRA was a key focus only in the (relatively few) cases where active unionization efforts were under way, or where long-established unions were clearly vulnerable to decertification. The broader managerial effort to weaken organized labor also involved the elaboration of a parallel universe that increasingly displaced the unionized sector of the economy. The human resource management (HRM) organizational model was basically designed to preempt unionization entirely. The large employers that adopted this approach in the post–World War II years deliberately incorporated the most attractive features of unionism into their own employment policies. They provided wages and fringe benefits comparable to those in the union sector, along with promises of long-term job security; they promulgated "open-door" policies and developed a variety of internal avenues for voicing grievances as an alternative to "adversarial" collective bargaining and industrial jurisprudence. This approach was by no means entirely new (see Jacoby 1997), but it became increasingly widespread in the 1970s and 1980s (Kochan, Katz, and McKersie 1986), in part because of its apparent synergies with the flexible new technologies that were being introduced into the workplace during these years. By the early 1990s, many elements of the HRM model had diffused so widely among employers that they were virtually standard business practice (Appelbaum and Batt 1994; Osterman 1994).

Many influential contemporary observers, most notably Michael Piore and Charles Sabel (1984; see also Block 1990; Zuboff 1988; Hirschhorn 1984), were optimistic that workers would benefit from both the decline of traditional mass production, with its notoriously alienating labor process, and the enhanced opportunities for participation in workplace decisionmaking that the HRM model seemed to embody. Captivated by the potentially humanizing and skill-enhancing applications of new technologies and the decentralization of production they facilitated, Piore and Sabel sketched out a vision of a democratic workplace in an economy guided by the logic of "flexible specialization." They saw deunionization as an inevitable aspect of the decline of the old industrial order, and they urged organized labor to abandon its long-standing mass-production-based focus on work rules and shop-floor control and define a more flexible role for itself in the newly emerging economic configuration. Thus, they applauded the embrace of "employee involvement" and other worker participation programs by the United Auto Workers (UAW) and a few other unions during the 1980s. Other commentators (for example, Heckscher 1988) echoed the call for unions to reinvent themselves and adapt to the organizational sea change that was sweeping across the business landscape.

Two decades later it seems indisputable that the promise Piore and Sabel and others saw for a more humane workplace to emerge in the post-industrial age has not been realized. Some firms, both in the new high-technology sector and in older manufacturing industries (often with union cooperation), did adopt high-performance work systems that genuinely fostered worker participation and training (Appelbaum et al. 2000). But by the end of the century this high-road managerial regime, coupling high wages and benefits with a focus on maximizing productivity and quality, had become increasingly exceptional in the United States. Instead, the prototypical workplace today is the low-road Wal-Mart Corporation, the nation's largest employer, infamous for minimizing labor costs by all possible means and for its unswerving commitment to "union avoidance."

The HRM model's widespread diffusion in the 1970s and 1980s was a major driver of deunionization. Yet this very success, ironically, sowed the seeds of the model's demise. As union density in the private sector spiraled downward, HRM's raison d'être melted away. The simultaneous dismantling of governmental regulation (which, like unionism, had taken wages out of competition in some key sectors) only intensified the problem. Before long, in more and more private-sector workplaces, the high wages that once had been the price of keeping unions out were ratcheted downward as the threat of unionism itself diminished. Similarly, pension programs (originating in the union sector and then imitated by nonunion HRM employers) began to deteriorate, while employers began to transfer more and more of the costs of health insurance to workers or to eliminate such benefits entirely. Low-wage jobs proliferated even as executive compensation soared, fueling the growth of income inequality.

Another striking aspect of the unraveling of the HRM model is the demise of long-term employment, once standard practice in many large firms, and the proliferation of explicitly impermanent relationships between employers and employees (Sennett 1998). One stark indicator of this shift is a survey conducted in the late 1990s by the Conference Board (1997), a business research group, which found that only 6 percent of corporate respondents agreed that "employees who are loyal to the company and further its business goals deserve an assurance of continued employment," down from 56 percent as recently as 1989 (Gosselin 2004). Although recent public discussion of declining employment security has focused mainly on middle management and other white-collar workers, the trend actually began at the lower levels of the labor market as a direct by-product of deunionization. Building on that foundation, employers then moved to externalize market risks at all levels of the job hierarchy through subcontracting, contingent employment, and other forms of casualization.

Not surprisingly, these changes have led to a precipitous fall in job satisfaction and morale, growing mistrust of employers, and a corresponding decline in worker commitment. As Peter Cappelli (1999, 122–36) puts it, the "happy worker" model that prevailed in the 1970s and 1980s—the notion, once conventional wisdom in management circles, that performance and productivity are tied to employee morale—now has been replaced with the "frightened worker" model, in which labor discipline is predicated on fear of job loss. From a different theoretical vantage point, this is what Michael Burawoy (1985) conceptualizes as a shift from a hegemonic to a despotic regime. If deunionization was a key driver of this change, the resulting increase in awareness of injustice in the workplace might also be expected to spark renewed interest in unionism.

REBUILDING LABOR: THE NEW UNIONISM

Deindustrialization, deregulation, and casualization, then, have all contributed to the sharp downturn in union density since the 1970s. But to what extent was that downturn also the result of problems *internal* to the labor movement? Chronic disunity among unions, inept leadership, and inadequate union responses to the radical environmental changes that emerged in this period surely played some role. In addition, internal organizational dynamics, as many commentators have noted, can make unions less effective over time. In Richard Lester's (1958) influential account, for example, unions gradually "mature," losing their initial dynamism and becoming increasingly bureaucratic and rigid. In Robert Michels's (1915/1962) classic theoretical formulation, similarly, unions inexorably succumb to the "iron law of oligarchy," so that political power is increasingly concentrated at the top and labor leaders become more conservative and less responsive to their membership. These claims are consistent with a more recent literature (for example, Moody 1997) that characterizes organized labor in the 1970s and 1980s as dominated by "business unionism" and oriented toward "servicing" members rather than organizing and mobilization. In this view, the current crisis reflects labor's bureaucratization, social isolation, and failure to engage its own constituency.

Rebuilding the labor movement will be impossible without renouncing what Steven Lopez (2004) calls "do-nothing unionism" and embracing the rank-and-file-intensive organizing strategies that, as Kate Bronfenbrenner (1997) demonstrates, offer an effective alternative approach. But for purposes of explaining the rapid deunionization that began in the 1970s, labor's internal difficulties seem secondary in importance—more a consequence than a cause of the decline. Even in the best of times, unions are shaped by their economic and political environment and reflect the structure of the enterprises whose employees make up their membership (see Offe and Wiesenthal 1980). When that structure is radically altered, unions inevitably face a serious crisis.

In this perspective, what is perhaps more remarkable than the sharp decline in union density is that substantial parts of the U.S. labor movement have succeeded in finding ways to reinvent themselves as "social movement unions" in recent years. John Sweeney's election to the AFL-CIO presidency in 1995 and other signs of labor movement revitalization in the intervening decade have surprised many observers, who had already written unions off as historical relics, hopelessly out of step with the post-industrial, globalized economy and with the "new" social movements focused on gender, ethnicity, race, sexuality, or environmental issues. Yet as Taylor Dark (2001) has argued, labor remains an influential political player, and in recent years it has proven itself capable of forging coalitions with those movements—as in the November 1999 "Battle of Seattle," where "Teamsters and Turtles" (and others) joined forces in protests against the World Trade Organization (WTO), and in the 2003 Immigrant Worker Freedom Ride as well.

Apparently contradicting the "iron law of oligarchy," moreover, the new unionism has developed within existing labor organizations, specifically the SEIU and other former AFL unions. If the labor movement's re-

vival in the 1990s came as a surprise, the particular shape it assumed was
even more unexpected. The most innovative and successful organizing
efforts emerged in geographical areas, among population groups, and in
organizational settings that are wholly unprecedented. Who could have
imagined that immigrant organizing in Los Angeles would be at the center of the nation's labor movement revitalization efforts? Or that the
unions that responded most energetically to recent political and economic transformations would be the old AFL craft and occupational
unions?

The AFL's historical record has long been underestimated, as a number of labor historians have pointed out (Brody 1964; Gordon 1999;
Greene 1998; Russell 2001; Tomlins 1979). Its positive achievements
were virtually obliterated from public memory in the aftermath of the
massive union upsurge of the 1930s and 1940s, when the CIO's progressive politics and dramatic grassroots mobilizations captured the imagination of the New Deal generation. Ever since, the industrial unions have
been almost universally considered the most progressive wing of organized labor. The prototype was the United Auto Workers (UAW), especially when it was led by the legendary Walter Reuther. Yet these former
CIO unions were decimated by huge membership losses in the wake of
deindustrialization in the 1980s. Since then, far from reviving, they have
circled the wagons, unable to extricate themselves from struggles over
outsourcing and the like.

The former AFL unions that have assumed prominence instead in recent years include building trades unions like the Carpenters and Laborers, the International Brotherhood of Teamsters, UNITE HERE, and,
above all, the SEIU. The latter's former head, John Sweeney, appointed so
many SEIU staffers to leadership posts in the AFL-CIO after he became
its president in 1995 that some insiders quipped that the federation should
now be called the "AFL-SEIU." Former AFL unions also form the core of
the CTW, whereas the critique of the AFL-CIO structure that led to the
2005 split met with fierce resistance from the old industrial unions.[9]

The division within the federation that led to Sweeney's ascent to
power in 1995 did not break down so neatly along AFL versus CIO lines.
At that time the Carpenters supported the old guard, while the UAW and
many of the other former CIO unions allied with the Sweeney insur-
gency, along with SEIU, HERE, and the Laborers (Dark 1999). A decade
later, however, it is striking that the SEIU and its CTW partners have
parted ways with the industrial unions on a variety of issues (including,
for example, the 2004 presidential primaries). More generally, the former

CIO unions seem increasingly backward-looking, while innovation and organizing energy is almost entirely concentrated on the AFL side. In this respect, Steve Early's (2004) anti-SEIU polemic "Reutherism Redux," which compares SEIU president Andy Stern to the UAW's Walter Reuther (and more generally, the SEIU to the UAW in its heyday), misses a crucial dimension of the new unionism, namely, the former AFL unions' central role.

Kim Voss and Rachel Sherman's (2000) incisive study of unions in the San Francisco Bay Area in the 1990s, one of the few attempts to specify the conditions under which union revitalization occurs, highlights three critical factors that facilitated local union innovation: an internal political crisis leading to leadership change, support from the International union, and the presence of leaders with activist experience in other social movements.[10] It is striking that all of the "full innovators" (as well as most of the "partial innovators") that Voss and Sherman examined were affiliates of SEIU and of the Hotel Employees and Restaurant Employees union (HERE). Yet they did not inquire into the reasons why the factors promoting innovation were present in *these* particular unions, both of which are former AFL affiliates.

One key explanation for the industrial unions' relative quiescence is simply their location in the manufacturing sector, which was so deeply affected by deindustrialization. Neither the building trades nor the service sector–based SEIU and HERE need worry that their members' jobs can be transferred to locations where labor is cheaper or more tractable (although the garment and textile workers in UNITE HERE, of course, *are* vulnerable in this way). SEIU also benefited from gaining an early foothold in the public sector, where union density remains relatively high and where a high concentration of female workers offered an opportunity to embrace the cause of gender equality, the first incarnation of a broader trend toward social movement unionism (Johnston 1994).[11]

Being concentrated in expanding sectors of the economy gives the former AFL unions an undeniable advantage. And a substantial (though difficult to calculate) part of SEIU's spectacular membership growth over recent decades is due to accretion; that is, to increased employment in already unionized units—particularly in health care—rather than to new organizing. Mergers with preexisting unions have also contributed to SEIU's growth. There is even some evidence that both absolute membership and union density have declined in recent years in some key SEIU (and other CTW) jurisdictions, despite their impressive record of organizing the unorganized (Hurd 2004).

Even taking this into account, however, the SEIU was easily the leader in innovation and growth in the 1990s. So it is worth asking: what else (besides insulation from the effects of deindustrialization) differentiates it and the other former AFL unions from those with roots in the CIO? One key factor is that SEIU and HERE, as well as the building trades unions, are occupationally based. As Cobble (1991b) has argued, in the post-industrial age, when workplaces are unstable and shifting entities, occupational unions have distinct advantages over those whose organizational units mirror the structure of the traditional industrial workplace. Interestingly, even though they otherwise resemble industrial unions, the garment unions—which were in the vanguard of the AFL's "new unionism" in the 1910s, then merged in 1995 to form UNITE, and later joined the CTW grouping as part of UNITE HERE—fit this pattern too. The subcontracting-based apparel industry bears little resemblance to the mass-production manufacturing that was the CIO's focus; it always had more in common with the construction sector, where workplaces were inherently unstable. Thus, the needle trades unions share many characteristics with those in the building trades—for example, portable benefits and a model of unionism predicated on taking wages out of competition in local labor markets, often by means of organizing tactics designed to recruit employers, rather than workers, into the union fold (see Piore and Sabel 1984, 115–20).

Their local market orientation also fostered a tradition of local autonomy in the AFL unions, in contrast to the centralized pattern bargaining that the CIO unions achieved in their heyday. As the historian David Brody (1967/2005, 42) has pointed out:

> The AFL rarely succeeded at the core of mass-production industry. But a vast peripheral field remained that was susceptible to—indeed, better suited to—the tactics of AFL unions, which were decentralized, with local unions dispersed across the economy and often equipped and motivated to carry on organizing work.

Against this background, it is ironic that SEIU and UNITE HERE are currently seeking to consolidate their market power at the regional, national, and even international level in a bid to strengthen their leverage vis-à-vis the multinational firms that now dominate such industries as building services, hotels, and health care. But the AFL national leaderships have always retained the ability to intervene in the affairs of their local affiliates through such means as trusteeships, which have been deployed far more frequently in the AFL than in the CIO unions (whose greater centralization historically made such mechanisms redundant). This dynamic underlies Voss and Sherman's (2000) finding that support from the International for local leadership change is a key factor facilitating union revitalization. In addition, as Brody (1967/2005, 42) notes, traditionally "AFL unions serviced their locals less than centralized CIO unions did, so proportionately more income at the national level was available for organizing work."

As is now well documented, many of the most successful initiatives of the SEIU have actually been "top-down" efforts, engineered not by the rank and file but by paid staff in the upper reaches of the union bureaucracy. Thus, "business unionism" has been the handmaiden of social movement unionism, not its antithesis! And the leaders who launched many of these initiatives often relied on trusteeships to do so: in the case of the Justice for Janitors campaign in Los Angeles, for example, trusteeship was the tool that ousted the old-guard local union leaders, who were staunchly opposed to the janitors' organizing effort. Although critics like Early (2004) paint such International intervention as blatantly undemocratic, this approach glosses over the complex and multilayered character of union leadership and the various political configurations that are possible across those layers. As Voss and Sherman (2000) show, when International leadership is progressive, it can be a powerful force promoting innovation at the local union level. On occasion this may involve the forcible displacement of secondary (local) leaders, but it can simultaneously open the door to rank-and-file participation, which otherwise may be held back by the corrupt local union "bosses" of the old AFL stereotypes.

Some commentators roundly condemn the SEIU's heavy reliance on "outsiders"—especially the college-educated organizers with no shop-floor experience who have helped staff several other unions' recent organizing efforts as well. Early (2004), for example, sees such outsiders as opportunists driven by personal ambition and ruthlessly hostile to any potential competitors. Yet the tradition of hiring "intellectuals" onto union staffs, and more generally recruiting talent from outside the labor movement, has contributed to the recent successes of SEIU and other CTW unions. The practice can be traced back for many decades in SEIU as well as in the garment unions that merged into UNITE (see Clark and Gray 2004; Gray 1981; more generally, see Mills 1948; Wilensky 1956). Although it was more unusual in the building trades, in the decades following World War II—the period of labor's most rapid expansion in Los Angeles—college graduates "found easy access to leadership positions" in the local Carpenters' and Painters' unions (Greenstone 1969, 157). Unions of every stripe have long hired lawyers from the outside, and union research departments have often been staffed by highly educated outsiders as well. But in the post–World War II years, the UAW and other former CIO unions had begun to make something of a fetish of recruiting their leaders (those in line positions if not always those in staff jobs) from the shop floor.[12] Although there may be valid reasons for this policy, it certainly has not saved the former CIO unions from bureaucratization or the other pitfalls of "business unionism." And it may have unintentionally deprived them of the creative energy and "strategic capacity," in Marshall Ganz's phrase (2000, 2004), that intellectual skills and/or experience in other social movements can bring to labor (see Piore 1994; Voss and Sherman 2000).

Outsiders often have been effective in dislodging old-guard union officials who are unable or unwilling to assume the risks involved in using new strategies and tactics or who justify avoiding the formidable task of organizing the unorganized by invoking the "servicing" needs of their existing members. And the recent ascension of leaders with both extensive formal education and activist experience in other movements to high-level positions in key unions has injected dynamism into the labor movement. It is no accident that three Ivy League–educated union presidents (including the SEIU's Andy Stern) were the main leaders of the dissident union grouping that led to the 2005 split in the labor movement (Greenhouse 2004). More generally, as chapter 4 as well as other recent research suggests (see again Voss and Sherman 2000), the most vibrant and innovative unions are those that *combine* social movement–style mobilization with carefully calibrated strategies that leverage the expertise of creative, professional leaders.

NEW UNION STRATEGIES

As the types of union growth strategies that were once embedded in the web of regulatory and legal institutions established in the New Deal era have become increasingly ineffective, labor has turned to new approaches. Organizing unorganized workers today increasingly occurs outside the framework of the National Labor Relations Board (NLRB), which has been virtually incapacitated after decades of employer manipulation. The once-conventional practice of unionizing one workplace at a time is also outmoded in the growing number of industries where highly competitive subcontracting has become widespread. This problem exists in all four of the cases analyzed in the pages that follow: in building services, residential construction, and garments, a union organizing victory at a single subcontracting firm would merely lead the affected building owner, housing developer, or apparel manufacturer to shift the work to nonunion subcontractors, putting the newly unionized firm out of business and its employees out of work. Traditional organizing is equally impractical in the intermodal trucking industry, both because of the large number of competing firms and because the owner-operators that dominate this sector of the industry are not legally classified as "employees" and thus are ineligible to vote in NLRB elections.

The SEIU and other CTW unions have developed an array of new strategies to address these problems. Rather than organizing individual work units, their focus is now on strategic organizing designed to take wages out of competition in an entire industry or sector—first in the local labor market but then over time on a regional, national, or even international basis. The unions engaged in this kind of organizing devote extensive resources to researching the power structure of the target industries in order to identify pressure points where union leverage can be exercised to win direct recognition from employers, thus sidestepping the NLRB electoral process entirely. They have built coalitions with community-based organizations, targeted key politicians, and developed sophisticated means of attracting media attention and public sympathy. In addition, these unions have launched "internal organizing" efforts to educate and mobilize their existing membership, arguing that the future welfare of current union members depends on organizing the unorganized.

In short, just as their location in expanding, nonmobile sectors of the economy positioned the former AFL unions to survive and grow even as their industrial union counterparts were paralyzed by deindustrialization, so too other distinctive characteristics facilitated their ability to develop these new organizing approaches. The AFL unions' experience prior to the establishment of the NLRB and the broader New Deal regulatory framework and their long-standing anti-statism and commitment to "pure and simple" unionism give these unions an edge over the industrial unions in the context of ascendant neoliberalism. Their traditional reliance on organizing strategies that focus on taking wages out of competition in local occupational labor markets is newly relevant as subcontracting has proliferated and cutthroat competition has been unleashed both in industries like building services and in deregulated sectors like trucking. By contrast, the industrial unions, from the outset, were accustomed to operating within oligopolistic industries where wage-based competition was historically rare. They have had enormous difficulty transcending the New Deal framework on which the CIO's initial growth was so heavily predicated.[13]

The willingness and ability of International leaders to intervene in the affairs of nominally autonomous local unions, as well as their recruitment of highly educated outsiders to augment leadership talent at all levels, further facilitated the former AFL unions' development of new strategies to confront the restructured political economy that emerged from the tectonic shifts of the 1970s and 1980s. The intellectual resources of outside staff recruits have generated sophisticated strategic research into the industries and sectors these unions targeted for organizing—research that often has proved critical to their success. Many of these outsiders also brought with them a vision of large-scale social change nurtured by previous activism in other social movements, from feminism to environmentalism to anti-imperialism; such visions also added vibrancy to the labor movement.

Criticisms of the top-down character of SEIU organizing and other such efforts by commentators like Early (2004) make much of the undemocratic aspect of the intervention of International leaders and the deployment of outsiders in strategic campaigns. The implication is that if only the legions of top union brass would step aside and allow the rank and file's natural leaders to take command, labor would no longer be so impotent. Yet in most cases top-down intervention has come at the expense not of the rank and file but rather of highly conservative old-guard secondary union leaders (few of whom attained their positions by democratic means) whose individual interests and culture of risk aversion often diverge from the interests of the workers they represent.

Moreover, the mobilization of the rank and file—both existing union members and the unorganized workers targeted for recruitment—has been central to the new unionism's success, as the immigrant organizing campaigns analyzed in chapter 4 illustrate. Some of these campaigns were initiated by International union staff, strategically designed to exert intensive pressure on powerful individuals and groups within the targeted industry in order to win union recognition; others began at the grassroots level, with limited involvement from established union organizations or leaders, at least initially. But analysis of these cases suggests that under current conditions a campaign is unlikely to succeed unless it involves *both* a strategic campaign *and* a bottom-up worker mobilization.

Regardless of how the effort begins (as either a leadership initiative or a bottom-up organizing effort), ultimately both components must be combined into a comprehensive strategy to neutralize employer power and extract a union victory. Where either the top-down or the bottom-up element is lacking, success is unlikely. Thus, the rank and file do have a vital role to play in labor revitalization—and in this arena immigrant workers have been a particularly dynamic force. But rank-and-file mobilization is best understood not as an alternative to but rather as complementary—and indeed integral—to the success of top-down strategic campaigns.

The janitors' case, along with other recent examples of low-wage immigrant organizing in Los Angeles and elsewhere, invites a reconsideration of basic questions about union structure and strategy. That the former AFL unions rather than their CIO counterparts have assumed center stage in these efforts to organize immigrants of color belies the old stereotype that paints the former as reflexively hostile toward racial and ethnic minorities. And the dichotomy between top-down and bottom-up forms of unionism also must be problematized. More generally, posing the question in terms of a normative hierarchy of different types of unionism seems less fruitful than a concrete assessment of the varied labor organizing strategies to win voice and power vis-à-vis employers, analyzing the conditions under which such efforts succeed or fail.

A vital starting point for rethinking these issues is to examine the historical record in light of contemporary developments. How did the unions actively engaged in organizing today recruit workers and consolidate their power in the first place? How were their strategies influenced by the political and economic conditions in which this initial organizing took place? And what were the roles of immigrants and native-born workers, respectively, in this earlier phase of union growth? Chapter 1 explores these questions for the four industries that are the empirical focus of this book: garments, trucking, construction, and building services. Reconstructing the historical logic of unionization in these industries not only offers some insight into the larger issues of union structure and strategy but also exposes the specific organizational legacies with which those who are currently struggling to rebuild the labor movement must grapple.

CHAPTER 1

THE "WICKED CITY": LABOR AND LOS ANGELES EXCEPTIONALISM

The first wave of significant union growth in Los Angeles took place in the 1930s and 1940s, and it must have been every bit as surprising to contemporaries as the 1990s labor resurgence. In the early years of the twentieth century, the city had hardly seemed fertile territory for union organizing. It was dominated by conservative, white, native-born residents and was notorious as a "company town" where employers were intransigently opposed to organized labor. Eager to attract investment, civic and business leaders actively promoted their city as "the Citadel of the Open Shop," as the president of the L.A. Chamber of Commerce proudly dubbed it in 1926 (Fogelson 1967, 130). Yet in the 1930s that citadel finally succumbed to the efforts of a new generation of unionists, and employers were compelled to accept collective bargaining in a range of occupations and industries. Organized labor's growth in the city accelerated during World War II, and after some fluctuations, by the mid-1950s the level of union density in Los Angeles reached its postwar peak at 37 percent—four percentage points above the U.S. average and only slightly below the level in California as a whole (see appendix A).

Intense labor struggles in the 1930s led to major organizing break-throughs in two of the industries that are our focus here, and in the other two such breakthroughs followed soon after. One of the first sectors where unionism gained a foothold in Los Angeles was garment manufacturing, starting in 1933 with a spirited strike that brought thousands of Mexican American women into the International Ladies' Garment Workers' Union. Two years later the ILGWU joined the newly established Committee on Industrial Organization (CIO) within the American Federation of Labor, which burst on the national scene in 1935 carrying the banner of union revitalization.[1] The ILGWU played a vanguard role in the 1930s cycle of union organizing in the City of Angels, as did the International Longshoremen's Association (ILA), which launched the massive 1934 strike that established collective bargaining for waterfront workers in all the Pacific Coast ports. Soon after, the ILA's West Coast locals joined the CIO, becoming the left-wing International Longshoremen's and Warehousemen's Union (ILWU).

The CIO was far less central to the labor movement in Los Angeles, however, than it was elsewhere in the country. The ILGWU and the ILWU were small islands of industrial unionism in a vast sea where the open shop still dominated. And when the big breakthrough for the L.A. labor movement did arrive a few years later, it was not the work of the unions affiliated with the CIO but rather that of the AFL-affiliated Teamsters' union. In 1937 the Teamsters deployed a bold secondary boycott strategy that leveraged union strength in northern California and Seattle to extract a collective bargaining agreement from trucking employers in greater Los Angeles. This effort proved spectacularly successful, but it bore little resemblance to the massive strike mobilizations that took place in mass-production settings elsewhere in the country during the 1930s. The Teamsters put most of their energy into generating direct economic pressure on employers, mainly by organizing their existing membership in the north to disrupt the business of the southern carriers—a strategy that required relatively limited participation from or recruitment of truckers in Los Angeles itself.

Even though it occurred just a few months after the UAW's historic 1937 triumph at General Motors after a months-long sit-down strike, the Teamsters' breakthrough in Los Angeles was rooted in a far more traditional approach to unionization, and one typical of the old AFL. It had several notable features. First of all, it was a form of unionism built around an occupational culture rather than centered in any fixed workplace site (see Cobble 1991b). Second, the union's success was predicated on its ability to take wages out of competition, in a variant of what Colin Gordon (1994) calls "regulatory unionism."[2] And third, although the broader change in the national climate for labor organizing could only have been a positive influence, the unionization of truckers in Los Angeles in no way relied on the New Deal institutional machinery established two years earlier by the National Labor Relations Act. Truckers did not vote to become unionized; rather, the Teamsters exerted direct leverage on the employers to win recognition and a collective bargaining agreement.

These same three elements were present in the next major union breakthrough in Los Angeles, which took place in 1941 when the AFL-affiliated building trades unions won a master labor agreement covering the bulk of southern California's construction industry. Here too occupational unionism, taking wages out of competition, and a non-NLRB organizing approach that focused on directly pressuring employers were key elements. And even the ILGWU's 1933 strike victory occurred in a highly competitive industry—similar to construction in that subcontracting was widespread—in which taking wages out of competition was a critical prerequisite for union success. Although the basis of organization in the garment case was industry rather than occupation, workplaces were unstable, shifting entities, as in construction and trucking. (And of course in 1933 the NLRB machinery did not exist.) Indeed, although the ILGWU was briefly affiliated with the CIO and had a relatively radical political pedigree as well, like the AFL-affiliated Teamsters and the building trades unions, it was a long-standing practitioner of regulatory "business unionism" (see Gordon 1994, 91, 100–4).

Only during World War II, as unionization spread still more widely through the L.A. workforce with the rapid expansion of aircraft and other defense industries, did the CIO gain a substantial membership in the region, and even then it lagged far behind the AFL. In the war years, moreover, much of the CIO's growth occurred as a result of "maintenance of membership" and other such wartime union security arrangements, rather than through the rank-and-file mobilization that had been more common in the 1930s. As unions consolidated their wartime gains, organized labor's strength in Los Angeles continued to grow during the late 1940s and 1950s. But once again the AFL, with its occupational rather than industrial workplace–based organizational structure, was the dominant player in the region.

Los Angeles janitors and other building service workers were among those drawn into the union fold in the immediate postwar years. The AFL-affiliated Building Service Employees' International Union (BSEIU, later to become the SEIU) launched a major organizing drive in Los Angeles starting in 1946. It was led by the legendary George Hardy, who would eventually become the union's national president. In this period, employer resistance was relatively weak, particularly in relation to the moderate style of unionism the BSEIU espoused. Hardy, who came to Los Angeles after the war from the union town of San Francisco, immediately saw the potential for the Southland as a powerhouse of service-sector unionism, and under his leadership the BSEIU recruited thousands of L.A. building service workers in the late 1940s and 1950s. His union developed a reputation for organizing "anything that moves," including hospital workers and government workers, initiatives that would later pay off handsomely. Politically, he was a liberal, "very much like . . . CIO officials in Detroit and Chicago" (Greenstone 1969, 154). Yet Hardy was squarely in the mainstream AFL tradition, organizing on an occupational basis, aiming to take wages out of competition, and seldom relying on NLRB elections. Under his leadership, the L.A. BSEIU typically pressured employers directly to win union recognition, seldom resorting to overt displays of worker militancy.

Nationally, the AFL unions differed from those in the fledgling CIO not only in their strategic and tactical approach to organizing but also in their political outlook. As the sociologist C. Wright Mills documented in his classic 1948 study *The New Men of Power*, CIO leaders were generally younger and better educated than their AFL counterparts and politically more progressive. The AFL unions were chronically plagued by gangsters and racketeers, who were virtually absent from the more centralized CIO unions; by contrast, Communists and other left-wingers were far more often associated with the CIO (Mills 1948, 68–73, 186, 289 and passim). Both types of unions grew rapidly in the years between the CIO's establishment in 1935 and the AFL-CIO merger twenty years later—if by different means. Their growth, however, was geographically uneven, with the AFL leading strongly in the West. And as David Greenstone (1969, 156) noted in his study of labor and politics, the L.A. AFL deviated in some respects from the national pattern:

> Like the Autoworkers in Detroit, nonfactory unions in Los Angeles faced both repression from employers and substantial exclusion from their city's nonpartisan electoral system. As a result, these unions only achieved a reliably secure position as a result of the Wagner Act and the creation of the NLRB. AFL unions in Los Angeles, therefore, resembled CIO unions elsewhere in the sense that they flourished only under the New Deal. . . . In Los Angeles, the rapid expansion of the labor movement after the Wagner Act was passed has created a new generation of nonfactory union leaders whose political views

were formed under Franklin Roosevelt. Consequently these leaders take for granted welfare-state politics, federal protection for unions, and the importance of supporting Democrats in national politics.

The dramatic mass mobilizations that were the CIO's trademark in the 1930s and 1940s, however, were rare in Los Angeles, and even when they did erupt, they produced relatively meager results. For example, the ILGWU's organizing efforts during the depression years had brought only about three thousand new members into the L.A. labor movement by 1937, whereas the Teamster campaign of that year yielded over twenty thousand—equal to the combined 1937 membership of some two dozen CIO unions then active in the city, according to one estimate (U.S. Senate 1940, part 64, 23613–14). Nationally too, as is often forgotten, AFL-affiliated unions had more members than their CIO counterparts in this period, but the balance was far more extreme on the West Coast, and in Los Angeles in particular, than in regions where the new industrial unionism took center stage. In 1955, when union density was at its postwar peak, and on the eve of the merger between the AFL and CIO, only 16 percent of Los Angeles union members were in CIO affiliates, compared to 29 percent of all union members in the United States (California Department of Industrial Relations, ULIC, 1956, 9, 16; see also Kennedy 1955). In this respect, Los Angeles resembled New York City, where AFL unions also predominated and where the CIO was thus relatively marginal (see Freeman 2000), although the New York labor movement's left-wing orientation had only the faintest echo in Los Angeles.

The ethnic and racial composition of midcentury Los Angeles, moreover, contrasted sharply with that of eastern and midwestern cities, where the working class was dominated by first- and second-generation immigrants from southern and eastern Europe. Indeed, these workers had formed the core constituency of both the "new unionism" that emerged in New York in the 1910s and the CIO union drives that swept through mass-production industry during the 1930s. In contrast, the white (or "Anglo," as it is still colloquially known) working class of Los Angeles was much more heavily native-born. The city's Chamber of Commerce explicitly promoted this fact in its efforts to promote industrial investment. Among other things, the chamber sponsored a speaking tour by Nobel Laureate Robert Millikan in the 1920s in which he called southern California "the westernmost outpost of Nordic civilization"; he then pointed out that the area had a "population which is twice as Anglo-Saxon as that existing in New York, Chicago, or any of the other great cities of this country" (quoted in Davis 1997, 376). During the nineteenth century and continuing into the first few decades of the twentieth, Los Angeles's rapid population growth was driven by internal migration, mostly that of whites from the rural Midwest. One result was that, as the historian Michael Kazin (1986, 379) has noted, "workplace hierarchies based on nationality seldom sprouted among whites—in sharp contrast to the steel mills, meat-packing plants, and textile factories of the East, where craftsmen, semi-skilled machine operators, and laborers often spoke different languages and rarely made common cause across a gulf of cultures."

African Americans were a significant presence in Los Angeles by 1930, however, and by that time immigration from Europe, Asia, and especially Mexico, although modest in scale by late-twentieth-century standards, had begun to have an impact on the city as well. During the Depression years, however, the influx of immigrants ground to a halt, and in the case of the single largest national group, it was actually reversed as massive repatriation and deportation campaigns reduced the city's Mexican American population by one-third (George Sánchez 1993, 12). Insofar as these non-Anglo groups were employed in the industries that were newly organized in the 1930s and 1940s, they joined the ranks of L.A. union members alongside their Anglo coworkers. At least half of the city's garment workers, recruited into the ILGWU in the 1930s, were Mexican American (Wuesthoff 1938, 109). Similarly, by 1950, 38 percent of Los Angeles's unionized janitors were African American. Both of these occupations included large numbers of women workers as well. Thus, the ILGWU and BSEIU belied the stereotypes of the AFL as exclusively white and male, even if the bulk of union members in Los Angeles in this era, concentrated in industries like trucking and construction, were indeed native-born white men (Greer 1959, 172–75).

The growth and revitalization of the U.S. labor movement in the 1930s and 1940s left its mark on Los Angeles, then, but organized labor developed a different profile there than it did in many other large cities, dominated as it was by the AFL unions. In part this reflected the unusual character of the economy in the region. Apart from extractive industries and railroads, enterprises tended to be relatively small. Moreover, prefiguring the late-twentieth-century "service economy," both employment and union membership were disproportionately concentrated in nonmanufacturing industries. With the important exception of aircraft and the related wartime industries that burgeoned in the 1940s and then became bulwarks of southern California's military-industrial complex during the cold war decades that followed, manufacturing was far less important in the regional economy than in the nation as a whole. Before the war, "cost, distance, and the slow development of power sources limited most California manufacturers to supplying consumer goods to a regional population that still lagged behind the concentrations found elsewhere in the nation" (Kazin 1986, 374).

To be sure, shipbuilding took off during World War I, with some multiplier effects in metalworking industries (Gordon 1954, 56). And while shipbuilding declined sharply after the war, in the 1920s and 1930s national manufacturers like Ford, General Motors, U.S. Steel, Goodyear, and Firestone, with direct encouragement from the local chamber of commerce, established satellite production facilities in the Southland (Davis 1997; Hise 2001). The growth of the automotive sector slowed during the Great Depression, although not even the economic crisis could stop the rapid growth of aircraft manufacturing (for which southern California's climate proved uniquely suitable) during the 1930s, when the groundwork was laid for that industry's spectacular expansion during and after World War II (Gordon 1954, 59–61).

But on the whole, in Los Angeles, as on the Pacific Coast generally, both employment and unionization remained concentrated in sectors like transportation, construction, services, and government—unlike most of the East and Midwest, where mass-production-based industrial unionism prevailed. In 1957 two-thirds of California's union members were in non-manufacturing industries, compared to only about half of union members in the United States as a whole at the time (Bernstein 1959, 531). As Van Dusen Kennedy noted in an insightful 1955 treatise on "nonfactory unionism," this had critical implications for the West Coast's labor movement. Jobs, and thus union members, tended to be dispersed geographically among a large number of relatively small employers. Standardization was limited and job content highly variable in many nonmanufacturing settings.

Moreover, as Kennedy (1955, 12) emphasized, nonfactory unions were relatively decentralized, with locals as the primary units, and their members had a "strong sense of occupational identity . . . coupled with a conservative political outlook or lack of working class orientation." Indeed, the AFL's tradition of craft or occupational—as opposed to industrial—unionism remained largely intact in this region. And as Kennedy further observed, the key functionary in the nonfactory union was the business agent, rather than the shop steward typically found in unionized factories, making for greater distance between members and officials. "The physical dispersal of the membership and their varying employment conditions could militate against the sense of group cohesion and community of interests which seem to foster [rank-and-file union] participation," Kennedy (1955, 28) observed. "The union member has good reason for thinking of his union as primarily an office activity and of himself as a taxpayer."

In Los Angeles the prevalence of nonfactory unionism and the predominance of native-born whites in the working-class population were mutually reinforcing and together made for a labor movement in which the AFL was the dominant presence. The irony was that the same AFL unions that had such a conservative reputation in the 1930s and 1940s would, decades later, position the new Los Angeles, with its vast population of working-class immigrants, at the leading edge of labor movement revitalization. The roots of this exceptional trajectory in U.S. labor history can be traced back a full century, to the years when Los Angeles first emerged as an important metropolis.

"THE CITADEL OF THE OPEN SHOP"

In sharp comparison to San Francisco, then a high-wage "union town," the economic and political elites of Los Angeles, under the leadership of *Los Angeles Times* proprietor Harrison Gray Otis, were unabashedly hostile to unionism in the early twentieth century. Contrary to popular myth, antilabor animus was not just Otis's personal idiosyncrasy but was woven into the very fabric of the city's political economy, as Carey McWilliams pointed out long ago (1946/1973, 276–77):

> Otis and his colleagues were quick to realize that the only chance to establish Los Angeles as an industrial center was to undercut the high wage structure of San Francisco. . . . Having land to burn, the Southland dangled the bait of "cheap homes" before the eyes of the prospective homeseekers. "While wages are low," the argument went, "homes are cheap." . . . From 1890 to 1910, wages were from twenty to thirty and in some categories, even forty percent lower than in San Francisco. It was precisely this margin that enabled Los Angeles to grow as an industrial center. Thus the maintenance of a cheap labor pool became an indispensable cog in the curious economics of the region. For the system to work, however, the labor market had to remain unorganized; otherwise it would become impossible to exploit the homeseeker element. The system required—it absolutely

demanded—a non-union open shop setup. It was this basic requirement, rather than the ferocity of General Otis, that really created the
open shop movement in Los Angeles.

The "homeseekers" to whom McWilliams refers here were native-
born migrants from the rural Midwest who were actively recruited by
the city's boosters in the early years of the twentieth century. Thanks
primarily to them, the population of Los Angeles grew at a phenomenal
rate, tripling between 1900 and 1910 and then doubling again in each of
the next two decades. "This continuous influx has caused the loose social
organization and the lack of social integration for which Los Angeles is
famous," one commentator observed in the 1950s, pointing out the implications for organized labor: "The labor unions have had a never-ending
job of organizing the unorganized" (Baisden 1958, 18).

The promotional efforts that attracted the steady flow of newcomers
emphasized leisure over work, touting the city's warm climate and promising a simple, relaxed way of life. Those who responded to the pitch were
disproportionately middle-aged and elderly, so that before World War II
Los Angeles had an unusually low proportion of young people in its population. This lopsided age distribution was another obstacle to union organizing. Moreover, many of the migrants were politically conservative
and saw organized labor as subversive, reinforcing the anti-unionism of
the city's employers (Fogelson 1967, 68–78, 84, 130–31).

Although, as in other large U.S. cities, Los Angeles's rapid population
growth in this period was fueled by migration, the new arrivals were
mostly internal migrants from other regions of the United States rather
than from abroad. And those whites who were foreign-born (about 15
percent of Los Angeles residents by 1930, compared to 33 percent of New
York City residents at that time) more often came from Canada or from
northern or western Europe than from the southern or eastern European
nations that supplied the vast bulk of immigrants to cities like Chicago
and New York, where unionism flourished in the pre–World War I era
(Fogelson 1967, 80).

Still, Los Angeles had a heterogeneous population in other respects.
By 1930 more than 13 percent of its 1.2 million residents were Latino,
Asian, or African American. As is still the case today, the largest non-Anglo group in the city was made up of Mexican Americans, who numbered
97,000 in 1930, or 8 percent of the population, according to the U.S. census.[3] In addition, 39,000 African Americans, 21,000 Japanese Americans,
and 3,000 Chinese Americans lived in Los Angeles at this time. (In con-

trast, less than 5 percent of New York City's 1930 population was non-white, and this group was overwhelmingly African American.) Los Angeles in 1930 was also home to 60,000 immigrants from southeastern Europe and 80,000 from northwestern Europe, who together made up about 12 percent of the population (Fogelson 1967, 76–82; George Sánchez 1993, 90). In short, "unlike most eastern and midwestern metropolises, which were divided between native [white] Americans and European immigrants, Los Angeles was divided between an overwhelming native white majority and a sizable colored [sic] minority" (Fogelson 1967, 83).

The city's extreme inhospitality to labor unionism also distinguished it from the nation's other large urban settlements in the early decades of the twentieth century. "There is probably no city in America where such unfriendly sentiment obtains against organized labor as in this beautiful city of Los Angeles," a printers' union official remarked in 1912 (Stimson 1955, 426). The standard point of reference was San Francisco, once the state's largest metropolis, where unions gained a foothold early and public sympathy for labor was widespread. In Los Angeles, by contrast, as the economist Ira Cross (1935, 268) pointed out in 1935, "almost a century passed [after the city's founding in 1781] before unions appeared, and at no time have they played an important part in the industrial or political life of the community." In 1910, 65 percent of California's union members lived in San Francisco, while only 8 percent were in Los Angeles (McWilliams 1949/1999, 145), even though the two cities had similarly sized populations at the time.[4]

If Los Angeles's working class was largely unorganized, the same could not be said of the city's employers. "The sentiment which has prevailed here [in Los Angeles] is that the owner of a business shall absolutely control it and be free to employ or discharge as he pleases," the radical journalist Lincoln Steffens, a San Francisco native, observed in 1911. "The conviction that this is right is more settled here than I ever saw it anywhere" (quoted in Baisden 1958, 15). In alliance with Otis and the *Times*, the Los Angeles Merchants' and Manufacturers' Association (M&M), founded in 1896, quickly became one of the nation's leading anti-union organizations. In conjunction with a variety of other employer organizations, the M&M brazenly and systematically promoted a wide array of anti-union tactics: "open-shop declarations, lockouts, black lists, discharges of union members, agencies for the importation and employment of nonunion workers, financial help to struck firms, economic pressure on employers friendly to labor, legislative lobbying and the like" (Stimson 1955, 256).

In the face of this determined and disciplined opposition, unionists in northern California who periodically attempted to organize their southern brethren made little headway. "Los Angeles, in spite of its name, is a wicked city and sadly in need of someone who can point out the benefits of trade union organization and the iniquities of rampant capitalism," the San Francisco building trades journal *Organized Labor* complained in July 1910 (quoted in Kazin 1987, 202). The catastrophic bombing of the *Los Angeles Times* building later that year, which killed twenty people, only served to dramatize labor's weakness, especially after two union men unexpectedly confessed to what Otis called "the crime of the century" in December 1911 (Stimson 1955, ch. 21).

The confession, which came four days before a mayoral election, was a devastating blow to the local labor movement and to the national AFL, which had staked its reputation on the claim that the accused men had been framed. AFL president Samuel Gompers himself reportedly wept at the news (Greene 1998, 224). This anticlimax also sealed the fate of the city's Socialist Party, whose candidate had won the mayoral primary but was now resoundingly defeated. The whole episode "aborted the labor movement in Los Angeles," McWilliams (1946/1973, 283) judiciously concluded. "It set back by twenty years a movement which, even in 1911, was dangerously retarded in relation to the growth of the community." Indeed, two decades later, despite sporadic efforts to revitalize organized labor in Los Angeles, little had changed. As Cross (1935, 287–88) summarized:

> There have been continuing and costly attempts to unionize the workers in various occupations [in Los Angeles], but for the most part with no tangible results. Strikes, usually insignificant in extent, have been called only to be lost because of the overwhelming supply of laborers and the anti-union attitude of employers, the newspapers, and the community.

Only in the 1930s, as unionism burgeoned all across the nation, did the labor movement finally pry open the heavily guarded gates of Los Angeles. As figure 1.1 shows, union membership in the city more than doubled from 1933, when it was under 20,000, to 1935, when it reached 45,000. Thus began "the sudden metamorphosis of Los Angeles," as the journalist Oliver Carlson (1938, 43) reported at the end of 1937, "from an open-shop paradise into a seething center of labor unrest." Rapid growth continued over the next few years, and by the end of the decade the city's

FIGURE 1.1   Union Members and "Gainful" Workers in Los Angeles, 1930 to 1950

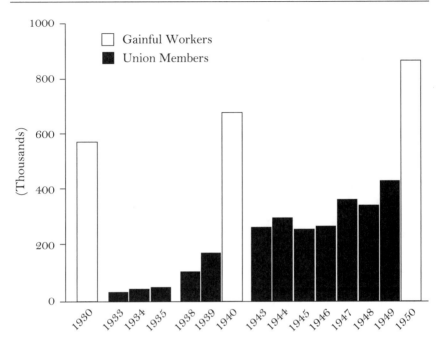

Sources: For union membership data, see appendix A; for gainful workers, U.S. Census.
Note: 1930 data are for nonagricultural gainful workers, age ten or older; 1940 data are for gainful workers, age fourteen or older; 1950 data are for the civilian labor force, age fourteen or older.

union ranks had grown to over 170,000 members—about 17 percent of the workforce (see appendix A). In 1939, Mayor Fletcher Bowron would state, "Even the most conservative manufacturers have come to realize that workers must organize, that bargaining cannot be with individuals, and that the effort to maintain the open shop is a lost cause" (Perry and Perry 1963, 521). As Los Angeles, already California's largest metropolis, grew explosively under the spur of the World War II economic boom, union membership continued to expand, reaching 431,000 by 1949, or 38 percent of the nonagricultural workforce (see figure 1.1 and appendix A).

Although organized labor made great progress in Los Angeles during this period, its trajectory diverged sharply from the heroic narrative that still dominates discussion of the broader labor resurgence that began in the Depression era. For it was not the new industrial unions associated with the breakaway CIO that made the biggest gains in Los Angeles, but rather the older, occupationally based, nonfactory unions tied to the AFL. Indeed, Christopher Tomlins's (1979) argument that the AFL's role in the national union resurgence of the 1930s is often underestimated applies with particular force to southern California. The CIO had established a modest beachhead in the region by the decade's end, most notably among the longshoremen at the port and to some extent in the embryonic manufacturing sector as well. But with only 50,000 dues-paying members in the city by 1939, the CIO was greatly overshadowed by the AFL, whose L.A. membership included some 120,000 workers at the time (Perry and Perry 1963, 495, 497). Numerically, the key organizing successes in Los Angeles in the 1930s were in the movie industry, with its AFL "silk stocking" and craft unions, and especially in such traditional AFL blue-collar jurisdictions as trucking and construction.[5] Leo Troy (1957, 4–5) found that in California as a whole only 12 percent of union members were CIO-affiliated in 1939, compared to 28 percent nationwide.[6]

AFL predominance in Los Angeles was due partly to the city's relatively modest manufacturing base, for the national CIO recruitment campaigns concentrated primarily on mass-production factories in this period. "In the absence of industrial employment, the number of clerical, domestic, and personal service employees increased by 90% during the 1920's," Carey McWilliams (1946/1973, 236–37) noted. "In no city in America has there been such a proliferation of wasteful and meaningless service occupations." As late as 1930, only 19 percent of the workforce in the five-county L.A. area was employed in manufacturing. Wholesale and retail trade accounted for 24 percent, another 28 percent were in service occupations, and construction and transportation had 7 and 9 percent, respectively (Coons and Miller 1942, 9; see also Fogelson 1967, 120–29). By contrast, nearly half the workforce in Detroit was employed in manufacturing in 1930. This was one fundamental reason why, as on the Pacific Coast generally, Los Angeles's labor movement was dominated by "nonfactory unionism" (Kennedy 1955).

The political and ideological legacy of Los Angeles's long history as an open-shop city also contributed to the predominance of the AFL over the CIO there. As we have seen, a persistent and powerful anti-union animus among the city's employers complemented a conservative and highly atomized working class with almost no previous experience of self-organization. As one commentator noted, "The AFL had a more 'conservative' reputation, and when an open shop was organized it was frequently preferred by both workers and management to the more 'radical' CIO" (Greer 1959, 22). In part this reflected the CIO's association with Communism, especially as personified by the colorful ILWU president, Harry Bridges. Frank Shaw, Los Angeles's mayor from 1933 until his recall in 1938, told an interviewer that "he had no animus toward the AF of L, which, unlike the CIO, did not indulge in violence, respected the sanctity of private property, and was not infested with Communists" (Baisden 1958, 171; see also Carlson 1938).

Even in industries where the CIO did gain a foothold in the region, unionism had a more conservative character than elsewhere in the nation and met with more ambivalence from workers, as the historian Becky Nicolaides reports in her study of South Gate, a blue-collar suburb of Los Angeles and the site of a General Motors assembly plant where the UAW organized in 1937. "Autoworkers in South Gate lacked the 'culture of unity' that characterized workers elsewhere in the 1930s, undergirding the CIO's success," she argues. "For the majority of workers, the union commanded a minimal commitment" (Nicolaides 2002, 82–83). And on the Los Angeles waterfront, where the aggressive, Communist-influenced, and (after 1937) CIO-affiliated longshoremen's union prevailed, port workers, "while militant on the job, were much less responsive to radical politics" than their northern California counterparts (Kimeldorf 1988, 14). Thus, while in San Francisco it was the huge left-led 1934 waterfront strike that turned the tide for organized labor, in the Southland the Teamsters' union, with its more conservative brand of unionism, would make the crucial breakthrough in 1937.

Thanks to "the phenomenal growth of the Teamsters in Washington [state] and California," Irving Bernstein (1959, 535) noted two decades later, "this organization's power over transportation has been used as a lever to unionize many nontrucking workers." In Los Angeles in particular, the Teamsters served as "a powerful organizational aid for other unions—generally AFL" (Greer 1959, 22), reinforcing the tilt in the local labor movement toward AFL unionism. The main beneficiaries of Teamster support in the late 1930s were the building trades unions, which had secured a strong base in the city's construction industry by the early 1940s. And after the war the BSEIU's campaign to organize janitors in Los Angeles would also rely heavily on support from the Teamsters' union. In all three of these cases the long-standing AFL tradition of organizing the employers was salient; rank-and-file workers did participate (and indeed, the efforts could not have succeeded without that participation), but their mobilization was not the centerpiece of union strategy.

Yet there was an alternative path that some segments of the L.A. labor movement ventured to explore in this period. The most significant case was the garment worker organizing that began in 1933 and that first established durable unionism in the city's apparel industry. The ILGWU, which would later briefly affiliate with the fledgling CIO, used a different mix of tactics from the standard AFL repertoire in this pioneering campaign. It made some efforts to pressure employers directly, but the main thrust of the organizing was extensive and overt rank-and-file worker mobilization—a phenomenon conspicuous by its absence in the processes by which Los Angeles's trucking, construction, and building service industries would be unionized over the years that followed.

The bulk of the garment industry workforce was comprised of first- and second-generation Mexican American immigrants, who joined the L.A. ILGWU in droves during the 1930s, alongside Jewish workers and a variety of other European immigrants. By contrast, the workforce in trucking and construction was made up largely of native-born whites, although small numbers of Mexican Americans, blacks, and foreign-born whites were present as well. The building service workforce was more diverse in composition, mainly owing to the strong representation of African Americans. But among our cases, only the garment industry had a predominantly foreign-born workforce in this period. Indeed, in some respects the ILGWU's successful campaigns in Los Angeles in the Depression era foreshadowed the dynamic Latino immigrant organizing of the late twentieth century. But in the 1930s the garment workers' union was an exception to the general pattern in the southern California labor movement, which was comprised mainly of native-born whites.

ORGANIZING LOS ANGELES GARMENT WORKERS IN THE 1930S

The garment industry, with its elaborate internal subcontracting systems and unstable, highly competitive economic conditions, has always been a challenging environment for labor organizing. Initially, only elite male craft workers like cutters and pressers were able to unionize successfully, taking advantage of employers' dependence on their skills. The majority of garment workers were more easily replaceable, and although the pervasiveness of extreme forms of exploitation in the industry made them highly prone to strike activity from the earliest period, building durable unionism was more difficult (Fraser 1991, 41). In a trade where undercapitalized sweatshops have always flourished, particularly among subcontractors, and cutthroat competition was the norm, organizing a single garment factory could easily drive it out of business rather than leading to any permanent improvement of wages or working conditions. The needle trades unions learned this lesson early: where they were successful, they organized on a sectoral or industrywide basis, taking wages out of competition and thus stabilizing the industry.

During the early twentieth century, a wave of mass strikes rippled through the New York and Chicago garment districts, starting with the legendary "Uprising of the Twenty Thousand" in New York in 1909–10 and the Hart, Schaffner, and Marx strike in Chicago that began in 1910 and soon galvanized that city's entire garment industry. These were landmark events in U.S. labor history that brought tens of thousands of immigrant workers, mostly women, into the union fold almost overnight and laid the groundwork for a new system of industrial relations in the needle trades. In what Steven Fraser (1983) memorably termed a "dress rehearsal for the New Deal," the ILGWU and its counterpart in the men's clothing industry, the Amalgamated Clothing Workers' (ACW) union, emerged as serious contenders for power in the 1910s.

Los Angeles's share of U.S. apparel manufacturing today is larger than that of any other city in the nation, but a century ago it was minuscule, and the development of garment worker unionism in the city lagged far behind New York and Chicago. The first ILGWU local in Los Angeles was not established until late 1910 or 1911, with a membership made up entirely of custom tailors. The ACW established its first local in the area even later, in 1920 (Perry and Perry 1963, 36). The less-skilled factory workers who by then made up the bulk of the garment unions' members "back east" remained unorganized in Los Angeles throughout this period, although the unions made sporadic attempts to recruit them as clothing manufacturing expanded in the city during the 1910s and 1920s. Thanks to steadfast employer opposition, on the one hand, and intense political factionalism inside the ILGWU, on the other, these efforts were seldom effective. By 1930 only about 5 percent of Los Angeles's 8,000 garment workers were unionized, nearly all of them in the cloak and suit trade, where skilled jobs were more plentiful and profit margins greater than in other parts of the industry (Wuesthoff 1938, 46–65; Laslett and Tyler 1989, 15–25).

Immediately after the passage in June 1933 of the National Industrial Recovery Act, which established minimum wages, maximum hours, and the right of workers to collectively bargain as government policy, the fortunes of the garment unions began to improve, both in southern California and throughout the nation. Now, almost a quarter-century after the mass strikes that brought industrial unionism to the needle trades in New York and Chicago, a similar drama was enacted in Los Angeles, albeit on a smaller, more peripheral stage. In the fall of 1933, two major ILGWU walkouts transformed labor relations in the city's garment industry. One of these strikes took place in the already partially unionized cloak and suit trade, yielding a closed-shop agreement that encompassed all the important firms in that sector. Simultaneously, some 3,000 workers, most of them Mexican American, launched a monthlong strike that established an enduring union presence in the dress industry for the first time. And in December 1933 the ACW launched a strike of 860 workers in support of workers at a men's clothing firm who were resisting a wage cut (Perry and Perry 1963, 251–58).

The 1933 ILGWU strikes in Los Angeles carried many echoes of the far better known "Uprising" that had erupted a generation earlier in New York (see Levine 1924). In both cases the strikers were immigrant women previously considered "unorganizable." Rose Pesotta, a Russian-Jewish organizer from the ILGWU's New York headquarters who was the chief strategist of the 1933 L.A. dress strike, encountered deep skepticism within the union about the idea of recruiting the first- and second-generation Mexican American women who made up the bulk of the garment industry workforce at the time.[7] Many in the ILGWU believed that "Mexican women could never be organized," she reported. "The skeptics reminded me that Los Angeles garment manufacturers preferred Mexicans to others because they would 'work for a pittance and could endure any sort of treatment.'" But Pesotta found that when the union actively solicited their participation, Mexican American workers responded enthusiastically. "We get them," she claimed, "because we are the only *Americanos* who take them in as equals. They may well become the backbone of our union on the West Coast" (Pesotta 1944, 21, 32).

In open-shop Los Angeles, efforts to approach employers directly in hopes of persuading them to sign labor agreements—as was often done in New York and Chicago—were patently ineffective. "We realized that none of the dress factory owners would consider meeting with us," Pesotta (1944, 30) later recalled. She focused her formidable energies, therefore, on mobilizing workers, visiting them in their homes, producing a bilingual newsletter and leaflets, organizing rallies, and broadcasting a Spanish radio program each evening to generate interest in the union. These initiatives generated a powerful dynamic, rooted in a curious transnational combination of Mexican immigrant culture and the Russian-Jewish radicalism that had galvanized the New York garment strikers a generation earlier—traditions directly embodied in Pesotta and other "outsider" ILGWU staffers. "World politics came to the Mexican immigrants of Southern California by way of Eastern Europe's shtetls, from which came most of the garment employers, ILGWU leaders, and Communists in the needle trades," observes the historian Douglas Monroy (1999, 238). "Pushed out of Mexico by the turmoil associated with the Mexican Revolution, Mexicans in *la costura*, as the needle trades were known, encountered the passions and spin-offs of the Russian Revolution in Southern California."

On September 27, 1933, a mass meeting of L.A. dress workers voted enthusiastically for a general strike if the employers refused to meet their demands, which included union recognition, minimum wages, a thirty-five-hour, five-day week, and basic grievance procedures (Pesotta 1944, 22–30). Just as in New York in 1909, the ILGWU's top leaders were wary of strike action, preferring other methods of union-building. But in 1933, once again, the rank and file (with Pesotta's support) ignored this advice (Laslett and Tyler 1989, 34). Like their New York counterparts a quarter-century earlier, immigrant women garment workers in Los Angeles proved to be determined fighters, impressing their allies in organized labor as well as the wider public with their spirit and militancy. They tirelessly picketed both in the city's factory district and in the nearby downtown shopping area, despite a formidable police presence and frequent arrests. The union provided strikers with regular meals at a commissary in a rented hall, as well as cash benefits to replace lost wages. Pesotta also skillfully orchestrated sympathetic media coverage for the strike. For example, after a Halloween party she organized, the press was alerted to a parade of three hundred costumed children marching through the garment center on behalf of their striking parents, generating excellent copy from the union's viewpoint (Pesotta 1944, 50–51).

In yet another echo of the earlier wave of organizing in New York, the L.A. walkout ended with an arbitrated settlement that embodied only the weakest imaginable version of the workers' demands. The employers, backed by the omnipresent M&M, had vigorously resisted the union's campaign (Vargas 2005, 86). But like the similar "Protocols of Peace" in New York in 1910, the 1933 agreement did establish a permanent foothold for the ILGWU in Los Angeles's previously unorganized dress industry. As Pesotta (1944, 61) summed it up, with this strike, "a new trail was blazed in the Los Angeles industrial wilderness." The union continued its organizing efforts over the next few years, gradually building up strength. By 1937, when it already was affiliated with the CIO, the ILGWU had 3,300 members in Los Angeles. Aside from skilled cutters and pressers, each with their own local union of a few hundred workers, the membership was evenly divided between the (mostly male) cloak and suit workers' local and the (mostly female) dress industry. By the end of the decade about 70 percent of the dress industry in Los Angeles and 100 percent of the cloak and suit trade was unionized, and the ILGWU had made inroads in other sectors (lingerie, cotton goods, knits) as well (Wuesthoff 1938, 106, 150; Laslett and Tyler 1989, 37–41). Meanwhile, in the men's clothing industry, the ACW's L.A. membership had grown to 1,500 by 1937 (U.S. Senate 1940, part 64, 23614).

Despite the repeatedly demonstrated militancy of its membership, the ILGWU in Los Angeles, as elsewhere in the nation, rapidly devolved into a highly bureaucratic organization. Control was centralized in the hands of social democratic Jewish male leaders, most of whom had once been skilled workers. These traditional craft unionists had a paternalistic view of women and Mexicans as vulnerable workers in need of union protection. They "came from or witnessed the sweatshops firsthand and did not want other people to have to work like that just because they were weak," Monroy (1999, 240–41) notes. "The ILGWU leaders numbered among those few gringos (and, because the Christian americanos called them bad names too, they were not completely gringos) who concerned themselves genuinely with Mexicans." Yet neither women nor Mexican Americans were represented in the union officialdom at a level remotely commensurate with their majority share of the membership.[8]

The ILGWU became disaffected with the CIO early on, and in 1940 it reaffiliated with the AFL (Morris 1958, 269). During the 1940s, its L.A. membership grew steadily, from 3,028 in 1940 to 6,957 four years later, and it peaked in 1950 at 12,165 (International Ladies' Garment Workers' Union, GEB and FSR, various years). By the 1940s, Los Angeles's unionized garment employers—following in the footsteps of their New York and Chicago counterparts a generation earlier—had come to see the advantages of union-led stabilization, which took wages out of competition and created a level playing field among the many small contractors that made up the industry. As this logic of regulatory unionism and labor-management cooperation took hold, the L.A. ILGWU came to rely more and more on organizing methods that did not involve direct worker mobilization. As Colin Gordon (1994, 102) notes, the fact that the union was "nominally socialist . . . only underscored the gap between ideology and practice."

As early as 1941, when the union struck the city's dress and sports-wear industries, the manager of the Dress Association of Los Angeles publicly indicated "that there was no real disagreement between the Association members and the ILGWU, but that the Garment Workers had called the strike against both the union and the non-union shops in order to produce such a show of strength that the nonunion shops might be more easily organized" (Tipton 1953, 47). Just after the war, when the union was approaching its peak strength, "as soon as new firms were established in cloak and suit they were automatically signed up by the ILGWU." Similarly, the ILGWU's 1948 industrywide strike (in which the ACW participated as well) succeeded partly because of "the support which both the Dress and Sportswear Employer Associations gave to the ILGWU in bringing hitherto unorganized shops under the union contract" (Laslett and Tyler 1989, 56, 59; Tipton 1953, 53).

By any measure, the garment unions made pioneering inroads in open-shop Los Angeles starting in the early 1930s. But their role in rank-and-file immigrant organizing, while prefigurative of developments later in the twentieth century, was highly atypical for this era. "The ILGWU and the Mexicans were the exception with the exceptions," Monroy (1999, 241) concludes, although, as he also notes, there were a few other modest industrial organizing efforts in 1930s Los Angeles that included Mexican American workers, notably in the furniture industry and along the waterfront. In the post–World War II years, as the labor movement expanded, the unions in Los Angeles would recruit whomever the employers hired, regardless of ethnicity or race. But in the period before the war, this was exceedingly rare. In those years the key breakthroughs for organized labor in southern California were in industries dominated by native-born white male workers, most importantly trucking and construction.

UNION GROWTH IN THE 1930S: THE TEAMSTERS TAKE LOS ANGELES

The Teamsters' union, founded in 1903 and conventionally considered one of the most conservative AFL affiliates (Craft and Peck 1998, 478), mounted a daring and ambitious challenge to the open shop in southern California during the 1930s, achieving a victory that paved the way for much of what followed. Trucking is a strategic sector for the labor movement in many urban areas, and this was nowhere more true than in Los Angeles, a "thinly settled and sprawling . . . [metropolis where] trucks are the very carriers of life for industry and business" (Greer 1959, 22; see also Gillingham 1956). Fully 83 percent of freight moved by truck in California in the mid-1950s (Bernstein 1957, 18). The southern California region's trucking industry was the largest in the West, overshadowing that of both the Pacific Northwest and northern California (Garnel 1972, 91).

Under the forceful leadership of Dave Beck, who would later become the union's national president, the Teamsters won a union-shop agreement in Los Angeles in late 1937 and signed up the vast majority of the city's for-hire truck drivers. By 1939 the International Brotherhood of Teamsters (IBT) boasted 20,000 to 25,000 paid-up members in the L.A. area, more than any other union (Garnel 1972, 161–64). Moreover, this breakthrough helped spur Teamster organization up and down the West Coast as well as nationally: IBT membership grew rapidly throughout the 1940s and 1950s, and by 1956 it was the largest union in the United States, with over 1.3 million members (Tomlins 1979, 1037). Not only was this achievement significant in its own right, but it also facilitated organizing in other industries and occupations, both in Los Angeles and nationally.

The Teamsters were not a new presence in Los Angeles in the 1930s. They had enjoyed some modest successes in the first decade of the twentieth century, winning union-shop agreements with all the city's major trucking firms and signing up some five hundred members by 1907. However, a disastrous truckers' strike that year, which galvanized the city's open-shop movement, all but destroyed the union. The Teamsters' union emerged from this crisis with its L.A. membership reduced to a mere thirty-five intrepid souls (Garnel 1972, 92–94). Despite occasional strikes and other reorganization efforts, the local union languished over the next two decades, when open-shop forces prevailed in the trucking industry, as in most others. In the 1930s, however, spurred by the passage of New Deal legislation, on the one hand, and by the example of the dramatic 1934 Pacific waterfront strike, on the other, the union began to prepare a new offensive.

The first breakthrough came in the aftermath of the 1934 longshoremen's strike, which many truckers supported and which emboldened the Teamsters to set up a new local in San Pedro, near the port of Los Angeles. Despite the fierce resistance of employers, orchestrated by the M&M and reinforced by extensive police protection for nonunion trucks, by 1936 the union had managed to recruit about two thousand members in greater Los Angeles (Perry and Perry (1963), 293, 411; Garnel 1972, 98–99, 145). To be sure, this achievement remained precarious in the face of unrelenting employer determination to crush the newly revitalized organization.

Soon afterward, however, the Teamsters, led by Dave Beck, finally gained the upper hand in Los Angeles. They did so by leveraging union strength in the San Francisco Bay Area and Seattle to exert pressure on trucking companies in southern California. As Donald Garnel (1972, 101) recounts in his definitive history of the expansion of the union on the West Coast in this period:

> Beck believed that the key to overcoming employer opposition to unionization of Los Angeles was to develop an entirely new approach. He recognized the futility of attempting to organize from within the city, where employer strength was still too great to be contested with the available resources. It was, therefore, necessary to develop a means of applying pressure in highly organized centers where the union was strong in such a way as to bring pressure to bear against the recalcitrant employers in areas where the union was weak. Beck sensed that there was a very high degree of economic interdependence throughout the economic system. He looked, therefore, for a common thread between the strongly anti-union areas and the strongly organized centers, a thread which could be tugged at in San Francisco, Oakland and Seattle, and felt in Los Angeles.

Beck's strategy was predicated on the fact that vast quantities of motor freight moved from Los Angeles to the north, where trucking carriers frequently "interlined," or exchanged loads. This long-standing practice was reinforced by the 1935 Motor Carrier Act, which froze the carriers' regional operating rights: a nonunion trucking firm could no longer legally haul its freight beyond its normal territory if a unionized carrier refused to interline with it. Thus, after consolidating the organization of long-distance highway drivers in the San Francisco Bay Area, where employer resistance was relatively weak, Beck was poised to attack the carriers in southern California using the leverage of the secondary boycott. Once the northern region of the state was solidly organized, "if a Los Angeles highway carrier resisted unionization, it would be prevented from making deliveries and picking up return freight in union strongholds along the Pacific Coast, especially in the Bay Area" (Garnel 1972, 146).

The secondary boycott, then, which the California state legislature tried to prohibit as early as 1941 (Taft 1968, 137) and which later would be outlawed nationally under the Taft-Hartley and Landrum-Griffin

Acts, was the key weapon in the Teamsters' arsenal in 1937. The union subsequently used this same "leap-frog organizing" technique in the Midwest and beyond (Brody 1967/2005, 42; see also James and James 1965, 98–100; Russell 2001, 46, 150). It was of a piece with the union's frequent reliance on "organizing from above," that is, directly persuading *employers* to sign an agreement without necessarily mobilizing workers on the ground. As Ralph C. and Estelle Dinerstein James's (1965, 143–44) account of the Teamsters puts it:

> On some occasions this top-down approach was chosen because employer opposition restrained the free expression of the workers' will. But in many cases it was simply cheaper, faster, and more effective to apply leverage against employers rather than to try persuading workers to vote for the Teamsters.

Moreover, Beck was a consummate pragmatist, to whom democratic rank-and-file unionism was anathema. As Garnel (1972, 74) argues:

> Beck was very distrustful of the ability of the rank and file to run a union efficiently. He saw the union as a benevolent dictatorship and the union leader as a benevolent dictator. . . . Beck believed that the workers knew what was best for themselves (and that a competent union leader could sense this without having to ask the membership), but they did not know how best to go about achieving their goals. Unions should, therefore, be run by "professional" union leaders appointed, rather than elected to their positions by individuals (such as himself) who had the capacity for determining good leadership ability. Elections were, therefore, just so much window dressing—a carry-over of an archaic practice that served no useful purpose. He was thus disdainful of the idea of rank-and-file leaders rising to the top through the election machinery. Instead, the top leader should choose the future leaders and then educate them.

Nor did Beck shrink from unorthodox or high-pressure tactics. Insofar as the Teamsters' West Coast campaign did engage in directly recruiting members, there were frequent reports of intimidation, coercion, and physical violence (see Garnel 1972, 74, 113–16, 150–55).[9]

From a strategic point of view, on the other hand, the Teamsters' L.A. campaign offers a more positive model. Rooted in a deep understanding of the dynamics of the trucking industry, it essentially aimed to make the cost to employers of resisting the union far greater than the cost of capitulation. The challenge the union faced was formidable, for the city's open-shop forces, led by the M&M, responded to the Teamsters' campaign with a threat to boycott any trucking firm that signed a union contract. The conflict rapidly escalated, and soon the parties were engaged in total war: "The M&M and its ally, the Chamber of Commerce, marshaled the resources of the entire business community to fight a union in a single industry. The Teamsters would retaliate by marshaling the resources of all of its locals throughout the coastal states to bring pressure to bear on the employers in Los Angeles" (Garnel 1972, 146).

Taking full advantage of the cutthroat competition prevailing in the trucking industry in the 1930s, the union chose a selective strike strategy directed at the single largest regional carrier, Pacific Freight Lines (PFL), a viciously anti-union firm, but one especially vulnerable to secondary boycott pressure. "While they [PFL] could lick us without question in the Los Angeles area," Beck told an interviewer several years later, "the minute that freight started moving north of Bakersfield and on into the Bay Area, we were absolutely in a position of greater economic strength than they were" (Garnel 1972, 148–49). The Teamsters began to build up membership among truckers in the L.A. harbor area in 1936, when Beck sent a team of organizers from northern California and Washington state to tackle the job. L.A. Central Labor Council secretary J. W. Buzzell characterized them as "a rough, tough cadre of 'muscle men' who would stop at little to achieve their ends" (Baisden 1958, 161). They reportedly stopped trucks on the highways and threatened nonunion drivers. They also picketed the docks, where they won cooperation from the (then still AFL-affiliated) ILA, whose longshore and warehouse members refused to cross the Teamsters' picket lines. When the Teamsters struck PFL in March 1937, the firm was caught in the vise of secondary boycott pressure both at the port and to the north. Its business rapidly hemorrhaged, and despite support from the M&M, the chamber of commerce, and the truckers' trade association, the company capitulated on June 2, 1937, after a nine-week strike.

Five months later, the Teamsters won a general master agreement for the entire southern California area from the Motor Truck Association (MTA). The victory included a union-shop agreement, but in an extraordinary testament to the power of the open-shop forces of Los Angeles, this part of the deal was "kept secret at the request of the MTA, which feared economic retaliation from the large industrial and commercial shippers, the M&M, and other anti-union groups in Los Angeles for having yielded to the union on so vital an issue" (Garnel 1972, 161–62). The agreement had a number of other unusual features as well. It covered a term of five and a half years and included both binding arbitration and no-strike, no-lockout provisions. This arrangement made sense in light of the fact that the Teamsters had triumphed through a process that involved minimal contact with southern California truckers themselves. As Garnel (1972, 229) explains, the union "desperately needed time to consolidate its gains and properly indoctrinate its new membership . . . [which included] large numbers of recent migrants from . . . rural traditionally anti-union sections of the country." By the mid-1950s, this had changed to the point where an academic observer could remark that in California the Teamsters' union "is in actuality what its name says it is— a brotherhood. Teamsters look after each other in fair weather and foul. . . . To my knowledge this is the only organization that refers to itself as 'the movement,' using the term as other unionists do when they talk about the whole of organized labor" (Bernstein 1957, 16).

Unionization brought stability to what had been an extremely competitive industry. In some regions, notably the northwest, the Teamsters even "initiated and staffed 'employer' associations where employers themselves were unwilling or unable to do so" (Gordon 1994, 109; see also James and James 1965, 92; Bernstein 1957, 15). Government regulation (in the shape of the 1935 Motor Carrier Act) was also an important influence here, but in this period enforcement was relatively weak. It was the union's master agreement that effectively took wages (which made up 35 to 55 percent of costs for most trucking firms) out of competition. Thus, the Teamsters helped establish order in an industry that had fallen victim to devastating cutthroat competition during the Depression—a prototypical case of regulatory unionism.

> In the 1930s, operators desperately trying to save businesses, cut truck rates until they frequently covered little more than out-of-pocket costs. To stave off impending disaster, wages were sent spiraling downward in hot pursuit of rates. Other cost items were pared to the bone and sometimes beyond. Proper maintenance of equipment, safety, and the like were ignored, as often out of necessity as ignorance. Squeezed by economic forces they did not understand, many operators, most of whom had as little formal education as their employees, failed to set aside enough for depreciation. The consequence was an astronomically high mortality rate among the carriers. (Garnel 1972, 294-95)

Trucking always had been an industry with low barriers to entry, and one in which many workers aimed to become business owners. "The typical employer with whom the Teamsters deal is small and often tiny, as in the case of the owner-operator," Irving Bernstein (1957, 13–14) noted. And as the historian Thaddeus Russell (2001, 43) points out, "The decentralized, entrepreneurial character of the trucking industry helped to create a culture of petit-bourgeois aspirations especially among Teamster leaders, many of whom identified with the employers." Indeed, the IBT had long allowed owner-operators to be union members (Cobble and Vosko 2000, 301–4). Both employers and the union were anxious to limit the potential for destructive competition; as late as the mid-1950s, the Teamsters' union in California had "numerous owner members and is profoundly concerned with keeping its employers solvent so as to protect its members' jobs" (Bernstein 1957, 15). Once the union established uniform wage rates, however, owner-operators and small firms were at a competitive disadvantage, and the industry became increasingly concentrated over time. Beck recognized this problem but was unapologetic. "There's no God-given right to every man to go into business," he declared, although this view probably was not shared by many Teamsters members (Garnel 1972, 295).

Having won acceptance in the industry, not always by entirely respectable means, the Teamsters proceeded to seek wider legitimacy. In a 1943 speech, Beck laid out his goals and objectives for the union in southern California. He argued for recruiting the best possible candidates for union staff jobs and paying them well. More generally, Beck argued that the union had to begin to "solve our problems by the use of brains rather than brawn," and he called on the Teamsters "to transfer your militancy . . . [to] the development of statistical bureaus, the use of legal talent, publicity channels of information" (*Southern California Teamster*, June 30, 1943, quoted in Baisden 1958, 228). By the mid-1950s, Beck had "imposed so fantastic a superstructure of committees, conferences, and divisions upon the union as to leave even a university president gasping in admiration," according to one contemporary (Bernstein 1957, 14).

The Teamsters not only led the way in winning union recognition in Los Angeles in the 1930s but also set high standards for collective bargaining agreements in the years that followed. Teamster drivers' hourly wages rose considerably faster than those of other unionized workers in the boom years between 1950 and 1964 (Levinson 1980, 119). And by the early 1960s, as a result of then-president James Hoffa's determined effort to establish centralized national bargaining in the industry, the long-standing wage differentials between truckers in the San Francisco Bay Area and those in Los Angeles had been dramatically reduced as well (James and James 1965, 194–203). In addition to securing higher wages, the IBT pioneered in winning paid vacations, pensions, and various other fringe benefits for its members. It was one of the first unions to negotiate employer-paid health and welfare plans in the post–World War II years, and by 1953 some 180,000 Teamster members and their dependents were covered by such plans (Gillingham 1956, 28). The union's organizing strategy, then, proved highly effective. The Teamsters not only succeeded in breaking the deeply entrenched power of the open shop in Los Angeles in the 1930s but also consistently delivered the goods for their members over the next few decades. They set the standard that other unions in the Los Angeles region would soon seek to emulate.

BUILDING UNIONISM IN THE LOS ANGELES CONSTRUCTION TRADES

The Teamsters' 1937 breakthrough, along with the labor movement's advances throughout the nation in this period, spurred a wave of union organizing in a variety of other industries in Los Angeles. "Labor began to stir on so many fronts that organizers were at a premium," a correspondent for *The Nation* reported in a piece entitled "Los Angeles Grows Up" at the end of 1937. "Desire for organization blossomed in groups hitherto looked upon as hopeless. . . . The lowly Mexican laborer earning five dollars a week became a union 'brother' of the famous screen hero" (Carlson 1938, 43).

After the Teamsters' victory, construction, which for many years had been the backbone of AFL unionism nationally, was the next blue-collar sector where unionization took off on a large scale in the region. In 1941, on the eve of U.S. entry into World War II, the largest construction employer association in southern California signed a master labor agreement with the building trades unions that included a closed-shop provision. Over the next few years, unionism was consolidated throughout the building trades, not only in Los Angeles but also throughout California.

Nationally, 25 percent of AFL membership during the 1930s and 1940s was in the building trades, and the largest AFL affiliate in this sector, the United Brotherhood of Carpenters and Joiners of America, had long since abandoned the orthodox craft union model for a more flexible and occupationally diverse "craft-industrial" form that embraced the selective organization of less-skilled workers in a wide array of jurisdictions (Tomlins 1979, 1027–30, 1039; Christie 1956). Not only in this pragmatic adaptation to changing conditions but in many other respects as well, building trades unionism closely resembled that of the Teamsters in this period. In both trucking and construction, barriers to business entry were minimal, and it was not unusual for workers to move into supervisory or subcontracting roles, blurring the class boundaries that might have fostered more radical forms of unionism.

"'Business unionism,' if by that term we understand conservative unionism, embodying a philosophy which is essentially opportunistic, has seen its most advanced development in the building trades," the economist William Haber (1930, 5) wrote in 1930. Indeed, the Carpenters' union, although originally founded by the socialist P. J. McGuire, was a bulwark of this type of unionism. It relied on professional organizers and business agents and took a conciliatory posture toward employers that sometimes "ripened into collusion and then rotted into flagrant racketeering" (Christie 1956, 123). Far from showing a commitment to interunion solidarity, the Carpenters were highly aggressive in jurisdictional disputes with other unions—much like the IBT.

Again like the Teamsters, the building trades unions had a history in Los Angeles going back several decades before their dramatic expansion in the late 1930s and early 1940s. The Carpenters chartered thirty-four new locals in the L.A. area between 1900 and 1904 alone, and by 1906 the largest of these had 2,500 members. Although like the rest of the city's labor movement, the building trades unions suffered in the aftermath of the abortive 1910 *Los Angeles Times* bombing, some 20 percent of the city's construction craftsmen remained organized even in 1912. At that point the Carpenters had more members than any other union in the city, a position they maintained throughout the 1910s and 1920s, when Los Angeles enjoyed a huge building boom (Bullock et al. 1982, 112–14, 125, 144–47).

But construction has always been among the most cyclically sensitive of industries. During the Great Depression, both employment and union membership in this sector collapsed, and by 1932 at least half of the building trades workers in Los Angeles were unemployed. The effects of this on the Carpenters and other construction unions were exacerbated by the influx of experienced workers from other parts of the country who undercut already reduced union wage scales. Membership plummeted so dramatically that by 1933 the city's Building and Construction Trades Council "was hardly more than a paper organization," and the few remaining union members "often hid their identification cards and buttons in order to get work at any wage" (Perry and Perry 1963, 230–31, 244–45, 260). Indeed, the only construction projects likely to employ union labor in the early 1930s were those in the public sector, thanks to hard-won "prevailing wage" laws that mandated union rates for such work.

But in the mid-1930s the local building trades unions launched a serious organizing drive, led by Cornelius "Neil" Haggerty, a leader of the L.A. Building and Construction Trades Council who later rose to head the state Building Trades Council and eventually to the national Building and Construction Trades Division of the AFL-CIO. He later recounted:

> I talked to general [union] presidents back in Washington, and they said, "It's just impossible. That's [Los Angeles,] the so-called white spot of the nation, non-unionwise. We've spent millions trying to organize it, and it can't be organized." So I forgot all about them and said, "All right, we'll get our own money." I went back [to Los Angeles] and called a meeting of the building trades. I told them that . . . if they would help me and be willing to work nights and Saturdays and Sundays, we could organize the city of Los Angeles and its environs. I sold it to most of the leadership of the movement.
>
> We arranged, number one, that we would stop the Saturday work. All our boys, non-union men, were working on Saturdays. They had to work seven days and seven nights a week to make a week's pay. That's how low the salary was that was being paid. So, we went around on Saturdays and talked to the men. We told them that if they would stop their Saturday work and just work five days a week . . . we could help get them a little more money than they were getting now.
>
> To make a long story short, we would have about 300 men come down to the labor temple on Saturday morning. They'd go out in five cars, five men to a car, under strict instructions just to talk to the boys on the job. If anybody got tough with them, forget about it and walk away. Don't use their hands or anything else, but just their tongue.
>
> It was amazing how that campaign took. . . . Later on the Merchants and Manufacturers decided that we were moving too fast and accomplishing too much. (Haggerty 1976, 23–24)

Indeed, this effort proved quite successful, and L.A. building trades union membership began to recover, especially after the Teamsters' 1937 victory at PFL and on the crest of the huge CIO-led national strike wave.

Over the next few years, "flying squads" of union members patrolled the city's construction sites, especially concentrating on residential housing, the sector where unionism was weakest. They recruited unorganized workers into their unions and also reached out to consumers, claiming that homes built with nonunion labor were of poor quality (Perry and Perry 1963, 453–55, 508).

But the linchpin of the building trades' organizing strategy was exerting pressure directly on employers, an approach similar to that used by the Teamsters. Through primary and secondary boycotts, they concentrated intense pressure on construction contractors to sign closed-shop agreements. Firms that resisted were placed on "unfair lists" and then picketed. This had long been standard operating procedure for building trades unions all over the country. The Carpenters' union, for example, was "a boycott-centered union," as the historian Robert A. Christie (1956, 302) noted. Well before the 1930s, the union "had ceased calling [its] field agents organizers," he recounted. "This was honest; they did not organize. They herded workers into their union through boycott and other secondary pressures." A 1939 L.A. contractor's affidavit described the standard tactics:

> That work was started on said job the morning of August 31, 1939; that shortly thereafter pickets bearing placards or shoulder sashes upon which appeared the term "Picket" and the insignia "AF of L" began pacing to and fro on the sidewalk in front and in the alley in rear . . . and stated . . . that if affiant would discharge the employees then at work on said job and employ only men who were members of one or more of defendant unions or organizations, or if affiant would require all said employees of plaintiff company engaged on said job to join one or more of defendant unions or organizations, all said pickets would be removed from the front and rear of said job, but that if affiant would not and did not comply with said request for complete unionization of said job, then said pickets would continue to picket said job and defendants and all of them would refuse to permit any member of said defendant unions or organizations to work on said job or to deliver any materials to said job. (U.S. Senate 1940, part 57, 21220)

The building trades organizing campaigns of the late 1930s made slow but steady progress. By the end of 1937, after several months of sustained effort, eighteen large contractors were still on the "unfair list" of the L.A.

Building and Construction Trades Council, but a number of others had come into the union fold. And by late 1939, the building trades' estimated membership in the city was twelve thousand—up from eight thousand in early 1937 (Perry and Perry 1963, 455, 508). But the big breakthrough came in 1940, when the unions launched a successful strike against the Griffith Construction Company, one of the region's largest building firms. This organizing effort involved not only a strike but direct employer pressure—at multiple levels—as Haggerty recounted decades later:

> One of the main contractors in the city . . . was Griffith Company. We went to Steve and I talked with him. I used to meet with him. I would go around and talk to these contractors, who were not union. Sometimes they'd buy me lunch, or give me a cigar. I didn't smoke cigars, but I always took it. . . . This time, Steve got the contract for the job. I went to him and I saw that he wasn't going to change his policies. [He was still] nonunion, open shop.
>
> I went back to the Columbia Broadcasting Company, CBS. It was their building, on Hollywood Boulevard. . . . I spoke to the general manager, Don something, and he said, "I'm sorry. Steve is a neighbor of mine and so I gave him the job." I said, "Well, you'll have a little trouble building the job." He said, "You're threatening us." I said, "No, sir, merely advising you that certain crafts aren't going to work on your job. If you can build this job without those crafts, well, you go right ahead."
>
> He found out in about three days that he couldn't. He couldn't get any electricity in there. He couldn't get the high power transformer he needed. So, he called me. There had been some unpleasantness, too, by the men themselves. . . . Anyway, we were lucky enough and handled things well enough so that we were able to get, after a while, complete organization of the building trades. (Haggerty 1976, 24–25)

Indeed, the success of the Griffith strike soon led to industrywide negotiations that in turn produced the first master labor agreement between the southern California chapter of the Association of General Contractors (AGC) and all the regional building trades unions, signed in 1941. The timing was propitious, for that same year the state legislature passed the "hot cargo" bill, designed to prohibit secondary boycotts (Taft 1968, 137). After the attack on Pearl Harbor in December 1941 led the United States to enter World War II, the building trades (along with the rest of organized labor) signed a no-strike pledge (Palladino 2005, 114–15). The war stimulated huge economic growth, including massive construction activity in and around Los Angeles; the 1941 master labor agreement ensured that the bulk of that work would be done by union workers.

Even without the war boom, this agreement would have been a landmark for the building trades. It included a closed-shop clause, binding arbitration, and union-controlled hiring hall arrangements, as well as no-strike and no-lockout provisions. Indeed, it "rapidly transformed construction labor relations from semi-organized confusion into responsible collective bargaining" (Bertram 1966, 34). As had occurred earlier in garments and trucking, and now in the building industry as well, unionism became the bulwark of stability in what previously had been a highly volatile, unstable sector of the economy. "For employers," as Colin Gordon (1994, 118) points out, "union recognition was a negligible price to pay for dependable access to skilled labor, guarantees against cutthroat bidding, and contract provision that prohibited union members from becoming contractors."

Because construction is a highly competitive, cyclically sensitive industry that often attracts speculative investment, employment tends to be irregular and highly insecure in the absence of unionism. Since work sites are by definition temporary, construction workers normally are hired on a "contingent" basis, meaning that the typical employer has no long-term commitment to any individual worker. Flexibility is an inherent requirement of labor deployment in this industry, for production is vulnerable not only to market uncertainties but also to vagaries of weather and seasonality. The elaborate subcontracting arrangements that are typical in construction spread these risks over a vast network of employers and workers. Thus, the modes of bureaucratic organization typical of modern mass production never took hold in the building industry, as Arthur Stinchcombe (1959) observed long ago. Instead, the industry has preserved older forms of work organization, of a sort recently revived in other settings and famously celebrated by Michael Piore and Charles Sabel (1984) as "flexible specialization."

Once collective bargaining becomes entrenched, however, organizational functions that management normally performs in other industries can be and often are administered by the unions, or jointly by labor and management. Thus, as the economist Daniel Quinn Mills (1972, 17) has noted, "the peculiar economic conditions and characteristics of employment in construction dictate that employers and unions are placed in a much more intimate relationship than in many other industries." Both workers and employers benefit from the rationalizing effects of unionism, which, by establishing hiring halls and other labor allocation mechanisms, takes wages out of competition, provides job security for workers, and guarantees a stable supply of skilled labor for employers. Indeed, the rise of industrywide collective bargaining in the L.A. construction industry in 1941 eliminated cutthroat competition, which had been especially widespread at the subcontractor level, where capital requirements were extremely low and small enterprises were constantly seeking a foothold.

As the benefits of unionism became increasingly apparent to employers, other contractor and home building trade associations signed on to the agreement first brokered by the AGC in 1941. The dramatic expansion of publicly funded construction projects in the early 1940s, which fell under prevailing wage laws, also encouraged the continued growth of unionization and helped spur the development of consolidated, regional collective bargaining in the industry (Bertram 1966, 35, 56). Nationally, according to some estimates, union density in construction grew from 65 percent in 1941 to 92 percent in 1947 (Palladino 2005, 129). By 1950 some 83,000 construction workers in Los Angeles were union members, more than in any other sector of the economy (California Department of Industrial Relations, ULIC, 1951). Statewide, the building trades made up 19 percent of California union members by 1957, compared with less than 12 percent nationally at the time (Bernstein 1959, 531). Construction workers' average earnings were well above those of manufacturing workers throughout the 1940s and 1950s in Los Angeles, and the pace of wage increases was also slightly greater than in manufacturing. By the end of the 1950s, fringe benefits like paid vacations and health, welfare, and pension plans were widely institutionalized as well (Bertram 1966, 147–49, 164).

Trucking and construction, then, were the two leading sectors of blue-collar unionization in Los Angeles in the pre–World War II period, in both cases located squarely within the AFL. The CIO's industrial unionism, despite its centrality to the national labor movement upsurge of the late 1930s, played a relatively marginal role in southern California. To be sure, as manufacturing expanded in the L.A. area in response to the huge economic stimulus provided by the war, the CIO would develop some strongholds in the region. But even manufacturing was never a CIO monopoly in this region. The AFL-affiliated International Association of Machinists (IAM) developed a large base in the aircraft industry, the International Brotherhood of Electrical Workers (IBEW) organized in electronics, and a variety of AFL unions recruited heavily in the burgeoning shipbuilding industry (Greer 1959, 22).

WARTIME UNION GROWTH AND POSTWAR CONSOLIDATION

Union membership grew rapidly in Los Angeles during and immediately following the war, as figure 1.1 shows. Most of the growth was in defense-related manufacturing, which swelled spectacularly with the wartime economic mobilization. Statewide, union membership increased 627 percent between 1940 and 1943 in the transportation equipment industry group (including aircraft and shipbuilding), which alone accounted for over one-third (36 percent) of all California union members in 1943. That year, the overall manufacturing sector, historically a relatively small component of both employment and union membership in the state, accounted for over half of all California union members. In Los Angeles, where manufacturing had expanded especially rapidly, transportation equipment had more union members than any other industry in 1943, surpassing even construction, which ranked second (California Department of Industrial Relations, ULIC, 1944).

However, in the CIO and AFL alike, workers in defense industries often became union members as a result of special wartime union security provisions like "maintenance of membership" agreements—the quid pro quo for the wartime no-strike pledge (Lichtenstein 1982)—rather than through the dramatic sit-down strikes and other workplace-focused organizing campaigns that fueled the CIO's growth elsewhere in the 1930s and 1940s.[10] Scott Greer (1959, 22) went so far as to suggest that many workers joined CIO unions in Los Angeles "because they could not get jobs in war work otherwise; they were in effect conscript union men." Thus, for both the CIO and AFL in Los Angeles in this period, expansion rarely depended on direct worker mobilization.

The labor movement continued its expansion in the region during the 1950s, as figure 1.2 shows. By 1955 the number of union members in Los Angeles was 722,000, or 37 percent of all wage and salary workers in the metropolitan area. This was the postwar peak of union density (although in absolute terms union membership would continue to grow) in Los Angeles, well above the national level and just below the level in the state, which was 39 percent in 1955. Although the labor movement was still much stronger in San Francisco (with 51 percent unionized at the 1955 peak), the north-south gap was now far narrower than in the prewar era

FIGURE 1.2   Union Density in Los Angeles, California, and the United
States, 1951 to 1970

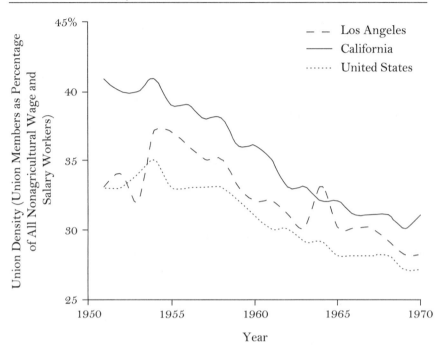

Source: See appendix A.

(California Department of Industrial Relations, ULIC, 1951, 10; 1956, 11).

Moreover, within the organized sector, union security was firmly entrenched. A 1946 survey found that 99 percent of union contracts in Los Angeles had closed-shop, union-shop, or maintenance-of-membership provisions. A year later, the closed shop was outlawed by the Taft-Hartley Act, but a similar survey in 1957 found that 89 percent of labor agreements in Los Angeles had either union-shop or maintenance-of-membership provisions (California Department of Industrial Relations, ULIC, 1947, 26; 1958, 23). On the whole, organized labor was now well established in Los Angeles, which no longer deserved its lingering reputation as an open-shop city.

In contrast to the prewar era, manufacturing had a central position in the postwar economy of southern California. In 1950, 28 percent of non-agricultural wage and salary workers in Los Angeles, and 33 percent of the city's union members, were employed in manufacturing. The figures increased somewhat with the stimulus provided by the Korean War and the consolidation of aerospace as a major industry in the region. By the mid-1950s manufacturing had stabilized at about 35 percent of L.A. nonagricultural employment and 37 percent of union membership (California Department of Industrial Relations, ULIC, 1951–57; CLSB, 1950–57).

Despite the growth of manufacturing, where the CIO was strongest nationally, the historic pattern of AFL predominance in the southern California labor movement remained intact. When the AFL and CIO merged in 1955, only 16 percent of Los Angeles's union members were in CIO-affiliated unions, about half the CIO's share of union membership in the United States at the time (29 percent), while over three-quarters (77 percent) were in AFL-affiliated unions, compared to 61 percent nationally.[11] The CIO membership that did exist in the region at this time was concentrated in industries like aircraft, autos, steel, and petroleum, as well as in communications. But the IAM, ILGWU, IBEW, and other AFL unions also had a strong presence in manufacturing (California Department of Industrial Relations, ULIC, 1956, 9), complementing the long-standing AFL dominance of the construction and transportation sectors. "In premerger terms, the Pacific Coast is predominantly AFL country," Irving Bernstein (1959, 534) wrote in 1959, adding:

> Of the 15 largest unions in California in 1957, only 2 were at one time CIO; the Auto Workers ranked 8th and the Steelworkers 10th. . . . These figures may overestimate the importance of the former CIO unions in the Pacific Coast labor movement, because much of their membership was concentrated in branch plants of nationwide steel, automobile, farm equipment, rubber, electrical and meatpacking companies. The unions that represent their employees locally, however, have looked for leadership to the centers of power in Pittsburgh, Detroit, Akron, Washington and Chicago.

Indeed, seven years after the AFL-CIO merger (in 1962), not a single official from a former CIO union held a full-time policymaking position in either the L.A. Central Labor Council or the statewide labor federation (Greenstone 1969, 146).

The Postwar Period and the Organization of Janitors

By the end of World War II, then, the industrial relations climate had been normalized in Los Angeles, which was no longer the extreme outlier it had been earlier. Employer resistance to unionism had by no means disappeared, but it was now far weaker than in the heyday of the open shop. As a result, the L.A. labor movement was poised to grow and prosper during the postwar period. Among the unions that made the greatest organizing inroads in Los Angeles in this era was the AFL-affiliated BSEIU. Nationally, the building service union's members included janitors, window washers, elevator operators, guards, and other service workers employed in apartment buildings, hotels, office buildings, and a variety of commercial establishments like theaters, bowling alleys, and supermarkets, as well as in some public-sector buildings. The BSEIU also pioneered in organizing hospital workers, who would eventually become a major part of the union's membership nationally (Fink 1977, 344–45).

In some respects the BSEIU was a typical AFL union, but its members hardly constituted a labor aristocracy. On the contrary, the union "represented what its old-timers characterized . . . as the dregs of the labor force," as Michael Piore (1994, 525) has observed. Concerned that so many of the office and apartment buildings that their members had constructed were being maintained by nonunion labor, the building trades unions had helped the janitors' organizing get started. Thus, the Plumbers' union sponsored the original petition for the BSEIU charter in 1920 (Ransom 1980, 2; see also Beadling et al. 1992, 5). "That these workers were organized at all was due to the fact that they worked in an industry in which other AFL craft unions were strong and, in the beginning at least, in which workers were, like those in the more traditional crafts, ethnic Catholics," Piore (1994, 525) noted. But African Americans were also a significant part of the janitors' union membership from the earliest period, and their representation would expand during and after World War II. Indeed, as Dorothy Sue Cobble (1997, 289) has argued, the BSEIU is a prime historical example that challenges "the standard historical portrait of the AFL as passive, stodgy, and little interested in reaching out to those beyond its ranks" (see also Jentz 2000).

The BSEIU was founded in 1921, building on the Chicago Flat Janitors' Union and a group of smaller AFL-chartered federal labor unions around the country. The Chicago apartment building janitors had been solidly organized for a decade. In 1918 they won a closed-shop agreement from the city's real estate board, and they enjoyed significant political influence in the city as well, working in close collaboration with the Teamsters and the building trades unions. Janitorial union membership in Chicago greatly overshadowed that in other cities in the 1920s, while the second-largest BSEIU local was made up of New York City elevator operators. The BSEIU had no presence whatsoever in open-shop Los Angeles in this period (Jentz 1997, 2000; Beadling et al. 1992).

After a slow start, the national union took off in the 1930s, with major strikes and organizing campaigns in New York City and San Francisco. Membership grew from ten thousand to forty thousand nationally between 1933 and 1937, mostly in New York, and then swelled to seventy thousand by 1940 (Beadling et al. 1992, 33–34). Whereas in the 1920s the building trades had helped the BSEIU get established, now it was the Teamsters who supplied the most critical support for BSEIU organizing. In both New York and San Francisco, truckers' refusal to make deliveries to buildings where janitors and other service workers were on strike helped to pressure employers into union recognition during the turbulent 1930s (Building Service Employees' International Union 1955, 53; Ransom 1980, 7).

Building on its breakthroughs in janitorial organizing in San Francisco, the BSEIU sought to extend its reach throughout California in the late 1930s. But in Los Angeles the union made little headway, except for workers covered by statewide contracts at the Fox movie theater chain and at the Bank of America (Ransom 1980, 7, 11). It did not help matters that in the late 1930s the national BSEIU fell into the hands of labor racketeers in Chicago and New York. However, after a brief reign, they were prosecuted and imprisoned, and in 1940 the union made a fresh start with a new, respectable leadership (Jentz 1997; Beadling et al. 1992). The BSEIU's representative in Los Angeles, Ray Finelli, was dismissed in May 1940. In early 1941 his replacement, John Mahoney, reported some modest success in recruiting bowling alley workers as well as in securing a contract with the American Building Maintenance company, which serviced Hollywood studio buildings (SEIU Executive Office Collection, Box 61, President [William L. McFetridge] to Ray Finelli, May 13, 1940, and John Mahoney to Paul B. David, February 11, 1941).

The BSEIU was squarely in the mainstream of AFL unionism in this period. As the union's own official narrative history (Beadling et al. 1992, 37) put it:

As an AFL member union, BSEIU had opposed the comparatively militant "pie in the sky" organizing favored by some unions, feeling that such an approach encouraged members to seek more than they could get. When some AFL unions had defected to the new and seemingly more militant CIO during the labor schism of 1935–36, BSEIU's allegiance was never in doubt. Such militance as the CIO espoused tended to confirm the public's view that organized labor could not act responsibly, McFetridge [then BSEIU president] felt, and he continued to preach a gospel of harmony between labor and management.

Like most unions, the BSEIU grew rapidly during World War II, and by 1945 its national membership had reached over 100,000. Its growth continued in the postwar years, with membership doubling between 1945 and 1950. It was in this period that the BSEIU began to make significant progress in organizing L.A. janitors and other building service workers. The union's leadership understood the strategic importance of expanding its activities in unorganized jurisdictions in the western United States. "[The] population of the U.S. is shifting to the West . . . we must organize in these places," vice president George Bradley reported to a BSEIU conference in 1946. "We are doing extensive organizational work in Southern California—it must be done to protect ourselves" (SEIU Executive Office Collection, Box 61, Conference of the International Union, October 21–22, 1946).

The L.A. organizing effort was spearheaded by Canadian-born George Hardy, whose roots were in the San Francisco janitors' union, in which his father Charles was a key leader. He was deeply influenced not only by his father but also by his firsthand observation of the 1934 San Francisco general strike, during which he was employed as a relief janitor at the longshoremen's hiring hall (Ransom 1980, 5). Hardy moved to southern California in 1946 along with three other unionists from the Bay Area to tackle the formidable task of expanding the union into the Southland. "Our Building Service 'doctors' in Los Angeles, most of whom learned medicine in San Francisco, have gone to work on the 'Openshopitis' and 'Scabitis' for which Los Angeles has so long been infamous," Hardy, who would later become the SEIU's president, boasted at the 1950 BSEIU convention. "In many instances we have found the right 'medicine' and effected cures." With the BSEIU's success in Los Angeles, he added, "have come tremendous improvements in wages, hours, and working conditions—wage increases that approximate 40 per cent during the past four years [1946 to 1950]." (Building Service Employees' International Union, *Proceedings*, 1950, 102–3).

Hardy was enthusiastic about the effort from the outset. "After looking over this town I am of the opinion it is ripe for organizing," he wrote to BSEIU president William McFetridge shortly after arriving in Los Angeles in April 1946. "I am staking all my money on it." Hardy went on to elaborate on the challenges involved:

> This city is so large, that it will take me quite a while to get rolling, so many places are two hours drive from the center of the city and contacting a few apartment janitors consumes your entire day. I feel that even with four of us from San Francisco down here, we must put on a lot more people and my budget will be rather high, but if we are to do a job, we just have to spend the money. . . . It is the best territory in the United States to tackle and if we click, we will be well repaid for our troubles. (SEIU Executive Office Collection, Box 61, George Hardy to William McFetridge, April 18, 1946)

Two months later, Hardy reported on his first victory, a contract for elevator operators and janitors at the Rosslyn Hotel obtained in cooperation with the Culinary and Hotel Service Workers' union, despite the strenuous opposition of the M&M. Although this brought only a handful of new members into the union, Hardy saw it as a major breakthrough. He wrote to BSEIU secretary-treasurer William Cooper thanking the International for its support and promised, "I am sure that once this overgrown village starts cracking, it will be well worth all the time, money and effort we are putting into it" (SEIU Executive Office Collection, Box 61; George Hardy to William McFetridge, July 11, 1946; George Hardy to William Cooper, July 22, 1946; *Service Employees News* 1, no. 2 [July 1946]: 1).

Although initially he found the going difficult relative to his previous organizing experience in San Francisco in the 1930s, Hardy's persistent efforts soon began to yield results. In 1945, just before he and his team arrived, there were three BSEIU locals in Los Angeles with about 2,800 members altogether; by 1950 there were eight locals, and membership had tripled. Expansion continued rapidly during the 1950s. Local 399, Los Angeles's flagship building service union, had 5,000 members in 1950, 7,000 in 1955, and 11,000 in 1960. By 1959 it was the second-largest local in the national BSEIU. In this period, the union also began to expand beyond building service workers, organizing in the public sector as well as among nurses and other health care workers. By 1960 the BSEIU had 20,000 members in Los Angeles, over one-third of them employed in the public sector (Beadling et al. 1992, 21, 34, 43; Building Service Employees' International Union, *Proceedings*, 1950, 10; 1955, 133; 1960, 190; Building Service Employees' International Union, *Report to Locals*, November 1950, 2).

The union built up membership in Los Angeles in the late 1940s and early 1950s primarily through a "shoe leather strategy," signing up workers in a wide variety of settings and then approaching their employers with demands for recognition and union contracts. Ever the pragmatist, Hardy used a wide variety of tactics to recruit new members. Shortly after his arrival in 1946, he reported to McFetridge:

> I am enclosing a typical picket line down here, they don't pull the people out on strike here, but the Union members down here stay on the job, and the picket line is placed outside. This way expenses are kepted [*sic*] down, no benefits are paid, and the strike is more effective but slow downs insided [*sic*] the plant. . . . It is new to me, having your people work behind your own picket lines, but it works. (SEIU Executive Office Collection, Box 61, George Hardy to William McFetridge, April 18, 1946)

Although he was open to any and all approaches to organizing, Hardy appears to have been more skeptical than many in the AFL about top-down, employer-focused methods. "Talks are going on to see if we can't work something out without trying to organize the workers," he reported in early 1947 in regard to efforts to organize hotel janitors in cooperation with the Culinary Workers. "However, these back door attempts don't usually pay off" (SEIU Executive Office Collection, Box 68, George Hardy to William McFetridge, January 11, 1947).

Early on, Hardy acquired a reputation for organizing "anything that moves." "It was almost like a religious belief," another BSEIU official later recalled. "He knew no fear, and he feared no competitors. . . . He saw organizing in everything. He supported anyone who was trying to organize." Under Hardy, the Los Angeles BSEIU cooperated with other unions, especially the Retail Clerks and the Culinary Workers, with whom they shared employers, and also leveraged Teamster support to pressure organizing targets by withholding trucking services. There were also some incidents of coercion and vandalism. "They managed through pretty much traditional efforts which involved a little strong arm stuff, maybe a few stink bombs here and there, to attract members and get some contracts going," one former SEIU official recalled. Another organizer noted that "sometimes they would load the toilets with something that turned almost to concrete" (Liebes 1998; see also Tsukashima 1998, 385–87; regarding similar tactics used by the Chicago Flat Janitors' Union, see Jentz 2000, 60).

BSEIU Local 399 recruited janitors employed in supermarkets, hotels, apartment buildings, auditoriums, YMCAs, department stores, private clubs, and hospitals, as well as those in its traditional jurisdiction in large downtown office buildings. Nonjanitorial workers were also part of the local, among them bowling alley "pin boys," pest control operatives, gardeners, and even nursery school teachers. BSEIU Local 193 also organized security guards, eventually including those employed by the Pinkerton company. Another local represented janitors and other blue-collar employees in public schools. The L.A. BSEIU negotiated dozens of contracts with a wide variety of employers in these varied settings. Hardy also exercised his entrepreneurial talents to add to the BSEIU's membership by affiliating existing independent unions, like the statewide carnival operators' union (McDermott, n.d.). The union made some early inroads into the public sector as well, even before collective bargaining rights had been established there. "We called it 'collective begging,'" one veteran SEIU officer recalled (Ransom 1980, 11; Eliaser 1998, 50–51; Building Service Employees' International Union, *Report to Locals*, various years; SEIU Executive Office Collection, Box 61, George Hardy to William McFetridge, August 6, 1946; McDermott, n.d.).

Hardy's determination to build the union in the Southland met with far less resistance from employers in this period than had been typical in the prewar years. "There was kind of a euphoric period after World War II, there were boom times, and the attitude was, 'Okay, we don't want labor war, we want labor peace,'" one SEIU official explained. "And we were in the AFL, we weren't a threat like the CIO." Indeed, although the union's organizing techniques did involve direct recruitment of rank-and-file workers, in this period it seldom mobilized them into overt displays of labor militancy. "In many cases we just went and signed up the people, then we'd go to the contractor and tell him, 'We've got your people.' And they didn't want a problem at the time," a staff member recalled. "I don't remember any big strikes."

From the start, a distinguishing feature of the Los Angeles BSEIU under Hardy's leadership was extensive reliance on research. As a former Local 399 president noted, "Most labor leaders of that day were afraid to hire as employees 'outside' educated staff," but Hardy, "realizing that if the union was to grow it would require 'mind-power' as well as rank and file 'manpower,'" recruited staff members directly from colleges and universities. "Research departments were created, and suddenly the 'Janitors' Union' had more intellectual prowess than any other union in the entire labor movement. In negotiations our research people knew more about the employers' business than they knew themselves" (McDermott, n.d., 2). Intellectuals could be found in the research departments of some CIO unions and as in-house legal counsel throughout the labor movement (see Wilensky 1956; Gray 1981), but in Hardy's BSEIU they were employed in a much wider variety of posts, even as business agents and local union presidents. In part this stemmed from the union's ambition to organize a broad swath of service occupations, in both the private and public sectors. "There were still unions that only staffed from below with limited horizons, not visions of the future or of representing everyone," one veteran staff member noted. "And then there were unions like SEIU that believed in getting trained people. It meant we got the cream of the crop." Reinforcing this practice was Hardy's strong commitment to membership education and training.

By the mid-1950s, the BSEIU had successfully organized about one-third of Los Angeles's large office buildings, according to a survey conducted by the Associated Building Managers. In this period, most building owners hired janitors and other service employees directly, rather than using outside contractors. In 1956 the same management survey found that 72 percent of the city's office cleaners, 88 percent of its elevator operators, and 76 percent of its watchmen were direct employees of building owners (Building Service Employees' International Union, *Report to Locals*, June 1956, 2). But the BSEIU also organized Los Angeles's janitorial contractors in this period, concentrating on those that were large and profitable enough to make concessions (Mines and Avina 1992, 435).

BSEIU members in Los Angeles benefited substantially from unionization. Janitorial jobs often had been structured as part-time work, but the union successfully pressed to transform them into full-time positions (Mines and Avina 1992, 436). Wages were boosted significantly, and by the mid-1950s health and welfare plans had become standard for BSEIU members in Los Angeles. For some, pension plans were added as well (Building Service Employees' International Union, *Proceedings*, 1955, 134). Wages and benefits still lagged behind New York, Chicago, and San Francisco, however, where union coverage in building services was more extensive (Building Service Employees' International Union, *Report to Locals*, October 1955, 2–3).

The BSEIU was notable for its racial and ethnic inclusiveness, a legacy that went back to the original Chicago Flat Janitors' union, in which immigrants and African Americans had been the majority of the membership and in which black leaders had been prominent from the outset (Jentz 1997, 7). Janitorial work in many of the cities where the BSEIU was strong had become an employment niche for African Americans by the 1940s and 1950s, and they were always a core component of the union's membership. In 1950 half the members of Los Angeles's main janitorial local were black, and another 9 percent were Mexican American (Greer 1959, 175).

Even more remarkably, given the long history of hostility toward Asian immigrants in the California labor movement, some eight hundred Japanese American gardeners became members of BSEIU Local 399 in Los Angeles in the early 1950s. This was an unusual case, however, in several respects. The previously independent gardeners, who had no love for organized labor, were incorporated into the union against their wishes through threats of violence, although afterward they did demand (and win) considerable autonomy within the local (Beadling et al. 1992, 41; Tsukashima 1998, 385–87).[12] This example captures the paradoxical character of the BSEIU in this period: in many respects, it was a mainstream AFL union that did not hesitate to use coercive organizing tactics, and yet its focus on "the dregs" of the labor force thrust it into direct confrontation with racial and ethnic divisions in the larger society.

Above all, the BSEIU was highly adaptable, a characteristic that would serve it well in later years, when organized labor would no longer be blessed with the favorable economic and political conditions of the immediate postwar period. Even in the 1940s and 1950s, the union was something of a hybrid, especially in California, where it flourished under the leadership of George Hardy. Under his influence, the BSEIU was also politically active in support of liberal Democrats (Greenstone 1969, 154). In this regard, and in its energetic commitment to organizing and inclusiveness, the BSEIU was often compared to the CIO, yet it was a decentralized union in which locals, as in most other AFL affiliates, enjoyed a great deal of autonomy.

In 1948 Hardy became the union's vice president for the West Coast, and later (in 1971) he was elected SEIU's International president. Unlike most of his counterparts in the CIO, Hardy from the start routinely hired "young fellas with college degrees," as a former BSEIU official recalled (see also Greenstone 1969, 154). This long tradition of hiring from out-side was among the critical factors that would later enable the SEIU to adapt more successfully than most other unions to the changing political and economic environment of the late twentieth century. The union cap-italized on the political creativity of activists formed by the protest move-ments of the 1960s and 1970s, from whose ranks the union gradually re-cruited a new generation of leaders. As Kim Voss and Rachel Sherman (2000) have shown, the role of such activists from other social move-ments was a key ingredient in the dynamic process of union innovation and revitalization that emerged in the 1980s and 1990s. The SEIU's growth in those years was also greatly aided by the fact that its jurisdic-tion coincided with the most dynamic sectors of the late-twentieth-cen-tury economy—service work, health care, and public employment. Yet the SEIU's ascent to its prominent position in the twenty-first-century U.S. labor movement also had deep historical roots in George Hardy's or-ganizing efforts in southern California in the 1940s and 1950s.

IMMIGRANTS, MINORITIES, AND UNIONISM IN LOS ANGELES

The BSEIU example already suggests the limits of the conventional dis-tinction between the AFL and the CIO in regard to the degree to which they included workers from socially disadvantaged racial and ethnic groups. To be sure, many AFL unions had a history of exclusionary be-havior that restricted access to skilled trades jobs to native-born white men. In California the AFL had a particularly notorious record of hostil-ity toward Chinese and Japanese immigrants, and although its history in relation to Mexican Americans and African Americans was more mixed, complaints had emerged from these quarters as well. The CIO in the 1930s offered an alternative, unambiguously inclusive form of organiza-tion: whereas the craft unions historically had won power by limiting ac-cess to skills to a narrow constituency, often bounded by categories like race, ethnicity, nativity, and gender, the new industrial unions aimed in-stead to recruit the largest possible proportion of the workforce in any given industry and to construct a unitary working-class identity that su-perseded all such categorical divisions (see Cohen 1990).

But the traditional dichotomy between craft and industrial unionism fails to capture the complex dynamics of labor movement activity in the 1930s and 1940s. As Cobble (1991a, 1997) and Tomlins (1979) have shown, many AFL affiliates had long since adapted their recruitment strategies to include less-skilled workers, pragmatically abandoning pure craft unionism in the face of changed workplace conditions. Our cases illustrate this process of adaptation quite well. Long before the 1930s, the Carpenters and many other building trades unions had shifted to a "craft-industrial" organizational form, taking in both skilled and unskilled workers in a wide variety of occupational categories. The Teamsters also deviated from strict craft union tradition, recruiting not only truck drivers but also warehouse workers and others in related fields. And the BSEIU, with its focus on janitorial and service occupations, from the outset focused its organizing on low-status, unskilled workers. Apart from the Carpenters and some of the other building trades unions, which recruited new workers mainly through kinship ties to their existing membership and were wary of expanding access to others (Palladino 2005, 143, 182), none of these unions excluded ethnic or immigrant workers in the period of mass union growth that began in the 1930s. In California the state Federation of Labor—then headed by Cornelius Haggerty, formerly head of the L.A. Building and Construction Trades Council—actively supported legislation prohibiting discrimination in building trades apprenticeship programs as early as 1951 (Palladino 2005, 152, 158). To be sure, unlike some of the CIO unions, the AFL's inclusionary approach was largely pragmatic and seldom part of any ideological commitment to building interracial or interethnic unity.

Mexican Americans and African Americans were the two largest non-Anglo groups in Los Angeles in these years.[13] The Mexican Americans were predominantly Spanish-speaking immigrants, although there was a significant U.S.-born group as well. In 1930 five times as many Mexican American families in Los Angeles were headed by foreign-born as by native-born persons. The native-born proportion increased over the following years, however, starting with the deportation and repatriation campaigns of the depression years and continuing until 1965, when mass immigration resumed (George Sánchez 1993, 70, 225; Laslett 1996, 63–66). By the end of World War II, Los Angeles had the largest urban population of Mexican descent outside of Mexico City, estimated at 300,000 (McWilliams 1946/1973, 316). Unlike Mexican Americans, of course, virtually all the city's African Americans were U.S.-born; and yet, because most were recent migrants from the rural South, they had much in common with their Mexican American counterparts. As Greer (1959, 21) noted, both groups were "the 'insulted and injured' who have left the land of their birth and heritage in response to the expanding economic system, the increasing wealth, of Los Angeles."

Before World War II, both African Americans and Mexican Americans were concentrated in the least desirable jobs in the regional economy. Many Mexican Americans worked in agriculture, then still the primary economic activity on much of the land that Los Angeles occupies today. Mexican American men also were employed as unskilled laborers, especially in construction, while women found jobs in domestic service and in the garment and food processing industries. Blacks were concentrated in domestic service and public-sector employment in the prewar period and were less likely than Mexican Americans to find work in construction and manufacturing (with some exceptions, like meatpacking). Opportunities expanded dramatically for both groups with the wartime economic boom, especially in defense industries. Thus, the growth of mass unionism in Los Angeles in the 1940s came to coincide with the movement of Mexican American and black workers out of agriculture and domestic service and into the mainstream of the blue-collar urban labor market.

As they began to organize in southern California during the 1930s and 1940s, AFL and CIO unions alike had little alternative but to recruit whomever employers had hired in the occupations or industries they targeted, regardless of race, ethnicity, or nativity. As Greer (1959, 29) noted, "Once men [sic] are working the union must organize them, no matter what their ethnic identification." In general, the membership composition of a given union closely mirrored that of its chosen jurisdiction, so that employers' hiring policies in the preunion era were the single most important factor determining the subsequent racial, ethnic, and national makeup of union membership.

Among our three AFL cases, only the BSEIU had an occupational jurisdiction in which African Americans were extensively employed in the nonunion era. As early as 1930, 29 percent of Los Angeles's janitors were black; the proportion rose steadily thereafter and by 1950 stood at 42 percent. African American representation in the city's trucking and construction workforce was much more modest. In 1930, 8 percent of all truck drivers in Los Angeles and Long Beach were African American. In construction, the skilled trades jobs remained overwhelmingly white preserves, but among unskilled laborers, blacks were relatively well represented. In 1940, on the eve of the industry's unionization, they made up only 1 percent of Los Angeles's carpenters and 2 percent of its painters, but they were 5 percent of cement finishers and plasterers and 10 percent of unskilled construction laborers (U.S. Department of Commerce 1933, vol. 5, 199–202; 1943, vol. 3, 244–45; 1952, vol. 2, 5-351-52).

The occupational distribution of Mexican Americans in Los Angeles overlapped with that of African Americans in some sectors, although the two groups also had separate employment niches. Because (unlike in 1930) the U.S. census did not enumerate Mexicans separately in 1940 and 1950, detailed data on their employment patterns are not available for those years.[14] Less than 1 percent of Los Angeles's janitors, and only about 6 percent of its truck drivers, were Mexican American in 1930. In the city's skilled construction jobs, Mexican Americans were also scarce, making up about 3 to 4 percent of painters and carpenters. On the other hand, about 38 percent of unskilled construction laborers were Mexican American in 1930.[15] Although precise figures are not available for the next few census years, qualitative evidence suggests that during the 1940s Mexican Americans moved into a wider range of jobs and increased their representation in sectors where they had established an early foothold.

As unionization took hold, both blacks and Mexican Americans were recruited alongside their coworkers in a wide range of occupations, more or less in proportion to their representation in employment. Greer's (1959) analysis of the ethnic composition of L.A. unions in 1950 found that blacks were 20 percent of the members of the Cement Finishers' union, 39 percent of the Laborers, 3 percent of the Painters, 12 percent of the Teamsters' warehouse division, 2 percent of the Teamsters' drivers' division, and 38 percent of the BSEIU. Greer also documented substantial Mexican American representation in union membership. Seven percent of the L.A. BSEIU, 15 percent of the Teamsters' warehouse division, and 10 percent of the Teamsters' drivers' division were Mexican American in 1950. In the city's building trades unions, Mexican Americans were still more numerous, accounting for 20 percent of the Painters, 10 percent of the Plasterers, 50 percent of the Cement Finishers, and 37 percent of the Laborers (Greer 1959, 172–73). Their inclusion in the building trades unions in this period was not entirely unprecedented: the AFL had organized Mexican American construction workers in Los Angeles before World War I, although, as with unionism generally in those years, the results proved fleeting (Arroyo 1981, 14, 22–23).

Many AFL unions in Los Angeles in the 1930s and 1940s, then, took in black and Mexican American workers in significant numbers, and in some instances their record in this regard was comparable to that of the CIO affiliates in the region. Although, among our cases, the Teamsters and building trades unions were predominantly comprised of native-born whites, even they had a significant minority of non-Anglo members by the late 1940s. Moreover, by 1950 African Americans and Mexican Americans together made up fully 45 percent of citywide BSEIU membership, and blacks alone accounted for as many as half the members in the downtown locals (Greer 1959, 172–75).

THE AFL'S DURABLE LEGACY

If the AFL unions were less exclusionary and more open to disadvantaged groups than in the standard stereotypes, they nevertheless differed from the CIO unions in several critical respects. Not only were most of them "nonfactory unions"—indeed, only 29 percent of AFL members, compared to 75 percent of their CIO counterparts, were employed in manufacturing in 1940 (Mills 1948, 61)—but also, as Cobble (1991a) emphasizes, they organized around occupational identities rather than within specific work sites or industries. To be sure, the archetypal AFL unions had originally recruited only within the most highly skilled craft occupations, most notably in the building trades. But by the mid-twentieth century this was far from typical: the AFL organized truck drivers, janitors, and many other fields along occupational lines, and in many contexts (including construction and garments) hybrid craft-industrial AFL unions had emerged.

In these less-skilled fields, where extensive training and a monopoly over skill could not be the source of union power (as was the case in pure craft unions), the AFL's occupational unions typically aspired to take wages out of competition by gaining control over the labor supply. To this end, they often succeeded in establishing hiring halls and closed-shop agreements (before the latter were made illegal under the 1947 Taft-Hartley Act). In many cases these arrangements were negotiated with local or regional employer associations (see Kennedy 1959). As Cobble (1991a, 1991b) points out, the AFL unions also elaborated rich occupational identities and cultures. They regularly monitored worker performance and disciplined members who failed to meet the standards. Another aspect of this occupational focus was the establishment of portable benefits and employment rights—in contrast to the CIO tradition of job rights tied to specific work sites.

Whereas the CIO unions tended to be centered in oligopolistic industries and mirrored those industries in their high degree of centralization, the AFL unions were typically decentralized and locally oriented—reflecting the fact that their jurisdictions were in highly competitive markets where work sites were often unstable (as in garments or construction), mobile (as in trucking), or relatively dispersed and small in scale (as in building services as well as garments). The AFL unions thus focused their organizing efforts on local (or at most regional) labor markets, and where they were successful, they became a key source of stabilization in those markets—examples of Gordon's (1994) "regulatory unionism." This approach also fostered a strong AFL tradition of local union autonomy. "The unions that have been most influential in the region have historically organized in essentially local product-market industries and have enjoyed a large measure of autonomy in relation to their internationals," Irving Bernstein (1959, 534) noted.

These unions also tended to be less "adversarial" in orientation than their CIO counterparts. They were deeply engaged in the problems of employers in their trades and mindful of the complex dynamics shaping the businesses in which their members were employed. Where they flourished, the AFL affiliates often had strong relationships with employers' associations and were in that sense quintessential "business unions." In occupations dominated by white males, like construction and trucking, where class boundaries between workers and employers were fluid, many union leaders were drawn from the more entrepreneurial and ambitious segment of the workforce. They were often politically and socially conservative, although "on the job site," as Palladino (2005, 170) notes of the building trades, "they were radicals."[16] By contrast, in low-wage AFL jurisdictions like building services and garments, where the workforce included large numbers of women and/or disadvantaged racial and ethnic groups, "business unionism" had a more progressive and yet simultaneously more paternalistic flavor. These unions relied heavily on recruiting "outsiders," many of them with extensive formal education, into the union staff and officialdom.

For both groups of AFL unions, "organizing" often focused as much on persuading employers to become part of the union as on directly mobilizing workers. The AFL also made extensive use of boycotts, secondary and otherwise. By contrast, the CIO more often focused on recruiting and mobilizing workers directly to win union recognition—initially through the mass strikes of the 1930s and later with more orderly efforts focused on the goal of winning NLRB representation elections. Both approaches were far less common in the AFL unions. Of course, they too ultimately had to engage and galvanize support from rank-and-file workers in order to succeed, but they tended to rely far more heavily on leadership-intensive strategies designed to pressure employers directly for union recognition than on bottom-up mobilization. The L.A. ILGWU in the early 1930s was an exception, perhaps because its organizing campaign took place before any cracks had been made in the city's open-shop regime, so that employer-focused tactics had no hope of success. However, within less than a decade the ILGWU's initial mobilization-based strategy was replaced by the more standard AFL focus on organizing employers.

The city's garment workforce in this period included large numbers of foreign-born Mexican Americans, and indeed, in many respects the 1933 ILGWU strike prefigured the wave of Latino immigrant organizing that would emerge in Los Angeles in the late twentieth century. By that time, the city's blue-collar workforce would be thoroughly dominated by immigrants—not only in the garment trade but also in a wide range of working-class jobs that had been native-born (and often Anglo) preserves in the earlier period of union growth. Moreover, as the next chapter documents, in all four of our cases the strength that organized labor had accumulated in the 1940s and 1950s would be deeply eroded in the 1970s and 1980s, with devastating consequences for wages, benefits, and working conditions. This transformation led native-born workers to abandon these occupations in droves, but then a new generation of unionists—again concentrated in the former AFL unions—would begin to organize the immigrants who replaced them. Faced with employers as hostile to unionism as in the open-shop era, in the 1990s these unions would engage in extensive rank-and-file mobilization among immigrants, as the ILGWU had done in the 1930s. But they would also carry forward the AFL legacy, drawing on the organizational repertoire established decades earlier. In that respect too the mid-twentieth-century L.A. labor movement was perhaps prefigurative, as Irving Bernstein (1959, 535) commented presciently in 1959:

> The development of unionism on the Pacific Coast may foreshadow the future of the American labor movement. If the latter is to continue to grow, it must penetrate those industries presently poorly organized, like trade, finance, insurance, services and government. . . . Success might lie in following the pattern that is already emerging on the Pacific Coast.

CHAPTER 2

TURNING THE CLOCK BACK: ANTI-UNION REACTION, THE RETURN OF THE SWEATSHOP, AND THE NEW IMMIGRATION

By the 1950s the labor movement in Los Angeles had expanded to the point that the city's historic reputation as a bulwark of the open shop had become anachronistic. "It is a prosperous movement," one contemporary noted, "one that has risen from the dead and today controls a substantial part of the workforce" (Greer 1959, 23). Union density in the L.A. metropolitan area reached a postwar peak of 37 percent of the nonagricultural labor force in 1955, still somewhat below the figure for the state of California that year, but comfortably above the national level of 33 percent (see appendix A and figure 1.2). "Historically, San Francisco was known as a 'union' town and Los Angeles as 'open shop,'" Bernstein (1959, 532) noted in 1959, "but this has long since ceased to be the case."

But if the city's labor movement was now normal in quantitative terms, it retained some unusual qualities, reflecting both the manner in which so much of its membership had been recruited during the 1930s and 1940s and the disproportionate weight of the AFL relative to the CIO. Organized labor in postwar Los Angeles was "a giant, whose bulk is obvious but whose effective strength remains to be determined" (Greer 1959, 23). Indeed, whether this giant could survive a serious test of its power was far from clear.

Such a test would not come for another two decades, and when it did arrive, the anti-union assault was not confined to Los Angeles but instead was national in scope. As the long postwar boom gave way to a prolonged period of economic difficulty in the mid-1970s, employers throughout the United States mounted a broad offensive against organized labor, both within the workplace and by means of public policy initiatives promoting deregulation and weakening established labor protections. In Los Angeles, as elsewhere, most unions proved to be poorly prepared for this challenge. Decades of prosperity had bred considerable complacency among labor leaders, and the bureaucratic regimes that had developed in many unions during the postwar decades were ill adapted to the suddenly transformed environment. Thus, the era of high-density unionism proved short-lived.

As early as the second half of the 1950s, union density began declining gradually all across the United States. In Los Angeles it fell from the 1955 peak of 37 percent of the workforce to 28 percent by 1970, although the absolute number of union members actually increased slightly over this period (see appendix A and figure 1.2).[1] The slippage in density during these years was largely due to expanded employment in nonunion sectors of the regional economy. The decline continued in the 1970s and 1980s; by then, erosion of union strength in industries where organized labor had once been firmly established was a more important contributing factor. Starting in the late 1970s, a massive corporate anti-union offensive combined with deregulation began to push private-sector unionization into a free fall. As figure 2.1 shows, during these years Los Angeles devolved once again into a citadel of the open shop, although this time it was hardly exceptional, as the wave of deunionization that began in the early 1970s left few regions of the United States untouched.[2]

All four of our cases were severely affected by these transformations. In the L. A. garment industry, unionism had always been somewhat tenuous, and erosion began far earlier than in the other cases. By the mid-1970s, the once-substantial unionized sector of the city's garment trade already had dwindled into virtual insignificance, and sweatshop conditions had reappeared even as Los Angeles was emerging as the nation's largest garment manufacturing center. With its classical cutthroat competition, intensified by layers of subcontracting that forced small subcontractors as well as workers themselves to absorb market risk, the nonunion garment industry effectively became a template for the new organizational forms that began to develop in other sectors of the regional economy as deunionization spread.

FIGURE 2.1   Union Density in Los Angeles, California, and the United
States, 1970 to 1987

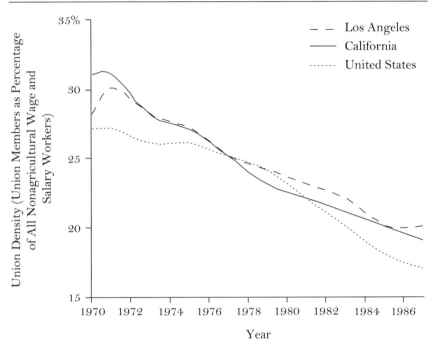

Source: See appendix A.

The next among our cases to undergo restructuring along these lines
was the residential construction industry, where union density declined
precipitously in the face of a vigorous employer attack starting in the
mid-1970s. During the economic recovery that followed the recession of
the early 1980s, residential construction in southern California was reconstituted on an entirely nonunion basis, with dramatic effects on wages
and benefits, and there was some modest erosion of union density in commercial construction as well. Meanwhile, the Teamsters' once-solid
strength among truck drivers at the Los Angeles–Long Beach port collapsed almost overnight as deregulation swept the industry in the early
1980s, and sweatshop-like wages and working conditions soon became
the norm among the independent contractors who took over the industry. Janitorial work also was deunionized in Los Angeles during the
1980s as rapid metropolitan growth and changing real estate ownership

patterns spurred extensive restructuring of employment arrangements in building services.

Labor costs make up a large proportion of total costs in all four of these industries, and as soon as the union-based system taking wages out of competition collapsed, cutthroat behavior and the intensive forms of labor exploitation classically associated with it rapidly reemerged. In all four cases, fringe benefits and job security evaporated along with the union wage premium, and previously stable jobs soon were replaced by a variety of casual, "contingent" employment arrangements. Under the newly fashionable banner of flexibility, labor practices of questionable legality began to flourish. Reports of all-cash wage payments, lack of overtime compensation, substandard pay for "training periods," and the like became commonplace in all four industries (as well as in others not examined here). What emerged was closer to nineteenth-century traditions of sweated labor than to the post-industrial model that was so widely touted in this period as a humane alternative to the old manufacturing-centered order, itself predicated on extensive unionization and government regulation.

Many commentators have linked the wave of deunionization that swept across the United States in this period to deindustrialization, itself a product of capital's enhanced ability to relocate operations offshore, especially in once-"basic" industries like auto and steel manufacturing. However, none of these four cases conforms to this model. Trucking, construction, and building services are all nontradable, place-bound industries, in Los Angeles as elsewhere. Even in garments, the local dynamic was one of deunionization without deindustrialization: although huge numbers of U.S. garment jobs were moved offshore during these years, at the same time the garment industry was expanding rapidly in Los Angeles, which soon became the nation's largest clothing production center. These data thus support Michael Goldfield's (1987) argument that the key dynamic driving union decline in this period was neither deindustrialization nor job relocation offshore, but a broader shift in the power balance between labor and capital.[3]

During this period of large-scale restructuring, Los Angeles's population, and with it the city's economy, continued to grow rapidly. This vigorous expansion provided a safety valve for unionized workers as their once-desirable jobs suddenly deteriorated. Rather than trying to swim against the tide of union decline, many simply moved horizontally into other high-wage (and in many cases still-unionized) positions.[4] Often once-unionized workers could do this without even changing their occupation. Thus, construction workers migrated from the residential sector of the industry into the booming (and still largely unionized) commercial sector; truckers moved from local, short-distance jobs to long-haul work in which unions were hanging on and conditions were better; and janitors moved from the private to the still-unionized public sector. Those able to make such transitions were overwhelmingly native-born workers, and except for janitors, many of whom were African American, most were "Anglos."

As these developments unfolded, Los Angeles became a magnet for the new immigration that gathered speed starting in the late 1960s. When native-born workers abandoned their formerly unionized jobs in such industries as trucking, residential construction, building services, and garments, employers turned for replacements to the vast new supply of foreign-born workers, mostly from Mexico and Central America. In garments, immigrants had always been a significant part of the labor force, but now they came to dominate it completely. And during the 1980s residential construction, local trucking, and private-sector janitorial work also became immigrant employment niches.

Thus, in an extraordinarily brief period, these four industries were utterly transformed. In all four, unionism was effectively destroyed, generating a precipitous decline in wages, fringe benefits, and job security—which in turn sparked an exodus of native-born workers. Latino immigrants eagerly filled the void even as employment arrangements rapidly devolved. First, in the garment trade, the virtual disappearance of union regulation together with growing reliance on a vulnerable immigrant workforce led to the revival of classic sweatshop conditions. In the residential building trades, labor recruitment, formerly organized by the unions, was increasingly taken over by opportunistic "labor barons" with ready access to newly arriving immigrants. Trucking at the port was restructured as an independent contracting system, and immigrant owner-operators, paid by the truckload rather than by the hour, poured into the field. In janitorial work, contract-cleaning firms—freed of union restrictions—increasingly turned over labor recruitment and management to Latino foremen and crew leaders.

Initially, the unions affected by these rather dramatic transformations offered surprisingly little by way of response. To make matters worse, despite the fact (documented in some detail later in this chapter) that de-unionization generally *preceded* the influx of foreign-born workers, many L.A. union leaders blamed the new immigrants for the decline of organized labor's influence. Attempts to organize the burgeoning immigrant workforce were few and far between, although this would change in the late 1980s and 1990s. Most veteran unionists viewed such organizing as extremely difficult, if not impossible, especially among the many immigrants who lacked legal documents. As a result, the demographic transformation of the workforce in those industries where unions once had been solidly entrenched became a convenient justification for labor's passivity, and the radical restructuring of work in all four of our cases proceeded unconstrained by any serious resistance from organized labor. By the late 1980s, it was difficult to imagine that these industries once had been union strongholds, with stable jobs, high wages, and extensive fringe benefits. Yet that had in fact been the situation in the immediate aftermath of the Second World War.

THE DECLINE OF ORGANIZED LABOR IN LOS ANGELES

After a decade of rapid growth, unionization in Los Angeles leveled off in the late 1940s, and organized labor entered a period of consolidation and relative stability. During the 1950s and early 1960s, overall union density in the city hovered in the 30 to 33 percent range. In some industries, however, most importantly construction and transportation, virtually all workers were organized. In 1955 there were 133,100 building trades union members in the L.A. area, nearly equal to the number of wage and salary workers (139,800) employed in the construction industry that year. Similarly, ten years later there were 119,200 union members, *more* than the number of workers (104,200) in the L.A. construction industry at that time (California Department of Industrial Relations, ULIC, 1956, 12, 41; 1966, 21; CLSB, 1965).[5] In southern California during the 1960s and 1970s, all drywallers in commercial construction and about 80 percent of those in residential were unionized. As one contractor recalled in an interview, "Back then, if you weren't union, you didn't work." Trucking also was unionized "wall to wall" in Los Angeles in the 1950s.[6] The trucking firms that serviced the Los Angeles–Long Beach port, in particular, were all under contract with the Teamsters. "You had to be union to get in on those docks," one trucker recalled.

Unionization was never so extensive in the building service or garment industries, but in both, organized labor had captured a substantial share of the market by the 1950s. A 1956 management survey found that service workers in 35 percent of Los Angeles's major office buildings were unionized (Building Service Employees' International Union, *Report to Locals,* June 1956, 2). Local 399 of the BSEIU had over 7,000 members in 1957, about half of whom were employed by building maintenance contractors (3,225) or directly by office building owners (385), while another large group (1,050) cleaned theaters and supermarkets (SEIU Research Department Historical Files Collection, "Local Composition Form," July 24, 1957). The BSEIU continued actively organizing L.A. building service workers for another decade, and by the late 1960s most janitors cleaning large office buildings in the downtown area were unionized, as were many of those cleaning buildings in outlying areas (Mines and Avina 1992, 435–36).

In the garment industry, union penetration was always more limited, yet by present-day standards the postwar years were the glory days. The ILGWU's L.A. membership peaked in 1950; in 1953 the union still claimed nearly ten thousand members in the city—nearly half the workforce in the women's garment industry (Laslett and Tyler 1989, 119). Two years later a state union membership survey found that 39 percent of the city's textile and apparel workers were organized (California Department of Industrial Relations, ULIC, 1956, 12, 25). "Even now when I walk around in downtown Los Angeles, I can show you where all the big manufacturers were," a garment union official recalled. "They used to be union, union, union . . . and now it's almost nothing."

Although there was considerable variation in pay rates by industry, union members consistently garnered substantially higher pay than their nonunion counterparts. In construction, a master labor agreement governed wages in this period. For drywallers, rates were high (nine cents per square foot installed), and the Carpenters' union carefully monitored building sites to ensure that premium rates were paid for especially difficult jobs, as the master contract required. Building trades workers also enjoyed extensive fringe benefits, including pensions, health insurance, and paid vacations. "For every dollar that we paid a man, we were paying another sixty-five cents between the taxes and the benefits and the workers' comp," one drywall contractor recalled. "Most of it was in the union benefit package." The union also trained drywall workers in a two-year apprenticeship program and ran hiring halls on which many employers relied for their labor supply.

In trucking too wages were impressive in this period. Nationally, truckers' average earnings were 38 percent higher than those of workers in manufacturing as late as 1980 (Perry 1986, 49); at the Los Angeles–Long Beach port during the 1960s and 1970s, truckers earned even more than the famously militant longshore workers with whom they interfaced daily. Although they were exempt from the minimum-wage and overtime provisions of the Fair Labor Standards Act, since the vast majority of truckers were Teamsters' union members in this period, they were protected by contractual rules governing hours and pay practices. They were paid by the hour and guaranteed forty hours' work per week. The union contracts also provided extensive fringe benefits, including paid holidays, paid vacations, health insurance, seniority rights governing layoffs, recalls, and shift preferences, as well as grievance procedures and other dispute resolution mechanisms.

Building service workers never earned as much as those in construction or trucking, but by 1975 unionized janitors in Los Angeles averaged $3.75 an hour—double the rates paid a decade earlier and well above the minimum wage (then $2.10)—and wages continued to rise over the next few years by about 50 cents an hour. In response to BSEIU demands, the city's cleaning contractors also had agreed to employ janitors on a full-time basis, rather than maintaining the part-time arrangements that had prevailed during the preunion era. Janitors' fringe benefits included eleven paid holidays, full medical coverage (Mines and Avina 1992, 436), and access to grievance and arbitration procedures. Even in the garment industry, workers in the unionized sector (mostly those making high-end tailored coats and suits) earned relatively good wages, with regular raises, and had union-managed health and pension benefits (International Ladies' Garment Workers' Union, GEB, 1974, 164).

By any standard, then, the L.A. labor movement was in relatively good health during the early postwar decades. Organized workers enjoyed high wages, fringe benefits, job security, and decent working conditions, and unions had established an array of administrative practices to support and maintain those arrangements. The one sign of trouble was the gradual decline in union density that was already under way by the late 1950s. The absolute number of union members in Los Angeles continued to grow, rising to over eighty thousand between 1955 and 1970, but the proportion of workers unionized fell sharply over this period (see appendix A and figure 1.2). This was largely because union recruitment failed to keep up with the expansion of the labor force (as was also the case at the state and national levels) in the most dynamic sectors of the economy. But as table 2.1 shows, previously unionized sectors also underwent deunionization in this period. The timing varied, but there was deterioration across the board.

The decline of union density was especially dramatic in the garment industry, where unionization had always been relatively tenuous. By

TABLE 2.1   Union Density in Los Angeles, 1955 to 1985, Selected Industries

	1955	1965	1975	1985
Construction				
Union members	133,100	119,200	89,500	70,400
All wage and salary workers	139,800	104,200	96,300	119,900
Union density	95%	100+%	93%	59%
Transportation and warehousing				
Union members	68,900	74,100	73,700	56,600
All wage and salary workers	75,700	84,800	105,800	124,000
Union density	91%	87%	70%	46%
Apparel and fabricated textile products				
Union members	16,100	11,700	9,800	7,900
All wage and salary workers	42,700	49,400	63,500	84,600
Union density	38%	24%	15%	9%
All manufacturing				
Union members	267,000	268,500	235,800	168,800
All wage and salary workers	696,400	759,400	766,100	900,700
Union density	38%	35%	31%	19%

Sources: California Department of Industrial Relations, ULIC and CLSB, various years; California Employment Development Department, CLMB, various years. All data are for July of the year indicated.

1974 the ILGWU claimed only 4,788 members in Los Angeles, half the number it had declared twenty years earlier (International Ladies' Garment Workers' Union, FSR, 1974, 228). As table 2.1 shows, in the city's apparel industry unionization dropped sharply in *absolute* terms between 1955 and 1985 even as employment grew rapidly. The result was dramatic: whereas in 1955 union density in the L.A. apparel industry had been equal to that in manufacturing as a whole, twenty years later it had dropped to less than half the level in manufacturing.

In construction, union membership had slipped to 93 percent of wage and salary employment by 1975, down from over 100 percent a decade earlier.[7] Indeed, by 1985 density would fall to only 59 percent. Nationally, construction was an early battleground in the broad corporate assault on unionism that would come to full fruition in the late 1970s and early 1980s. As Marc Linder (2000) has shown, the gains made by the building trades unions in the 1960s, taking advantage of the tight labor market of the Vietnam War years, generated a fierce backlash from employers (see also Palladino 2005). That backlash led in turn to the sharp slippage in union density in Los Angeles's construction industry between 1965 and 1985 (see table 2.1).

In the transportation and warehousing sector, union membership increased slightly in absolute terms in Los Angeles between 1955 and 1975, but density fell from 91 to 70 percent. Nonunion trucking had expanded gradually all over the United States during these years. The legal prohibition on secondary boycotts under the Taft-Hartley Act of 1947 and the Landrum-Griffin Act of 1959 made it difficult for the Teamsters to organize the new nonunion carriers, while rapid increases in union wage levels in this period deepened trucking employers' motivation to avoid unionization and helped stimulate increasing use of owner-operators (Levinson 1980, 135–39). As in construction, the decline that began in this period accelerated sharply in the 1980s, so that union density had fallen to only 46 percent by 1985—half the level of thirty years before.

Building services was a partial exception to the general deunionization trend of this period. No precise union density data are available for L.A. janitorial workers in this period, but the available evidence suggests that it was on a different timeline from the cases shown in table 2.1. By 1973 the flagship SEIU local in Los Angeles, Local 399, had nearly tripled its membership over the 1957 level. Much of this growth was due to extensive new organizing among hospital workers, but the local also had 5,300 members in its building maintenance division in 1973 (up from 3,225 in 1957) and another 2,000 or so performing janitorial jobs in supermarkets, industrial facilities, and other commercial buildings (SEIU George Hardy Collection, Box 42, Folder: "Local 399 June–July 1973." "Breakdown of Local 399 Membership by Division," July 31, 1973). Deunionization would come to building services eventually, but the process seems to have begun a decade or so later than in the cases shown in table 2.1.

Even in the fields where a drop in density was palpable over the 1955 to 1975 period, however, a sense of crisis in labor's ranks was conspicuously absent, both in Los Angeles and nationally. That would not change until labor's power came under direct and sustained attack throughout the private sector during the late 1970s and especially in the 1980s. Despite the gradual erosion of union density that began in the late 1950s, complacency was the order of the day, so that labor leaders were woefully ill prepared to respond to the more daunting challenges that emerged in the late 1970s and 1980s.

Yet the roots of the crisis that finally came to a head in those years lay buried in earlier developments. Beneath the apparent stability of the immediate postwar period lay a variety of managerial efforts to restore the pre–New Deal order. The backlash began with the 1947 Taft-Hartley Act, which rolled back many of the gains labor had made over the preceding decade, and with the McCarthy-era purges, which eliminated many progressives from union leadership in the late 1940s and early 1950s. Management in the United States had never fully accepted organized labor's legitimacy and actively sought to limit union power even in the mid-twentieth century, when density was at its peak (Harris 1982; Lichtenstein 2002). Still, until the late 1970s the material gains that labor had made in earlier decades were largely preserved within the unionized sector, even as that sector steadily declined in importance relative to the workforce as a whole.

By the 1980s, however, some of the nation's most powerful and high-profile unions had suffered massive membership losses, and even in settings where they were able to hold on to their members, they had been forced to make extensive concessions. In the manufacturing sector, as plant closings devastated whole communities, the erosion of union power was especially dramatic and attracted extensive public attention around the nation. But deunionization was not simply a by-product of deindustrialization. Indeed, in Los Angeles, as table 2.1 shows, manufacturing employment actually *increased* between 1975 and 1985, yet union density within that sector fell precipitously. And the broad anti-union offensive targeted not only manufacturing but many other sectors (among them, construction, transportation, and services) where capital lacked the ability to shift operations around the globe. At the same time, carefully coordinated, highly successful business efforts to dismantle the structures of governmental regulation that had been established in the 1930s and 1940s also contributed to the decline of organized labor.

DEUNIONIZATION WITHOUT DEINDUSTRIALIZATION IN THE LOS ANGELES GARMENT INDUSTRY

Among our four cases, the only one in which operations can be relocated easily is garment manufacturing. Indeed, starting in the 1970s, domestic employment in this industry declined sharply as apparel production increasingly was shifted offshore. This in turn led to rapid erosion of union strength in the industry, a trajectory that conforms to the conventional wisdom linking globalization to deindustrialization and deunionization. But in contrast to the United States as a whole, in Los Angeles garment industry deunionization was accompanied by massive employment *growth.* Even as apparel makers were fleeing the more highly unionized East and Midwest, Los Angeles developed into the nation's largest garment production center, supplying the growing West Coast retail market as well as meeting increased national demand for casual clothing.

Labor unions often benefit from employment growth in sectors where they have established a foothold, but that was not the case in the postwar L.A. garment industry. On the contrary, the ILGWU, the union whose jurisdiction (women's clothing) was in the most rapidly growing segment of the local industry, steadily lost ground in the postwar years. Its share of all wage and salary workers in the L.A. apparel sector plummeted from 32 percent in 1950 to 11 percent in 1971 and continued to fall after 1971, both in absolute and relative terms, as table 2.2 shows. By 1992 the ILGWU's membership had fallen to only 2 percent of the city's apparel workforce.[8] Even that figure may overstate the presence of unionism in the industry, for by 1992 the ILGWU's L.A. membership included workers in a wide variety of industries.

In the same period, garment industry employment took off in Los Angeles. Between 1971 and 1992, the number of garment workers there nearly doubled, in sharp contrast to New York City, where it fell by over one-third during those years (Nutter 1997) and where, by the late 1990s, 30 to 40 percent of the industry was still unionized (Levitan 1998, 60). By this time, Los Angeles had replaced New York as the nation's largest garment production center (Bonacich and Appelbaum 2000, 16–18). But unlike New York, where the unions managed to retain a significant (although shrinking) presence, in Los Angeles the industry expanded on an entirely nonunion basis.

In the U.S. garment industry, and above all in its burgeoning L.A. branch, recent decades have witnessed the revival of low wages and sweatshop conditions reminiscent of those that flourished a century ago. Directly paralleling the union's decline, U.S. apparel workers' earnings fell dramatically, from 85 percent of average weekly wages for manufacturing workers in 1947 to 55 percent by the early 1980s (Ross 2004, 98). In the absence of effective governmental regulation—or as Robert Ross (2004, 147) puts it, after three decades of "unilateral disarmament in the fight against labor lawbreakers"—and with unionism rapidly evaporating, legally mandated minimum-wage and overtime pay requirements soon came to be honored in the breach rather than the observance. For

TABLE 2.2   ILGWU Membership in Los Angeles, 1947 to 1992

Year	ILGWU L.A. Membership	Total ILGWU Membership (U.S. and Canada)	L.A. Members as Percentage of Total ILGWU	Wage and Salary Workers in L.A. Apparel and Textile Products Industry	L.A. ILGWU Members as Percentage of L.A. Apparel Workers
1947	9,646	379,197	2.5	NA	NA
1950	12,165	422,510	2.9	38,300	31.8
1953	9,912	430,830	2.3	42,400	23.4
1956	9,342	445,093	2.1	42,600	21.9
1959	9,246	442,901	2.1	42,300	21.9
1962	7,661	443,122	1.7	46,300	16.5
1965	6,287	442,318	1.4	49,400	15.5
1968	5,865	451,192	1.3	50,800	11.5
1971	6,217	442,333	1.4	55,500	11.2
1974	4,788	428,734	1.1	67,800	7.1
1977	3,958	365,346	1.1	74,100	5.3
1980	3,700	340,951	1.1	75,200	4.9
1983	3,232	282,559	1.1	73,200	4.4
1986	2,985	219,001	1.4	81,200	3.7
1989	2,046	165,170	1.2	92,200	2.2
1992	2,114	137,315	1.5	98,800	2.1

Sources: International Ladies' Garment Workers' Union, FSR, various years; California Department of Industrial Relations, ULIC and CLSB, various years; California Employment Development Department, CLMB, various years. Employment data are for July of the year indicated.

the same reasons, working conditions deteriorated rapidly as well. The health insurance and other fringe benefits that the ILGWU had won for its members in an earlier era are nowhere to be found in the vast nonunion sector of the industry today. As early as 1980, a detailed study of Hispanic garment workers in Los Angeles found that the vast majority were undocumented immigrants, 39 percent of whom were paid less than the minimum wage. Overtime pay violations were common, and few workers had fringe benefits of any kind. Less than 5 percent of this group were offered employer-provided health insurance, and only 6 percent had paid sick leave (Maram 1980, 31–35).

Government inspections, similarly, have uncovered extensive labor law violations in the L.A. garment industry. A 1994 study based on random inspections of California garment shops by a team of federal and state investigators found over half in violation of minimum-wage laws, while over two-thirds failed to comply with overtime pay laws. Fully 90 percent of the shops surveyed had violated health and safety regulations, including a few especially egregious cases where fire exits were locked or blocked. Record-keeping violations were documented in 73 percent of these shops, with 30 percent found to be illegally paying workers in cash. Illegal industrial homework (typically associated with child labor) was distributed by 15 percent of the factories surveyed, and investigators found a few cases of child labor in the shops themselves as well, with thirteen-year-olds working nine-hour days. This study was statewide in scope, but it "found the most widespread abuses in Los Angeles and Orange counties" (Silverstein 1994, D1). Subsequent investigations have found similarly extensive legal violations (for a summary, see Ross 2004, 31–32).

By the 1980s and 1990s, then, subminimum pay levels had become standard practice in the L.A. garment industry. Occasionally, far more extreme complaints surfaced. In some instances, workers simply were not paid at all: after weeks of work with wage payment deferred, their shop would unceremoniously close and the owner would disappear (Bonacich and Appelbaum 2000, 182; Soldatenko 1992, 271–74). The most spectacular example of such abusive practices was the slave labor operation discovered in El Monte (just east of Los Angeles) in 1995, where seventy-two Thai garment workers were found sewing clothes for up to eighteen hours a day in a small apartment building enclosed by barbed wire and patrolled by armed guards (Su 1997).

The apparel industry, with its extensive reliance on subcontracting, is in some respects a paradigm of "flexible production." In garment manufacturing, however, contracting out is hardly a recent innovation. "The apparel industry . . . has used contracting out for decades and has developed this flexible production system to a fine art," Edna Bonacich and Richard Appelbaum (2000, 12) observe. For more than a century, indeed, the industry has relied on extensive subcontracting chains that force small employers as well as workers themselves to absorb market risk— always high in this industry given the ever-fickle whims of fashion. Cutthroat competition has long prevailed among the subcontractors who handle the cutting and sewing that is the industry's lifeblood. In turn, subcontractors have relied consistently on piecework pay systems to transfer market risk to workers (simultaneously minimizing the costs associated with low productivity, a chronic problem in this low-wage, high-turnover industry).

Historically, these dynamics have combined to encourage sweated labor in the garment trade—a tendency that has been curbed only episodically, either by unionization extensive enough to take wages out of competition and/or by effective regulatory measures that mandated minimum wages and maximum hours and banned industrial homework. As early as the 1930s, when both unionization and regulation were on the rise, manufacturers and contractors in New York City, the garment industry's historic center, responded by relocating production to lower-cost areas in the Northeast. Later, as unions successfully organized workers in that region, U.S. clothing production increasingly moved south and west, and ultimately offshore (Waldinger 1986, ch. 3).

The shift in the domestic industry's center of gravity from New York, where as late as the mid-1990s a significant share of apparel production remained unionized, to Los Angeles, where the union presence is virtually nonexistent, highlights the importance of deunionization in the recent deterioration of wages and working conditions. It is no accident that illegal sweatshop employment practices have been especially widespread in Los Angeles, where governmental regulation was never as institutionalized as in New York. Although the New Deal–era national regulatory laws are still on the books, enforcement has declined sharply in recent decades. As Michael Piore (1997, 140) observes, "The return of the sweatshop in recent years thus appears to be primarily the product of the decline of government regulation and diminishing union strength."

Globalization adds to the downward spiral as U.S. garment contractors are increasingly pitted against competitors in countries where wage standards are far lower. The ever-present threat of capital mobility also makes it difficult for workers to organize or otherwise challenge low pay or sweatshop conditions. However, globalization offers at best a limited explanation for the deterioration of conditions in the industry over recent decades. For one thing, offshore garment manufacturing mostly involves segments of the industry suited to long production runs, for which demand is relatively predictable, whereas more fashion-sensitive items are often still produced domestically (Bonacich and Appelbaum 2000). Ironically, although basic wages are higher in the United States, sweatshop conditions may be *more* widespread in the highly decentralized domestic industry than offshore, where mass production in large factories is more common, facilitating both state regulation and the recently established "monitoring" systems that are meant to provide a check on at least the most egregious labor rights violations.

Perhaps the best evidence that globalization and enhanced capital mobility are not the primary forces driving the deterioration of the pay and working conditions of U.S. workers in recent decades is the fact that in many nonmobile industries, where offshore production is not an option, sweatshop conditions similar to those in the garment trade also emerged in the 1970s and 1980s. A case in point is the construction industry—like apparel, a sector where subcontracting has a long tradition and cutthroat competition has historically flourished in the absence of unionism.

THE ANTI-UNION OFFENSIVE AND CASUALIZATION IN CONSTRUCTION

As Linder (2000) has shown, the national corporate anti-union assault generally associated with the 1980s was foreshadowed by developments in the construction industry during the Vietnam War years. Building trades union wage demands escalated in the late 1960s, stimulated by low unemployment in the absence of wage and price controls. In response, the nation's major construction firms, along with their largest industrial customers, launched a full-scale anti-union offensive in the early 1970s. Nonunion "merit shop" contractors began aggressively bidding on jobs, not only in suburban and southern markets where unions were weak but in highly unionized areas as well. They benefited from new construction technologies that facilitated the employment of fewer skilled workers, as well as a key NLRB decision in 1973 that sanctioned the use of "double-breasted" firms—that is, those with both union and nonunion subsidiaries (Palladino 2005, 176). As the recession of the mid-1970s further weakened labor's bargaining power, the open-shop firms boldly underbid their unionized competitors and increasingly put the building trades on the defensive. The unions responded by reopening their contracts and "giving back" some past gains, paving the way for the broader wave of concession bargaining in basic industry that rippled across the nation in the 1980s.

The employers' attack on the building trades unions proved extremely effective. Nationally, union density in construction was cut in half between 1970 and 1990, falling from 42 to 22 percent; the residential sector was particularly hard hit (Allen 1994, 426). A key player in the open-shop offensive was the Associated Builders and Contractors (ABC), whose largest chapter was in Los Angeles (Galenson 1983, 381; Bourdon and Levitt 1980, 114–16). Indeed, the ABC explicitly targeted Los Angeles as the "proving ground" for its deunionization efforts; by the late 1970s, some three hundred contractors in that city had withdrawn from collective bargaining agreements and announced plans to subcontract work to nonunion firms (Palladino 2005, 185).

Construction in Los Angeles had been completely unionized in the mid-1960s, and density remained high through the late 1970s (see table 2.1). As a Carpenters' union official declared in 1969, "There isn't a nail driven in this area that isn't driven by a union man with a union card in his pocket" (Haggerty 1976, 25). By 1987, however, the last year for which such data are available, union density in construction had plummeted to only 53 percent (California Department of Industrial Relations, ULIC, 1989, 28). The turning point was the deep recession of the early 1980s, when the building industry came to a virtual standstill. During the subsequent recovery, it became obvious that the open-shop sector had gained the upper hand: a 1984 survey found that nonunion general contractors accounted for three-fourths of residential and one-third of commercial and industrial construction in the eleven-county southern California region (Berkman 1986).

The open-shop movement was orchestrated by the industry's big players; smaller contractors often preferred to remain in the union fold as long as they could. "There's no union contractor I know of that by choice would go open shop for the hell of it," the president of the Associated General Contractors stated in 1981. "It's a lot easier for him to stay union as long as he can compete," since the union provides a reliable supply of trained workers and sets uniform wage scales. "But the minute he starts to lose work and his business is threatened, he will go double-breasted or open shop. That's all there is to it. He has to" (*Engineering News-Record* 1981, 26). Indeed, as the nonunion sector grew, "the prices dropped out from underneath the union contractors," one employer recalled in an interview, "and so they were unable to compete. . . . Some double-breasted and went nonunion, but most of them went out of business." The open-shop contractors initially profited handsomely by bidding against union firms, but once the union sector had shrunk, they were increasingly squeezed by competition from other open-shop operations.

Initially, the unions offered little resistance to this shift, especially in the residential sector. "Residential construction was not a primary battleground between unions and antiunion employers, but rather was abandoned to nonunion employers by default," Linder (2000, 180) concludes. The AFL-CIO's national Building and Construction Trades Department did launch a pilot organizing campaign in 1978 that focused on Los Angeles and claimed some success (Palladino 2005, 185–88). Yet there was significant reticence about this effort on the part of many of the local unions in the region. Insofar as the unions maintained their grip on commercial construction in the region, many local union leaders did not perceive the triumph of the ABC-led open-shop movement in the residential sector as a major threat, especially in cases where their members readily found new work in the burgeoning commercial sector. "In the 1980s, we had tremendous growth in the commercial industry," a local union official recalled in an interview. "We were building twenty-, thirty-story buildings. It was just work for us, and that's all we cared about. [Residential] is a lost industry, we'll just concentrate on commercial."

Not surprisingly, deunionization led to rapid deterioration in wages, conditions, and benefits, especially in the residential sector. Pay rates were cut by as much as half over the course of the 1980s, overtime work remained common but was rarely properly compensated, and fringe benefits became a distant memory. "Once the union was actually broken out of the business," a contractor frankly stated, "these guys were taking a screwing, it was as simple as that." A variety of unscrupulous and illegal practices that had been relatively rare in the union era began to emerge as competition among contractors increasingly spun out of control. Reports surfaced of workers being paid on an all-cash basis, and there were even some accounts of payment in drugs. At a 1988 hearing, a union contractor laid out the economic logic of payment in cash to the Orange County Human Relations Commission as follows:

> The average $10-an-hour employee may take home $8 out of that $10 that he earns after the taxes and the FICA and so on is deducted. Well, the typical cash-paying employer will say, "Look, I'll pay you $8.50 in cash, you're going to be $.50 better off." That saves him $1.50 right off the bat. That's just the tip of the iceberg. What else is he saving? He saves all his share of the payroll taxes that go on top of that: workers' compensation insurance and the other legal requirements, easily another $2.50. By not putting this work on the books, he's saving his obligation to the State and Federal taxes that he owes, easily another $1.00. You're talking $6.00 an hour in savings. I want to ask any subcontractor out there if he can work on 60% of his labor payroll. . . . Obviously, you cannot compete with him. (Orange County Human Relations Commission 1989, 16)

This type of cost-cutting was especially common in the labor-intensive drywall and carpentry trades. "The carpenters is typically where contractors are really going to try and cheat," one unionist explained:

There's so much man-hours concentrated in the average stick-built job on carpenters, that's where they can chop the dollars out of a job. In other words, "Let's make a decision, we won't cheap it on the electricians and the plumbers, that's where we get our lawsuits flowing from, and if those things go wrong, you got a problem. But who knows bad drywall? Who knows the framing doesn't have enough nails in it?" you know. That will pass inspection now anyway, inspectors are getting looser. So they take a big hit.

Under these conditions, union workers began to leave the residential trades; indeed, most never returned after the 1980 to 1982 recession.

With the union increasingly out of the picture, employers transferred the tasks of labor recruitment, training, and deployment to a cadre of "labor barons" (also known as labor brokers, coyotes, contratistas, or patrons) who replaced the union as a source of labor supply. These were Latino entrepreneurs, experienced craft workers themselves, who moved into the vacuum created by the union's collapse and began to recruit immigrant workers into the industry, drawing on extensive social and kinship networks in the immigrant community. "They [immigrant workers] didn't speak English, or very little," one contractor explained in an interview.

You had the rise of the Hispanic that was bilingual, was a little sharper than the rest of them, and he very quickly realized that he could put himself in the position of being a labor baron and not have to touch a tool and make a lot more money than anybody working. So he was the guy that would contact the drywall contractor and say, "Gee, I control fifty drywall hangers, you know. I'll run your work for you." . . . I have no respect for them [labor barons]. They cheat their people, they cheat the drywall contractor, they cheat everybody. In many cases they will add people to the payroll that don't even exist, just put dead men on the payroll. And then they just take the check down to the local check cashing place where they'll cash anybody's check and, you know, pay the small fee, and they'll cash five or six checks in different names. Other times they'll have guys take a check for x number of dollars, cash the check, and give them back a certain amount of it in cash. It's very hard to control. Obviously we cannot follow a man down to cash his check and make sure he puts the money in his own pocket.

A union staffer described similar abuses that became common in this period:

> They were controlling pools of thirty and forty people, living off
> these guys. They would give them twenty, thirty bucks a day. They
> could get away with this, because in Mexico you're lucky if you were
> making $30 a week. And to come here and make $30 a day, you're a
> king, you know. And some of these patrons had a big house and he
> had them live with him and he'd charge them rent. So he's whacking
> 'em twice. He charges 'em gas to go to work and he charges 'em for
> living with him.

Like sweatshops in the garment trade, the labor baron system in construction was not entirely new: such arrangements had been common in
the preunion era (see Montgomery 1987, ch. 2) and had persisted on the
margins of the industry later on, even when the workforce was largely
native-born and white (see Haber 1930, 217, 511). But in the 1980s, with
the virtual collapse of the union and the ensuing shift to immigrant labor,
such practices once again became pervasive in the mainstream of the residential construction industry. And changes in U.S. immigration policy—specifically the introduction of employer sanctions in 1986—would
soon make this type of subcontracting even more attractive to employers
(Massey, Durand, and Malone 2002, 120–24).

The whole setup had many advantages from the contractors' point of
view. Not only were they spared the tasks of labor recruitment, but all
the headaches of union work rules, grievances, and bureaucratic bottle-
necks were now gone, costs were lower, and market risks were external-
ized. As a contractor explained, "If you're going to bid so much money to
do an operation and you don't use a labor baron, and you pay out these
dollars, you may run over cost. Where if you just put it out as so much
money and let them worry about getting it done, you've already locked in
your margin."

In an industry where labor accounts for more than half of total production costs, the potential savings to employers from this set of arrangements were enormous. To be sure, with the labor barons acting as middlemen, the contractors themselves became increasingly "disconnected
from the people that were actually doing the work," as one put it in an interview. But a more flexible system of labor deployment was difficult to
imagine, and it quickly became institutionalized once unionism was effectively eliminated from the residential sector of the industry. Even as employers benefited, workers paid a heavy price for this new regime. Not
only were their earnings sharply reduced, but they also were forced to absorb the industry's market-related risks to an unprecedented degree,

without any of the advantages previously secured by unionism. Residential construction, then, like the garment industry, had effectively reverted to the age of cutthroat competition and to a system predicated on the ability to exploit cheap, "flexible," nonunion labor. Similar changes were brewing in other industries as well.

DEREGULATION AND THE RESTRUCTURING OF TRUCKING

The same neoliberal business interests that helped orchestrate the open-shop offensive within the construction industry also lobbied successfully to reconfigure the nation's political and legal environment during the 1970s. Among the most far-reaching of the changes they were able to put into place was deregulation, most notably in the transportation and communications sectors. In the case of trucking, deregulation had devastating effects on workers, directly undermining organized labor's previous gains, reducing wages sharply, and setting in motion rapid devolution of working conditions at the micro level. The systems of worker recruitment, compensation, and deployment were radically transformed as much of the trucking industry came to resemble what Michael Belzer (2000) has aptly labeled "sweatshops on wheels."

Advocates of trucking deregulation included the National Association of Manufacturers (NAM) (also a major player in the earlier effort to de-unionize the construction industry) and the major industrial shippers. Their initial successes took the form of a series of administrative actions in the late 1970s and then culminated in the Motor Carrier Act of 1980, the key legislation deregulating the trucking industry. The advocates of deregulation explicitly targeted unionism as an obstacle to market efficiency. It is noteworthy, however, that trucking employers, along with the Teamsters' union, strongly opposed deregulation (Moore 1986, 17–18).

With deregulation, along with rising fuel costs and the deep recession of the early 1980s, "trucking changed from an almost completely unionized industry, following a centrally-bargained pattern, to a partially unionized industry" (Belzer 1994, 260). Unionization fell from 60 percent of the nation's truckers in 1980 to only 25 percent by century's end (Belzer 2000, 21, 28). The decline was especially rapid in the early 1980s, by one estimate falling by half between 1981 and 1985 alone (Rose 1987, 1162; Perry 1986, 110). Even within the segment of the industry that remained unionized, wages and benefits were deeply eroded by national-level concession bargaining in the early 1980s, while many employers dropped out of the national master freight agreements entirely, extracting even greater givebacks at the local level (Rose 1987, 1157).

As in construction, union decline proceeded unevenly: while unions retained a foothold in long-distance trucking, many other segments of the industry—among them the short-haul trucking that served shippers in the massive Los Angeles–Long Beach port—soon became dominated by nonunion owner-operators who labored long hours for relatively low pay without any of the extensive fringe benefits that had once been standard features of Teamster contracts.

With wages no longer taken out of competition, "low wages, long hours, and unsafe and unsanitary working conditions have returned to trucking" (Belzer 2000, 7). As deregulation advocates promised, ground shipping prices did decline as the basis of competition in the industry shifted from quality of service to price. But the vast bulk of these savings—an estimated 80 percent (Belzer 2000, 45)—came not from increased efficiency but instead from sharply reduced wages and the elimination of fringe benefits. Costs and risks were increasingly transferred to workers in the deregulated environment as small firms contracting work out to owner-operators began to replace the larger, unionized trucking companies that had once dominated the industry.

The segment of the trucking industry servicing the port of Los Angeles and Long Beach followed this pattern to the letter. Prior to deregulation, a few large firms had dominated drayage in the harbor area, and virtually all their employees had been represented by the Teamsters. After 1980, however, midsized and small companies began competing for the work. As a trucking firm executive explained:

> In 1980 a lot of middle- to upper-management employees of trucking companies lost their jobs because their companies went out of business. So they decided, "Hmm, I'll just start hiring owner-operators, independent contractors, and I'll get myself a license to operate and I'll cut the going rates by twenty percent." With deregulation, you could start a trucking company and operate out of a phone booth. All these people needed—the entrepreneurial people here—was "How do I get enough drivers to buy enough trucks?" Used trucks, actually, because they put them all in used trucks, okay?

At the same time, and paralleling developments in the construction industry, the large unionized firms soon began "double-breasting"—in other words, setting up nonunion subsidiaries—and they also encouraged workers to become independent contractors. The idea of being an owner-operator had widespread appeal. "You had people coming into the industry who saw this as an opportunity," one trucker recalled. "They thought, 'Hey, I'll be my own boss!'. . . So everybody got their trucks. Everybody's mother got their trucks." As a trucking executive noted, this arrangement also had considerable appeal for employers:

> The advantage of the owner-operator independent contractor for a company who hires those drivers is that it becomes a non-asset-based company. They do not own the equipment. They do not have employees that they have to guarantee work for. And if that employee doesn't have work, you're not responsible for unemployment insurance and so forth, because he's not an employee, okay?

Thus, the large unionized firms rapidly disappeared from the harbor. The Teamsters did attempt to reorganize port truckers in the early 1980s under these changed conditions, but after a few years they abandoned the effort.

The rates paid by steamship companies to have cargo containers trucked from the harbor to various local destinations fell sharply with this transition—by as much as half, according to some industry insiders. These savings came largely at the expense of the truckers themselves, who now were paid by the load rather than hourly and who received no income while they waited for work, often for as long as half a day, in huge lines at the shipping terminals. "They would contract that particular work out to a driver, and he would be paid a set amount of money for taking that can [freight container] from Los Angeles to the harbor," a former union truck driver recalled. "Whereas [before,] we got paid for dead time, we got an hourly rate. [After 1980,] we just couldn't compete. We were getting chewed up. I mean, why am I going to pay a union carrier x amount of money when I could get a guy for half the amount?"

Although costs for shippers definitely declined, far from illustrating the virtues of unfettered market competition, the harbor trucking industry in the aftermath of deregulation stands out as a spectacular example of the *inefficiencies* that can result. Trucking congestion has grown steadily worse with the rapid increase in the volume of goods flowing through what is now the nation's largest port and is a grave concern for shippers, trucking employers, and drivers alike. But despite periodic appeals for rationalization (especially a centralized dispatching system), market anarchy persists. The deregulated industry depends largely on the exploitation of truckers themselves, who are forced to absorb the costs of inefficiency in the form of unpaid hours spent waiting for jobs.

As independent contractors, the drivers also bear most of the market risks. They not only absorb all the costs of owning and maintaining a truck but also are vulnerable to unpredictable fluctuations in fuel prices, fines for overweight containers, and other such factors entirely beyond their control. The health insurance, pension plans, sick pay, and paid vacations that unionized truckers enjoyed before 1980 have since become a distant dream. Once they have purchased a truck (which involves monthly loan payments as well as insurance, repairs, fuel, and so forth), most owner-operators find that they can make ends meet only by working excessively long hours, often compromising safety in the process. Even with the long hours, by the mid-1990s port truckers' net incomes had declined to about $20,000 a year once they had met all their expenses. In this regard, they are like truck drivers in the nonunion sector nationally, who, as Belzer (2000, 152) reports, typically earn little more than the minimum wage.

At the Los Angeles–Long Beach port, many trucking firms have been accused in recent years of taking advantage of immigrant drivers with limited proficiency in English and imposing hefty charges for liability insurance, workers' compensation, and other such items as payroll deductions, even though the workers are owner-operators (Mongelluzzo 1994). Some trucking companies depend on Latino middlemen, who play a role similar to that of the labor brokers in the construction industry— recruiting immigrant drivers and assisting them in purchasing trucks, obtaining insurance, and so forth, in exchange for a substantial portion of their pay.

Like their counterparts in the garment trades and residential construction, today the trucking firms—and more importantly, their clients, the commercial shippers and retailers who dominate the port—obtain highly flexible labor at greatly reduced costs under this new regime. Immigrant truck drivers, nominally independent contractors but tied to their de facto employers through elaborate arrangements that involve loans, insurance, and other business necessities, absorb the costs of the new flexibility, with Latino middlemen often acting as exploitative intermediaries. Far from the post-industrial utopia imagined by apostles of the new economy, trucking deregulation has instead heralded a return to classic sweatshop conditions.

"FLEXIBILITY" AND RESTRUCTURING IN BUILDING SERVICES

Deunionization began somewhat later in building services than in our other cases. The janitorial membership of SEIU Local 399 in Los Angeles had climbed steadily over the postwar period, reaching five thousand by 1978, and SEIU also had a large and rapidly growing membership among L.A. hospital workers. Wages for the city's unionized janitors attained an all-time high of $12 an hour in 1982, accompanied by extensive fringe benefits. The 1980s brought an office building boom to Los Angeles in the aftermath of the recession that opened the decade, a context in which janitorial unionization might have been expected to further expand and prosper. Instead, by 1985 Local 399's building service membership had fallen to a mere eighteen hundred workers, only about 8 percent of the city's growing janitorial workforce. The union contract signed in 1983 included major wage concessions, part of a desperate effort to hold on to the remaining membership in building services (Mines and Avina 1992, 435–37).

The combination of the expansion of the nonunion sector and concessions in the union sector sent real wages for the city's janitors into a tailspin: they fell 36 percent from 1983 to 1988 alone (Bernstein 1989). Total office space in Los Angeles doubled over the decade that ended in 1994, but the number of janitors increased by only 25 percent (Service Employees International Union 1995, 11). Thus, janitors found themselves cleaning more space for less pay. The result was a sharp decline in cleaning costs, which fell from $1.87 per square foot per year in 1979 for the city's downtown buildings to $1.08 in 1993 (in constant dollars), even as cleaning contractors' revenues rose (Service Employees International Union 1995, 10).

For firms that specialize in janitorial services, direct labor is the single largest component of total operating costs—over 50 percent for the larger cleaning contractors, which enjoy economies of scale on overhead and other expenses (Building Service Contractors' Association International 1995, 19). Thus, in contrast to industries like garment manufacturing, where it is the small enterprises that have the greatest incentives to reduce labor costs, in building services the very largest firms are in such a position. In the 1970s and 1980s, as national and even international firms came to dominate the building service industry, efforts to cut costs by avoiding the influence of the union began to emerge. Nonunion build-

ing maintenance firms surfaced in Los Angeles in the 1970s, undercutting the unionized cleaning contractors with discounted prices, especially
in outlying areas of the city. As the nonunion sector grew, it put growing
competitive pressure on the unionized firms, whose costs were inevitably
higher. As early as 1971, the president of one major union firm complained to Local 399:

> We have a serious problem in the city of Los Angeles. It is growing
> in intensity and becomes more alarming every week. I am referring
> again to nonunion competition over which, it appears, the union has
> no control. So that makes two of us. We have estimated that we have
> lost about $1,000,000 a year to non-union competitors. (SEIU
> George Hardy Collection, Box 41, Folder: "Local 399, Aug. 1971," A.
> H. Wittenberg Jr. to Michael McDermott, July 30, 1971)

Foreshadowing later developments, the nonunion cleaning companies
were already beginning to hire immigrants in the 1970s and were "dele-
gating a great deal of decision-making power to Hispanic crew leaders,
who typically recruit, hire, fire and pay workers" (Mines and Avina 1992,
432; see also Johnston 1994, 160).

Entering the market for office cleaning requires minimal capital, and
indeed, there are many small "mom-and-pop" companies in the business.
But precious few owners of major buildings are willing to entrust their
valuable properties to such firms. Rather, they tend to contract with the
larger, more reputable companies. After a group of midsized, nonunion
cleaning firms aggressively moved into the market in the late 1970s and
early 1980s, disrupting the old equilibrium whereby unionization had
taken wages out of competition, more and more of the unionized firms set
up nonunion "double-breasts." Faced with this, Local 399 was forced to
grant concessions to hold on to its remaining janitorial membership, by
now reduced to a hard core in downtown Los Angeles.

The union did launch some efforts to organize the new nonunion firms
in the early 1980s but made little headway. Even when the SEIU was able
to win NLRB elections among janitors (it won three between 1981 and
1985), its organizing efforts were constantly stymied: building owners
could simply terminate their contracts with the newly unionized cleaning
firm (such contracts typically have thirty-day cancellation clauses) and
arrange to obtain the needed services from a nonunion firm instead
(Mines and Avina 1992, 438; Waldinger et al. 1998, 105). The strike
weapon was also undermined. As one Local 399 staffer put it, "We used

to walk out to settle our differences, but now if we go out, we don't get back in" (Mines and Avina 1992, 439).

Freed of the constraints that had accompanied unionization, cleaning contractors increasingly turned over responsibility for hiring and firing and for managing day-to-day operations to first-line supervisors. As in the construction and trucking cases, Latino intermediaries now emerged as key players, prized for their ability to tap into and control the immigrant labor supply that rapidly came to dominate the janitorial workforce. And as in those other cases, the absence of union regulation combined with a relatively informal, decentralized form of management soon gave rise to unscrupulous and often illegal practices that exploited the vulnerability of the new immigrant workforce.

In mid-2000, the *Los Angeles Times* labor reporter Nancy Cleeland (2000b) wrote a detailed exposé of such practices in one segment of the janitorial industry: the nonunion subcontractors hired to clean supermarkets and other large retail establishments:

> He works the midnight shift seven nights a week, stripping, waxing and buffing the floors. . . . He says he earns far less than the minimum wage, and just laughs when asked about overtime pay for his 56-hour weeks. Strong chemicals make his nose bleed, burn his fingers and eat the soles of his cheap sneakers. He operates powerful, potentially dangerous machines but isn't protected by workers' compensation insurance. . . . Not only are many janitors earning subminimum wages—about $550 to $750 twice a month for 56-hour weeks—they are also untaxed. Typically paid in cash or personal checks, with no deductions for Social Security, Medicare or federal and state income tax, they are part of a thriving underground economy that robs billions of dollars from U.S. and California treasuries every year. . . . [None of the workers interviewed] could name the company for whom they worked. They knew only the subcontractor, who showed up twice a month to pay them in personal checks. They told of wrapping steel wool pads around their sneakers when stripping floors, to keep from slipping on the slick chemicals. They told of weeks they went unpaid, of arbitrary schedule changes.

Another case that came to public attention involved an office cleaning company firm that pleaded guilty in court to failing to pay overtime and keep legally required records. One of the employees involved complained that he was forced to work up to nineteen hours without a break and was paid neither the minimum wage nor overtime (Fausset 2001).

One common practice in the nonunion sector of the industry was to demand that newly hired janitors turn over their first month's pay to the supervisor to secure their jobs. Some supervisors reportedly extracted sexual favors from female janitors on the same basis. Health and safety protection was nonexistent for janitors working with dangerous chemicals and heavy machinery, and unpaid overtime was common (Gardetta 1993, 17). One janitor told the *Los Angeles Times* that he had worked for five weeks full-time for no pay, in a "training program." After that, when he refused his supervisor's demand of a $150 payoff out of his first paycheck to keep the job, he was summarily fired (Ybarra 1988).

Cynthia Cranford (2001, 97) describes other employment practices, most of them illegal, used by cleaning firms:

> Working for more hours than one was paid, and earning less than the minimum wage, was very common in this industry and was achieved in multiple ways. Cleaners often worked by the piece, rather than by the hour. . . . Cleaners were also encouraged to bring family members to "help" with the work without being paid. And many janitors worked for weeks without pay, to "practice" in order to get a "recommendation." . . . Cleaners were also pressured to prepare their supplies before they clocked in and to work different split shifts, clocking in under different names at each shift. Cleaners were often paid in cash or by personal check in order to avoid detection of such violations [and] to avoid having to pay social security.

Thus, in janitorial work, as in the other three cases, classic sweatshop conditions became endemic in the wake of deunionization. In addition to earning sharply reduced wages and seeing fringe benefits disappear, janitors were subjected to a variety of illegal and highly exploitative practices, similar to those facing garment workers, residential construction workers, and others in the deregulated, nonunion, low-wage labor markets of Los Angeles—labor markets increasingly dominated by foreign-born workers.

INCORPORATING IMMIGRANT LABOR

Workers and union officials, as well as less self-interested commentators, have sometimes attributed the precipitous decline of unionism that took place in Los Angeles during the late 1970s and early 1980s to the increased availability of "cheap" immigrant labor. In this view, a large influx of foreign-born workers—particularly those with limited education who find employment in relatively low-skilled jobs—inevitably depresses wages, especially for the less-educated and for ethnic and racial minorities. The economist Vernon Briggs (2001, 174), for example, argues that "unskilled and poor" immigrants, "by their presence . . . impoverish similarly situated native-born workers and their families in the same local labor markets." George Borjas (1999, 82–85) offers a more nuanced analysis but comes to essentially the same conclusion, attributing a large share of the recent growth in U.S. income inequality to immigration. Noting that the sharp decline in union density took place in the very same period as the surge in immigration, Briggs (2001, 175) extends the argument to suggest that "the revival of mass immigration is likely to be a contributing factor to the decline in unionism."

The strong correlation between declining union density and increasing immigration since the mid-1960s does not, however, mean that the causal arrow should be drawn in the way that these commentators presume. On the contrary, there is evidence to suggest that it operated in precisely the opposite direction: that deunionization—which, as we have already seen, typically leads to deterioration in wages, benefits, and working conditions—provokes native-born workers to abandon no-longer desirable jobs, at which point immigrants then fill the vacancies. That is precisely what appears to have happened in the four cases examined here. Apart from the qualitative evidence summarized earlier, the timing of the immigrant influx, considered alongside selected comparisons between the labor market in Los Angeles and in other parts of the United States, provides support for this interpretation.[9]

When deunionization took off in the late 1970s and 1980s, it affected many parts of the United States that lacked any significant supply of immigrant labor. California generally, and Los Angeles in particular, attracted a disproportionate share of the immigrants who arrived in this period; most of the rest were concentrated in a few other regions (Portes and Rumbaut 1990, 34–42; Massey, Durand, and Malone 2002, 59–60, 106–7, 126–27). But union decline, and the accompanying deterioration in compensation and working conditions, was by no means confined to such immigrant-rich labor markets. That fact already casts doubt on the notion that the increased availability of immigrant labor was an important cause of deunionization.[10]

Moreover, in some areas of the United States where a large supply of immigrants *was* available in this period, such as New York City, union decline was relatively modest in some of the very same industries where rapid deunionization had radically transformed labor conditions in Los Angeles. In the janitorial case, for example, deunionization was geographically uneven: the SEIU was able to maintain its grip on building services in its historic strongholds of New York, Chicago, and San Francisco, even as it collapsed in Los Angeles and several other cities. But immigrants moved into the New York metropolitan area's building service workforce to almost the same degree as they did in Los Angeles. By 1990, 57 percent of New York City's janitors were foreign-born, compared to 64 percent of those in Los Angeles.[11] Yet because the vast majority of both native- and foreign-born janitors in New York were union members, in 1990 they earned $7,000 more annually than their Los Angeles counterparts (Waldinger et al. 1998, 108). The influx of immigrants in this case had no apparent effect on the strength of the union.

Similarly, immigrants made up 68 percent of the workforce in the New York City garment industry by 1990 (compared to 81 percent in Los Angeles).[12] By then, the garment unions already had been greatly weakened by the wave of outsourcing that shifted production from New York to other parts of the country (especially Los Angeles) as well as abroad, but most of the garment workers who remained employed in New York were union members. In 1989 the ILGWU had seventy thousand members in the city (Freeman 2000, 308), compared to two thousand in Los Angeles (see table 2.2), and most of them were employed outside the garment industry. At this time, moreover, Los Angeles was already overtaking New York in the overall level of garment industry employment (Bonacich and Appelbaum 2000, 17–18; Levitan 1998, 24). Thus, as in the janitorial case, it is difficult to sustain a claim that immigration led to union decline.

In construction and trucking, meanwhile, union decline was under way on a national scale at a time when immigration was still highly concentrated in a few gateway cities. In the case of construction, as discussed earlier, rapid deunionization began in the 1970s and accelerated in early 1980s. At this point, however, major urban immigrant receiving areas like New York and Chicago were *more* likely to retain a significant union presence, relative to the Sunbelt or the booming suburban and exurban areas, where immigration flows had not yet appeared. Moreover, the construction workforce was surprisingly stable in terms of race, ethnicity, and nativity during these years. Nationally, 90.6 percent of unionized construction workers were white in 1977–78, and the figure was only slightly lower—89.0 percent—in 1989. In the nonunion sector too, whites made up 91 percent of the workforce at both the beginning and end of this period of rapid union decline (Allen 1994, 415).[13] These data are difficult to reconcile with the hypothesis that immigration was a key force driving union decline.

In the trucking industry, similarly, there was minimal change in the ethnic and racial makeup of the workforce at the national level prior to the dramatic deunionization that followed deregulation in the 1980s. In 1970, 80.9 percent of truckers in the United States were native-born whites; in 1980, the figure was virtually unchanged at 81.0 percent. Only *after* 1980 did immigrants (as well as African Americans) enter trucking in significant numbers (see table 2.3 and appendix B).[14]

Foreign-born workers did pour into the labor market in all four of the L.A. cases examined here. Yet the timing of this transition from native-born to immigrant employment suggests that the immigrant influx was more a *consequence* than a *cause* of deunionization. As the collapse of union power removed the floor under wages and opened the door to the super-exploitative employment practices documented earlier, many native-born workers left for greener pastures, whereupon immigrant workers moved into the newly vacated positions.

Table 2.3 shows the growth in the immigrant share of the L.A. work-force for all four cases from 1970 to 2000, drawing on U.S. census data. In the trucking and drywall occupations, immigrant Latino employment rose modestly from 1970 to 1980, but after 1980 it skyrocketed—that is, *after* the unions had effectively collapsed (owing, as already discussed, to deregulation in trucking and the recession of 1980 to 1982 in construction). Significantly, total employment in both these fields expanded rapidly in the 1980s, with nearly all the growth occurring among foreign-born Latinos.

The influx of immigrants into Los Angeles's trucking and drywall jobs was even more extreme in the sectors where the immigrant organizing efforts of the 1990s occurred, namely, residential drywalling and port trucking. Unfortunately, the U.S. census data on which table 2.3 draws cannot be disaggregated to this level of detail. However, virtually all my informants noted that in Los Angeles's commercial construction industry, where unionism remained largely intact, the immigrant presence was minimal in the 1980s, while in the residential sector, where unionism had evaporated entirely by the end of the 1980 to 1982 recession, the work-force rapidly became dominated by Latino immigrants during the 1980s. The 40.2 percent figure in table 2.3 for foreign-born Hispanic drywallers in 1990 includes both commercial and residential construction and thus

TABLE 2.3 Employment in Selected Occupations in the Five-County Los Angeles Area, by Race, Ethnicity, and Nativity, 1970 to 2000

Occupation	1970	1980	1990	2000
Drywallers				
Native-born white	77.5%	68.1%	42.9%	24.1%
Foreign-born white	3.2	2.9	1.7	0.5
Native-born black	3.2	3.2	1.7	2.3
Native-born Hispanic	9.7	12.9	11.9	14.9
Foreign-born Hispanic	**6.4**	**9.0**	**40.2**	**55.7**
Other	0.0	3.9	1.7	2.5
Population estimate	3,107	6,204	10,843	6,758
Truckers				
Native-born white	72.3%	60.2%	43.8%	32.4%
Foreign-born white	3.1	3.3	3.8	3.0
Native-born black	6.4	8.8	7.2	6.7
Native-born Hispanic	11.9	14.3	14.5	15.8
Foreign-born Hispanic	**4.6**	**10.5**	**26.1**	**34.5**
Other	1.7	2.9	4.6	7.6
Population estimate	74,862	100,947	138,275	150,722
Garment workers				
Native-born white	24.3%	15.8%	11.3%	6.2%
Foreign-born white	10.2	4.2	2.6	1.8
Native-born black	10.3	3.7	2.0	0.9
Native-born Hispanic	14.1	9.2	5.0	5.6
Foreign-born Hispanic	**32.6**	**55.1**	**65.3**	**63.2**
Foreign-born Asian	5.4	10.0	12.3	19.4
Other	3.1	2.0	1.5	2.9
Population estimate	39,094	64,573	88,146	82,442
Janitors				
Native-born white	46.7%	34.9%	18.5%	12.6%
Foreign-born white	5.3	4.1	2.3	1.5
Native-born black	24.0	15.8	7.3	5.2
Native-born Hispanic	11.8	11.6	9.3	11.3
Foreign-born Hispanic	**10.3**	**28.9**	**56.2**	**63.4**
Other	1.9	4.7	6.4	6.0
Population estimate	31,794	46,519	63,844	68,037

Source: U.S. Census Bureau, integrated public use microdata series (IPUMS), version 3.0. For 1970: 1 percent form 1 metro sample; for 1980 and 1990: 5 percent state sample; for 2000: 5 percent census sample. All estimates are calculated using person-level weights. In all cases except trucking, the data are for wage and salary workers in the labor force only (trucking includes the self-employed) for the five-county Los Angeles metropolitan area (Los Angeles, Orange, Ventura, Riverside, and San Bernardino Counties), except for 1980, which also includes Imperial County. Because of significant changes in the industry and occupational classification systems in 1980 and in 2000, all estimates have been adjusted to reflect the most recent (2000) U.S. census classification system. See appendix B for more details on the data and methodology. Thanks to Christine Schwartz for meticulous research assistance with this data analysis.

Note: The categories "white" and "black" include only non-Hispanics.

greatly understates the change for the residential sector. Similarly, the 26.1 percent figure in table 2.3 for the immigrant Latino proportion of truckers in 1990 includes all types of trucking in the L.A. region, whereas by all accounts the immigrant influx was far greater among the short-haul truck drivers working in the harbor area than in the industry as a whole.

In short, even if the availability of a vast pool of immigrant labor accelerated the shift to low-road employment practices, the timing for both construction and trucking in Los Angeles suggests that immigrant employment was more a consequence than a cause of the change. The garment and building service industries present a more complex picture, however, for in both there was significant employment growth among Latino immigrants (and in the garment case among Asian immigrants too) before 1980. In the garment industry, this growth probably reflects the fact that the deunionization process began far earlier than in the other cases and was in fact virtually complete by 1980 (see tables 2.1 and 2.2). Here, as in drywall and trucking, the extensive entry of immigrants into the field took place *after* the unions had been crippled; the only difference was that both processes took place at an earlier time. As table 2.3 shows, as late as 1970 nearly half (48.7 percent) of the L.A.-area garment workforce was made up of native-born workers (half of them non-Latino whites), a surprisingly high figure given the industry's traditional reliance on immigrant labor in a wide variety of times and places.

The janitorial case is the most ambiguous of the four, since deunionization of this industry occurred somewhat later than in the other cases. Yet, as table 2.3 shows, there was substantial growth in immigrant janitorial employment in greater Los Angeles as early as the 1970s. Although it is difficult to be certain, the most likely explanation is that the early immigrant influx reflected the initial emergence of the nonunion sector during the 1970s. As noted earlier, unionized building service employers had complained about being undercut by nonunion contractors as early as 1971. The qualitative evidence also suggests that new nonunion contractors relied on immigrant labor from the outset, especially in outlying areas of this sprawling metropolis (Mines and Avina 1992, 429, 439). If this interpretation is correct, the data in table 2.3 may simply reflect the fact that the nonunion sector of the building service industry was already substantial in the five-county L.A. area by 1980, even if the collapse of janitorial unionism in the downtown core would not become apparent until the 1983 collective bargaining round. In any event, after 1980 the immigrant influx accelerated rapidly, even in the janitorial case.

Figure 2.2 summarizes the data on the growth of immigrant Latino employment in these four occupations, comparing Los Angeles to the United States as a whole. In all four cases, the increase in immigrant employment occurred earlier and was more extensive in Los Angeles than in the nation as a whole. This is not surprising, given Los Angeles's prominence as a premier immigrant gateway city and the later dispersion of immigrant flows into more and more parts of the United States (see Massey, Durand, and Malone 2002, 126–28; Frey 2002). And this comparison further reinforces the point about the relative timing of deunionization and immigration, since by the time immigrants became a significant presence in the nation as a whole, union decline was already ancient history.

By century's end, then, low-wage immigrant Latinos made up the majority of workers in all four of these occupations, a dramatic change that took place in only two decades (although the specific timing varied among the cases). Indeed, once employers began to hire immigrants, their numbers grew rapidly, thanks to the resilient social and kinship networks on which employers typically relied for recruiting new workers (See Waldinger and Lichter 2003). "It was like an atomic explosion going on," one residential construction contractor told us. "I mean, one guy would get in and he'd bring two or three relatives, make a crew, and then one or two guys would split off that crew and make two new crews, and before you know it, you had this huge amount of people here." More generally, the supply of immigrant labor was plentiful and growing. As one building service executive boasted, "We could get 150 Mexican workers in 24 hours" (Mines and Avina 1992, 432).

As Douglas Massey and his colleagues (2002) have shown, the wave of new legislation that began in 1986 with the Immigration Reform and Control Act (IRCA), despite its announced intention of restricting immigration, instead had the opposite effect, leading to growth and stabilization of the immigrant labor supply. Moreover, they argue, "the post-IRCA regime of immigration enforcement lowered wages and working conditions . . . exacerbating income inequality, encouraging subcontracting, and generally promoting the informalization of hiring" (Massey, Durand, and Malone 2002, 126).[15]

Employers rapidly came to view immigrants as highly desirable workers. "You know, the good old days of the Anglo-Saxon worker, there were good sides to it and there were bad sides to it. Communication was good. Work ethic was bad," one drywall contractor declared:

FIGURE 2.2 Immigrant Latino Employment in Selected Occupations, Los Angeles and the United States, 1970 to 2000

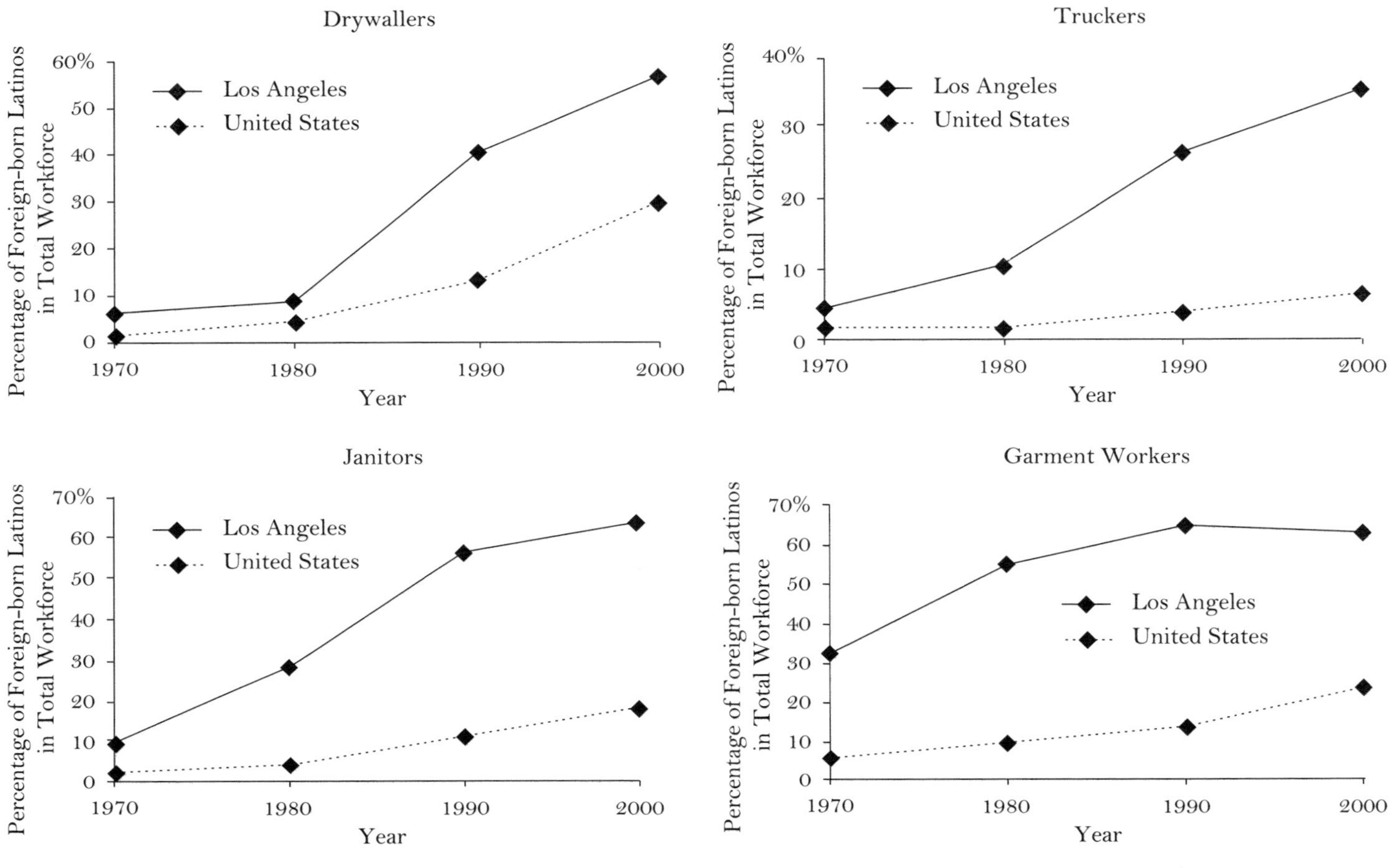

Source: U.S. Census Bureau, integrated public use microdata series (IPUMS), version 3.0. See table 2.3 and appendix B for details.

The drywall trade, being a piecework operation, it has always been a haven for people who cannot get to work at eight o'clock every day. The white guys, you had no communication problem. But unfortunately, there was a higher-than-desirable percentage of the alcoholics, the drug users, the problem personalities. When John Smith wanted to show up at nine, ten o'clock and then miss two days during the week, the Hispanics were there wanting to work. Willing to work. Showing up early. Working all day. Drug use is almost nonexistent. Drinking on the job—in the drywall trade they like their beer, but generally speaking, you don't find them drinking during working hours, and they don't stick around the jobs and drink. Those two issues I think are much better under Hispanic labor than they ever were under the white Anglo. A lot of the so-called white Anglos that worked in the trade, not all of them, but a great percentage of them, were not the most desirable. So you really got the bottom of the work status in the white Anglos. Where in the Hispanic, you're getting mainstream, you're getting more of the family-oriented. For them, it was a good job. It was a much better job than picking strawberries. So you got a better class of worker.

Managers in other immigrant-employing industries expressed similar views. "If I could find another labor force as reliable . . . as Mexicans, I would use it," an executive in the building service industry declared in the early 1990s. "But I can't." And a manager at a unionized janitorial firm complained, "There are plenty of people on the union benches, but they are rejects" (Mines and Avina 1992, 433; see also Waldinger and Lichter 2003).

Thus, all four of these occupations were radically transformed in the final decades of the twentieth century. In an earlier era, thanks to unionization, native-born white male truckers and construction workers with limited formal education had won high wages, extensive fringe benefits, and good working conditions. Garment and janitorial workers were several notches below those labor aristocrats on the occupational ladder, a status reflected in their greater internal diversity, with many more women as well as African Americans and Latinos. But even their jobs had provided superior wages, benefits, and working conditions in the glory days of organized labor in Los Angeles.

In the 1970s and 1980s, however, everything changed. Employers relentlessly attacked unionism and extracted cost savings and "flexibility" from the workforce—both directly by means of wage and benefit cuts and indirectly by introducing new organizational forms that forced workers to absorb more market risk. In all four of our cases, wages fell sharply, fringe benefits evaporated, and working conditions deteriorated, in many instances reaching scandalous levels reminiscent of pre–New Deal sweatshops. Faced with these circumstances, native-born workers began to abandon these fields, and immigrants from Mexico and Central America rapidly replaced them. Upper-level managers looked the other way while the Latino "labor barons" and supervisors to whom they had transferred responsibility for labor recruitment and management engaged in a variety of unsavory and often illegal labor practices. The immigrant newcomers at first appeared—to friend and foe alike—willing to tolerate the various forms of exploitation that were rapidly becoming standard practice in all these occupations. Virtually no one expected them to mount an organized response. Yet starting in the late 1980s, they would surprise everyone by doing precisely that.

CHAPTER 3

ORGANIZING THE "UNORGANIZABLE":
IMMIGRANT UNIONIZATION AND LABOR
REVITALIZATION IN THE 1990S

"Next to the abundant economic opportunities available to wage earners in this country, immigration has been the factor most guilty of the incohesiveness of American labor," Selig Perlman (1928, 168) wrote in his classic 1928 treatise on the labor movement, adding:

> To workers employed in a given industry, a new wave of immigrants, generally of a new nationality, meant a competitive menace to be fought off. . . . For, by the worker's job consciousness, the strongest animosity was felt not for the employer who had initiated or stimulated the new immigrant wave, but for the immigrants who came and took the jobs.

In keeping with this long historical tradition, the initial response of unionists to the foreign-born workers who poured into Los Angeles's newly restructured industries and occupations during the late 1970s and early 1980s was openly hostile. They saw the new arrivals as excessively docile, compliant, and uncritical of low wages and degraded conditions—a threat to the standards that organized labor had won at great expense in earlier years. Despite the fact that, as the last chapter showed, employer-driven deunionization and an exodus of native-born workers had *preceded* the influx of immigrants into these fields of employment, the newcomers were widely regarded, by workers and union leaders alike, as interlopers.

Few L.A. unions made any effort to organize immigrants in these early years, and if they considered it at all, most labor leaders believed it to be an impossible task. "The leadership could not interact with the workforce that was coming here," one building trades official later recalled. "At the beginning they [union leaders] thought, 'They're lazy. They're uneducated. They don't speak the language. They're just going to come here and take the money and run.' All the stereotypical things that you've always heard, all those things were said." Even unionists who were more sympathetic to immigrants tended to agree that organizing them was a hopeless quest. The prevailing assumption was that the new arrivals from Mexico and Central America were content with the low wages and poor conditions that native-born workers found unacceptable, since the immigrants' workplace standards were based on their experience south of the border. Moreover, for the large numbers of undocumented migrants, fear of deportation was presumed to be an insurmountable obstacle to unionization, given the risks entailed in organizing. The typical attitude among unionists, one informant explained, was, "No, you can never organize those guys. You're beating your head against the concrete."

At first, the lone dissenter from this view in the L.A. labor movement was the ILGWU, which had been engaged in organizing foreign-born workers, including Mexican Americans, for most of its history. In the 1970s it became the first union in the region to actively recruit the new immigrants. As Cristina Vasquez, then an ILGWU organizer, recalled:

> At that time there were all kinds of problems organizing Latino immigrant workers. Nobody else wanted to organize them. Hardly anyone thought it was possible. The County Federation of Labor at the time was busy blaming immigrants for the decline of unions and for falling wages. No other union that I know of was organizing immigrants. It was only us. . . . One time, we brought a group of Latino workers to an L.A. County membership meeting. The union people were asking very racist questions like, "Where's your green card?" "You're not supposed to be here." "You're working for lower wages." (Milkman and Wong 2000b, 7–9)

As we have seen, deunionization had begun relatively early in the city's garment industry, sparking a membership crisis for the union that helped motivate it to launch these new organizing efforts. But the campaigns the ILGWU undertook in this period did not target the city's rapidly burgeoning nonunion garment sector. Instead, they involved an assortment of low-wage industries, ranging from furniture to mattresses to auto parts. "We were just beating the bushes to see who would come out," Vasquez recalled. "We were building a union of immigrant workers more than a garment workers' union." Moreover, the union's successes in this period tended to be short-lived:

> We were winning elections, but we couldn't convert them into contracts. It was like a revolving door. We were bringing members in through one door and other members were going out through the other door. . . . Our membership went down very dramatically starting in the late 1970s, even though we were doing more immigrant organizing than anyone else. (Milkman and Wong 2000b, 10)

If the ILGWU's efforts proved frustrating, they were instructive nonetheless. For one thing, organizers quickly learned that the new immigrants were highly receptive to unionism, once the possibility was presented to them. This would have a major impact on the local labor movement, for many of the staff who worked for the ILGWU during these early years would later be hired by other unions in Los Angeles and help to lead the immigrant organizing that swept across the region in the late 1980s and early 1990s.

The "revolving door" phenomenon that Vasquez lamented also influenced the thinking of these pioneering organizers. It exposed the futility of organizing isolated workplaces—"hot shops," in union parlance—simply because their workers were unusually disgruntled. Recognizing that unionizing a single establishment in a competitive industry could be counterproductive if it undermined the viability of the business and thus put union members out of work, many organizers turned to a more strategic approach that targeted whole industries or sectors, with the aim of taking wages out of competition in the local labor market. From this perspective, it was a short step to imagine rebuilding unionism in sectors where labor had historically been strong.

In addition to the ILGWU, another crucible for the new generation of organizers that would become the cadre of the new labor movement in Los Angeles during the 1990s was the United Farm Workers (UFW), whose victories in the 1960s and 1970s were still emblazoned in public memory as a high-profile example of successful immigrant organizing.

California's massive agricultural sector was a world apart from urban, industrial Los Angeles, and yet the workforce casualization described in the last chapter was strongly reminiscent of the employment regime long institutionalized in agriculture. Like farm workers, the vast majority of Los Angeles's immigrant industrial, service, and construction workers were Mexican-born migrants. Like farm workers, they were no longer being hired by conventional employers but by immigrant middlemen who acted as labor contractors and often took on supervisory responsibility as well. Like farm workers, the new urban immigrant workers were paid low wages, often in cash, with minimal if any fringe benefits, and faced substandard working conditions. Thus, UFW veterans who later became active in efforts to unionize urban immigrant workers in southern California found themselves on familiar territory in quite a few respects.

By the late 1980s, as more and more organizers became aware of the potential for immigrant unionization, the once-conventional wisdom about "unorganizability" began to dissolve. Indeed, in Los Angeles, and sometimes elsewhere as well, unionists were increasingly persuaded that foreign-born workers were actually far *easier* to recruit than natives, and by the 1990s that revisionist view would be widely echoed in public commentary as well as inside the labor movement. In February 2000 this shift would lead to a historic reversal in the national AFL-CIO's official policy stance on immigration, which had been strongly tilted in favor of restriction for over a century. Now, led by its once-marginal southern California branch, organized labor suddenly emerged as a leading advocate of amnesty for the undocumented and as a defender of immigrant rights more generally.

Starting in the late 1980s, L.A. unionists launched a series of immigrant organizing initiatives in a direct response to the devastating effects of casualization and restructuring described in the last chapter. The ILGWU had pioneered such efforts precisely because these labor market transformations appeared earlier in the garment industry than in other sectors and generated the internal sense of crisis within the union that Voss and Sherman (2000) have identified as a key precondition for labor revitalization. A similar sense of crisis soon engulfed other unions in Los Angeles as well. The fact that former AFL affiliates had long dominated the regional labor movement facilitated L.A. unionists' ability to adapt to the transformed conditions of the 1980s; as argued in chapter 1, such unions were better equipped than their CIO counterparts to tackle the daunting task of organizing the low-road employers that now dominated the regional economy.

Another key comparative advantage for the late-twentieth-century L.A. labor movement was the fact that the new immigration was so highly concentrated in southern California. The region's massive and relatively homogeneous Latino immigrant working class proved highly receptive to unionization efforts for several reasons. First, the newcomers were deeply enmeshed in social networks that often became a key resource for union mobilization. Second, they had a more collectively oriented worldview than most native-born workers—a worldview in which unionism was a familiar, or at least comfortable, option. Finally, they shared an ongoing experience of stigmatization in the face of open hostility from the native-born—and often explicitly nativist—community. In all of these respects, the transnational migrant workers of late-twentieth-century Los Angeles had much in common with earlier generations of working-class immigrants to the United States. As Mae Ngai (2004, 270) so eloquently puts it, today's immigrants "travel with the ghosts of migrants past." Likewise, the challenges that the new immigration presented to the U.S. labor movement in the 1990s had many historical antecedents.

IMMIGRANT UNIONISM, PAST AND PRESENT

From the earliest period, the U.S. labor movement had been deeply engaged in political wrangling over immigration and consistently came down on the side of restrictionist policies in the early decades of the twentieth century (see Ngai 2004). And yet organized labor's growth during its formative years had been predicated largely on recruiting immigrants and their offspring, who made up a huge proportion of the working class in the urban and industrial regions of the country that were the primary sites of union-building. Ironically, in this era U.S. labor leaders were disproportionately foreign-born themselves, even when anti-immigrant sentiments within the unions were at their height.

Like their counterparts in the 1970s and 1980s, many of the craft unionists who dominated the AFL in the late nineteenth and early twentieth centuries were intensely hostile to the "new" immigrants who were then arriving in massive numbers from southern and eastern Europe. Chinese and other Asian immigrants were the objects of even more extreme exclusionary impulses in this period, with Californians leading the charge (Mink 1986). Labor's anti-immigrant animus was reinforced by employers' frequent deployment of foreign-born workers as strikebreakers and by the fact that the newcomers had come to dominate the ranks of the unskilled in many industries. At the same time, some labor organizers sought to directly recruit foreign-born workers into union ranks, with lasting results in a few industries (notably, coal mining and clothing). But most unionists continued to view immigrants as "unorganizable" and were active in the political coalition seeking restrictions on immigration (Greene 1998; Haus 2002).

Nevertheless, apart from the Chinese Exclusion Act of 1882 and a series of more obscure barriers to the entry of other Asian nationalities that were erected in the years that followed, immigration to the United States remained essentially open prior to the 1920s. Only 1 percent of the 25 million Europeans who sought entry between 1880 and World War I were barred. The proponents of restriction did not achieve their goal until 1924, when the Johnson-Reed Act imposed a new system of "national origins" quotas—from which, however, Mexico and the rest of the Western Hemisphere remained exempt. This abrupt policy reversal was fueled by the resurgent nationalism and antiradicalism stimulated by World War I and the Russian Revolution, as well as by the new labor-saving technologies that reduced the demand for industrial workers (Ngai 2004).

Despite a widespread belief among labor leaders that southern and eastern European immigrants were "unorganizable," there was no lack of interest in unionism on the part of the new immigrants themselves in the pre-1924 years. On the contrary, they often responded enthusiastically when the opportunity to organize arose. Thus, the economist Issac A. Hourwich (1912, 34) noted in 1912 that "immigrants from Southern and Eastern Europe are the backbone of some of the strongest labor unions." And during the huge steel organizing drives of World War I, "the great initial response came from the immigrant steelworkers. They were the first to crowd the mass meetings and sign up for membership," noted David Brody (1960, 223). "In contrast, the natives were, according to all reports, an unenthusiastic lot." In meatpacking too, "organizers found the foreign-born much easier to organize than the native-born" (Barrett 1987, 195).

As would once again be the case in the late twentieth century, highly elaborated social networks and left-wing, collectivist political worldviews played central roles in this earlier wave of immigrant unionism. "Not only were foreign-born workers prominent among the strikers in the coal, steel, textile, clothing, oil, lumber, maritime and other industries" during the World War I strike wave, the historian David Montgomery (1986, 329, 346) notes, but "their patterns of collective mobilization were also usually based on ethnic communities . . . [in which] both commitment to trade unionism and a heavy sprinkling of revolutionary rhetoric were easy to detect." In the needle trades too, especially among left-wing eastern European Jews, "it was within the immigrant working-class community that the roots of labor militance took hold and spread" (Glenn 1990, 178). Indeed, the ILGWU and the Amalgamated Clothing Workers—both of which were famous for their attention to community issues beyond the workplace—were among the few unions that opposed restrictive immigration policy in this era (Haus 2002, 51).

Both for the largely Slavic immigrants in steel and meatpacking and for the Jewish garment workers—as for English and German immigrants half a century earlier (see Brody 1993, 110–11)—receptivity to unionization efforts was often rooted in prior experiences with strikes and labor organization in Europe (Hourwich 1912, 349–51; Glenn 1990, 178–85). Selig Perlman (1928, 192–93) went so far as to credit the very existence of the nineteenth-century American labor movement to the influence of foreign-born workers who brought an "imported socialistic class-consciousness" with them from Europe. Indeed, American labor leaders of this era, from Samuel Gompers on, were disproportionately foreign-born. When the sociologist Pitirim Sorokin and his students analyzed the 1925 edition of *American Labor Who's Who*, they found that nearly one-third (32.7 percent) of the labor leaders listed were immigrants—more than double the foreign-born proportion of the nation's population at that time. Significantly, Russia was the leading supplier of these immigrant labor leaders, followed by England and Wales and then by Germany (Sorokin et al. 1927, 389–90).

Of course, not all immigrants of this era were veterans of labor or radical movements at home, and ethnic parochialism and fragmentation among workers at times posed serious impediments to organization. But what held back immigrant organizing in the early twentieth century was seldom antipathy toward or disinterest in unionism among immigrants themselves. Rather, it was a mix of employer resistance bolstered by strong state support and the fact that so many AFL leaders—especially those in the orthodox craft unions for whom the idea of recruiting unskilled workers was still anathema—saw immigrants as a threat to established standards rather than as a potential constituency.

The picture changed dramatically in the 1930s, however, when industrial unionism finally took off and both the AFL and CIO affiliates enjoyed a decades-long surge of sustained growth. As Lizabeth Cohen (1990) has argued, the homogenizing effects of popular culture in the 1920s, along with the CIO's deliberate efforts in the following decade to

build a "culture of unity" that would preempt ethnic and racial fragmentation, yielded powerful results once economic and political conditions
were transformed by the New Deal. Now CIO union leaders aimed "to
meet workers on their ethnic, or racial, ground and pull them into a self-
consciously common culture that transcended those distinctions" (Cohen
1990, 339). The available evidence, albeit fragmentary, suggests that
second-generation immigrants from southern and eastern Europe predominated among CIO activists (Cohen 1990, 324–25; Friedlander
1975). And as more and more AFL affiliates metamorphosed into quasi-
industrial unions in these years, they too increasingly took in first- and
second-generation immigrant workers.

Paradoxically, the upsurge of unionism in the 1930s and 1940s was
not only a force for broad economic and social transformation but also a
primary vehicle of immigrant assimilation. The economic improvements
won by the labor movement in this era brought foreign-born rank-and-
file workers squarely into the middle-class mainstream for the first time.
Organized labor also provided opportunities for individual mobility:
those with the requisite leadership skills could now become career union
officials. More generally, as Michael Piore (1979, 156–57) has insight-
fully suggested, unionism in this era was "part of the process through
which ethnic communities coalesced and the second-generation communities expressed their resentment against the job characteristics that the
parental communities, with a different motivation and a different attitude
toward the labor market, had come to accept."

As chapter 1 documented, southern California was home to relatively
few immigrants from southern and eastern Europe in this period, and the
new CIO unions were concentrated mainly in the Midwest. But the 1930s
wave of unionization did help foster assimilation and Americanization
among California's Mexican Americans, then as now the region's single
largest immigrant group. Carey McWilliams's (1946/1973, 316–17) account of this process has some striking parallels to Piore's analysis of the
social dynamic affecting European counterparts on the other side of the
continent:

> From 1907 to 1940 . . . immigrant Mexicans were admirable work-
> ers, docile and obliging . . . difficult to organize because of the lan-
> guage barrier and the prejudice against them. . . . By 1940 a large
> second-generation group had reached the threshold of maturity,
> American-born children of the immigrants who had crossed the bor-
> der after 1920. By no means so docile and tractable as their parents,

the second-generation Mexicans are typical cultural hybrids . . .
[and] have shown every indication of profound social unrest.

Just as it did for European immigrants in the Midwest, organized labor brought California's Mexican Americans substantial improvements
in economic status in the 1930s and 1940s, as well as new opportunities
for leadership. Even when it had an explicitly left-wing character, as was
often the case, unionism among Mexican Americans in Los Angeles "involved at its core an attempt by the children of the immigrant generation
and those who had arrived in the United States as youngsters to inte-
grate themselves into American society," the historian George Sánchez
(1993, 249) argues. "Ironically, such labor and political activity often
served as the greatest 'Americanizing agent' of the 1930s and 1940s."

Yet the situation of European Americans and Mexican Americans diverged sharply in one crucial dimension: the marking of Mexicans as
racial "others" became increasingly salient in this period, whereas the opposite was true for Europeans. The 1924 Johnson-Reed Act, which
barred all but a few Europeans from legally entering the United States,
did not apply to Mexicans (nor to immigrants from the rest of the Western Hemisphere). Yet in the decades that followed its passage, the descendants of European immigrants were increasingly incorporated into
the "white" population—in part through the leveling effects of mass
unionization. In the same period, by contrast, Mexican immigrants were
discursively and administratively reconstituted as "illegal aliens" through
a complex and highly racialized regulatory regime. This process culminated in the introduction of the bracero program in 1948, but it was already
well under way in the 1920s and 1930s through bureaucratic initiatives on
the part of border agents, who acted largely at the behest of agricultural
capitalists in the Southwest, as Mae Ngai (2004, ch. 4) has shown.

In this context, it is not surprising that the most outstanding examples
of Mexican American unionism in the 1930s and 1940s emerged in agriculture. Despite the fact that neither these early mobilization efforts nor
the high-profile campaigns of the UFW in the 1960s and 1970s would
succeed in establishing durable collective bargaining in this sector over
the long term (see Martin 1996), the farm workers' organizing victories
became an enduring symbol of the transformative potential of unionism
for Mexican immigrant communities in California. The UFW also provided valuable training for a new generation of activists, some of whom
later became involved in urban immigrant labor organizing. As Marshall
Ganz, Kim Voss, and their colleagues (2004) have shown, the UFW also

served as an important "bridge" organization between the social movements of the 1960s and 1970s and late-twentieth-century unionism in California.

Mexican American activists also experimented directly in the 1970s with labor organizing in urban settings, where unlike farm workers, who were typically newcomers, settled immigrants and their descendants were frequently employed. Both the UFW and these lesser-known urban organizing drives attracted the energies of political activists influenced by the civil rights movement and the New Left—a group that included the college-educated children of the generation of Mexican Americans who had been unionized in the 1930s (Gutiérrez 1995, ch. 6). In the postwar boom years, California's Mexican Americans had made substantial gains in income, occupational status, and educational attainment, narrowing the gap with the white majority, thanks in large part to the direct and indirect effects of unionization (Gutiérrez 1998, 312). But just as these developments were taking shape, a new immigration policy was crystallizing that would radically transform the composition of the Latino community.

THE POST-1965 WAVE OF IMMIGRATION

The Hart-Celler Act of 1965 set the stage for a massive influx of newcomers that would rapidly enlarge the population of southern California over the decades that followed. Even as it expanded immigrant access to the United States in other respects, nominally this legislation imposed quotas on Mexico and the rest of the Western Hemisphere for the first time. Nevertheless, in the aftermath of its passage, millions of new Latino immigrants crossed the U.S.-Mexico border, in many cases without documents and with few economic or educational resources. Partly because of the exploding demand for low-wage labor in southern California in the 1970s, the region became the destination of choice for the new arrivals, a phenomenon amplified by the effects of chain migration. Douglas Massey and his colleagues (2002, 59) found that 70 percent of all Mexican immigrants who came to the United States between 1965 and 1985 went to California, with about 40 percent of the total heading to the southern part of the state and fully 30 percent to Los Angeles.

Immigration concerns were not particularly prominent on the agenda of organized labor in the period of relative prosperity that gave rise to the 1965 legislation. But the AFL-CIO did join the liberal reform coalition that orchestrated the loosening of the restrictionist regime that unions had so enthusiastically supported four decades earlier—albeit with some lingering concerns about protecting labor standards (Ngai 2004, 243–58). Two decades later, however, when forces favoring new restrictions on immigration reemerged and won passage of the 1986 Immigration Reform and Control Act (IRCA), unionists once again shifted with the political winds. By now organized labor was facing a far more difficult environment than in 1965: unions were under widespread attack from employers, and they also faced a hostile political regime in Washington, D.C. The AFL-CIO, in any case, strongly supported IRCA, which combined an amnesty for most undocumented immigrants with a new provision for "employer sanctions"—penalties on employers who knowingly hired undocumented workers (Briggs 2001, 163–64).[1]

IRCA was followed by additional immigration legislation in 1990 and 1996 intended to restrict new immigration, but none of these laws stemmed the massive influx of newcomers. On the contrary, the number of immigrants entering the United States actually increased in the late 1980s and 1990s. Moreover, until 1994—when the passage of Proposition 187 in California signaled the state's hostility toward the newcomers and "Operation Gatekeeper" suddenly militarized the San Diego–Tijuana border area—most of the newcomers were still choosing California (and in most cases southern California) as their destination (Massey, Durand, and Malone 2002, 106–7).

Indeed, in the post-1965 period the L.A. region became home to a vast new immigrant workforce, most of them low-wage Latinos from Mexico and Central America. These new arrivals rapidly became the majority group in all four of our case-study occupations, as shown in table 3.1, which draws on U.S. census data from 1990 and 2000. Although all four fields attracted newcomers from various parts of the world, by 1990 Latinos already were by far the dominant group, most of them Mexican-born, with a substantial portion from Central and South America as well. In 1990, as the table also shows, most had been in the United States for less than ten years, and they were somewhat younger than the average worker in the same occupation.

By 2000, however, the number of recent arrivals had declined substantially, and their average age had increased as well, suggesting some stabilization of the workforce over the course of the decade. These changes are consistent with the broader effects of the tightening of the U.S.-Mexico border in the mid-1990s, which, as Massey and his colleagues (2002, 128–33) have shown, unintentionally led many sojourners who had previously been moving back and forth between their countries of origin and

TABLE 3.1   Characteristics of Immigrant Workers in Selected Occupations in the Five-County Los Angeles Area, 1990 and 2000

	Drywallers		Truckers		Garment Workers		Janitors	
	1990	2000	1990	2000	1990	2000	1990	2000
Place of birth								
Mexico	80.0%	89.4%	54.0%	58.0%	54.3%	55.9%	58.1%	68.7%
Central or South America	10.5	9.6	21.9	20.8	21.6	16.6	26.4	21.4
Years since arrival in the United States								
Less than five years	44.1	17.9	20.6	7.2	33.6	19.7	34.7	17.1
Less than ten years	75.9	36.3	46.6	21.8	60.9	43.2	61.0	35.7
Average age (years)								
Foreign-born Latinos in this occupation	28.0	32.5	32.5	36.8	32.2	35.1	33.8	38.0
All workers in this occupation	30.8	34.0	35.4	38.6	34.3	37.1	36.0	38.8
Percentage with less than eight years' education								
Foreign-born Latinos in this occupation	44.4%	39.2%	39.9%	32.6%	55.7%	56.7%	52.6%	52.6%
All workers in this occupation	20.0	23.2	12.7	13.3	41.7	43.0	34.3	37.1
Mean annual earnings (1999 dollars)								
Foreign-born Latino males	$21,955	$25,469	$26,923	$30,079	$16,392	$16,329	$17,204	$18,131
Native-born white males	$38,600	$34,753	$40,056	$35,244	$75,870	$77,704	$26,206	$22,461

Source: U.S. Census Bureau, integrated public use microdata series (IPUMS), version 3.0. See table 2.3 and appendix B for details on data and methods.

the United States to settle permanently in the north. Meanwhile, in the late 1980s and early 1990s, many previously undocumented immigrants obtained legal status through IRCA's amnesty provisions; they too were less likely to return to their home countries.

The table also shows that a disproportionate share of immigrant Latinos in all four of these occupations had less than eight years of formal education in both census years. Their annual earnings (shown only for males) were also consistently lower than those of native-born whites in the same fields, although the gap narrowed between 1990 and 2000. Among drywallers and truckers, immigrants' earnings rose modestly over the decade, even as, in both these cases as well as that of janitors, the earnings of native-born whites deteriorated. This is consistent with Lisa Catanzarite's (2002) finding that in "brown-collar" occupations where Latino immigrants are disproportionately represented, both foreign- and native-born workers often experience wage penalties.[2]

THE MYTH OF IMMIGRANT "UNORGANIZABILITY"

Could these impoverished, poorly educated newcomers be organized into labor unions? At first, both unionists and outside observers presumed that the answer was an unequivocal no. After all, many immigrants were (or imagined themselves to be) mere sojourners, visiting the United States for a short period in order to earn some money to support their families back home, and should thus be reluctant to assume the considerable risks involved in unionization. And even if wages and working conditions seemed poor by U.S. standards, immigrants were presumed to be using a different standard of comparison, one based on their experience in their countries of origin, against which the jobs north of the border might not look so bad. Finally, especially for the huge numbers of undocumented migrants, fear of apprehension and deportation by the immigration authorities was seen as a strong disincentive to become engaged in the high-risk and often publicly visible activities involved in struggles for union recognition.

For a long time this was the prevailing view. As Hector Delgado (1993) reported over a decade ago, most academic commentators and unionists at that time viewed undocumented workers as "unorganizable." Delgado went so far as to suggest that "the unorganizability of undocumented workers because of their legal status has become a 'pseudofact'" (Delgado 1993, 10, citing Merton 1959).

There is extensive qualitative evidence that employers tend to view immigrants—documented or not—as more tractable than natives, and thus uninterested in unionization. Roger Waldinger and Michael Lichter (2003, 155–80) have documented this perspective in detail, based on interviews with employers in several L.A. industries. They report that many employers regard native-born workers as "lazy," prone to "whining," and possessed of a strong sense of entitlement; immigrants, by contrast, are seen as eager, superior, and subservient workers who are willing to work hard at any job, even for low wages. As one employer told Waldinger and Lichter, immigrants are "willing to work for a dollar. They don't have an attitude of 'you owe me a job.' They'll give eight hours' work for eight hours' pay, and they're happy doing it." These employers considered the most recent arrivals (those most likely to be undocumented) as especially highly motivated workers who evaluated wages and working conditions by the standards of their home countries. "Compared to where they came from, this is paradise!" one employer exclaimed (Waldinger and Lichter 2003, 162). Employers, like many labor organizers and outside observers, simply took it for granted that immigrants lacked any interest in unionization—although they would soon be proven mistaken.

To the extent that immigrant workers did seek to improve their lot by means of collective bargaining, it may seem reasonable to expect that the undocumented would be fearful about the risks involved in union organizing, particularly those actions involving confrontations with state authority. Yet in practice, any such fear seems to be less of an obstacle to organization than is often presumed. Delgado was the first to investigate this issue directly through his study of a successful 1985 ILGWU union drive among undocumented Latino immigrants at an L.A. waterbed mattress factory. "Undocumented workers' fear of the 'migra' [the U.S. Immigration and Naturalization Service (INS)]," he reported, "did not make them any more difficult to organize than native workers or immigrant workers with papers."

> Workers reported giving little thought to their citizenship status and the possibility of an INS raid of the plant. . . . [One worker] claimed that he had never been afraid of the INS, adding, "I've never seen them here. Only in Tijuana." [Another] said that he had a better chance of "getting hit by a car"—and he didn't worry about [that] either. . . . In response to the prospect of deportation, . . . workers responded that if deported they would have simply returned (in some cases, "after a short vacation"). Julia Real [pseudonym], a

sewer, commented, "They're not going to kill you! The worse [*sic*] thing they can do is send me home, and I'll come back!" (Delgado 1993, 61, 63)

Although recent efforts to tighten restrictions on immigration may have altered the climate since Delgado did his pioneering fieldwork, among the dozens of unionists we interviewed in the late 1990s, none endorsed the view that the undocumented are "unorganizable," despite extensive concerns about the danger of deportation and notwithstanding employers' regular efforts to exploit such fears by orchestrating INS raids in the midst of organizing campaigns. As one janitorial organizer noted, the risks involved in unionizing looked different from the perspective of many immigrant workers than from that of the native-born. "There, if you were for a union, they killed you," she noted in regard to the role of Salvadorans. "Here, you lose a job for $4.25 an hour [the minimum wage at the time of this interview]" (Milkman and Wong 2000b, 24).

By the 1990s many organizers had come to believe that foreign-born workers, especially Latinos, were unusually responsive to unionization efforts. "It's not true that immigrants are hard to organize," a San Francisco hotel union organizer declared. "They are more supportive of unions than native workers" (Wells 2000, 120). An L.A. janitors' union activist was more emphatic: "We Latino workers are a bomb waiting to explode!" (Waldinger et al. 1998, 117).

Attitudinal data regarding the relative receptivity of immigrants and natives to union organizing efforts are fragmentary. But the available evidence suggests that, contrary to popular belief, immigrants tend to be more pro-union than natives and that both Latinos and Asians (regardless of nativity) tend to be more pro-union than whites, although less so than African Americans. In the 1994 national Worker Representation and Participation Survey (WRPS), for example, 51 percent of Latino respondents nationwide (regardless of nativity) who were not union members indicated that they would vote for a union if a representation election were held in their workplaces, compared to 35 percent of non-Latinos. The figures were similar for Asian American respondents, 49 percent of whom said they would vote for a union, compared to 35 percent of non-Asians. African American respondents expressed even stronger support for unionism in this survey, with 64 percent indicating that they would vote for a union, compared to 32 percent of non–African American respondents.[3]

Other studies also have found evidence of relatively strong pro-union attitudes among Latino workers, regardless of immigrant status (for an early review, see DeFreitas 1993, 289, 293). Although Latinos are not quite as pro-union as African Americans, both groups are consistently more positive toward unionism than whites. And analysis of actual union representation election results also suggests that union organizing efforts tend to be more successful in workplaces that employ predominantly nonwhite workers (Bronfenbrenner and Hickey 2004, 36–37).

A variety of data from California specifically indicate that the state's Latino population is relatively favorably disposed toward unionism. In the 1998 statewide referendum on the anti-union Proposition 226, which would have required unions to obtain members' permission to spend dues money on politics, 75 percent of Latino voters opposed the measure, compared to only 53 percent of voters overall (Del Olmo 1998). And in a 2001–2002 statewide survey of California workers, 67 percent of non-union Latino respondents indicated that they would vote for unionization, double the rate for nonunion Anglo respondents (33 percent). Only African Americans had stronger pro-union preferences (74 percent) in this survey. Whereas few earlier studies examined such attitudes by nativity, this one found more pro-union sentiment among immigrants (most of whom were Latino) than among natives: 66 percent of noncitizen respondents (regardless of ethnicity) expressed a preference for unionization, compared to 54 percent of foreign-born citizens and 42 percent of native-born respondents (Weir 2002, 121).[4]

The notion that workplaces with large concentrations of foreign-born workers are especially promising unionization targets can be found in recent journalistic and academic accounts as well, and not only in California. For example, in an article on a 1999 strike in a meatpacking plant where 90 percent of the workers were foreign-born, a *New York Times* reporter attributed the strike's success to "the receptivity that many immigrants feel toward union activity and their growing confidence that . . . the potential benefits of pressing for better wages and working conditions outweigh any risks" (Verhovek 1999). Similarly, the *Times* account of the union victory at the Fieldcrest Cannon textile plant in Kannapolis, North Carolina, that same year—a historic achievement in that several previous efforts to unionize that plant had failed—attributed the success in part to the "growing numbers of immigrants in the work force who tend to be more likely to support unionization" (Firestone 1999). Leon Fink (2003, 180) offers a more provocative insight in his study of Guatemalan immigrants' unionizing success in a poultry processing plant in

North Carolina: "For workers steeped in a personalistic relationship to authority—as is classically the case in the Latin American countryside—the cold expediency of U.S. industrial relations invited alternative if not outright oppositional forms of loyalty."

Such positive constructions of the potential for immigrant unionization represent a sharp break from the earlier view of immigrants as vulnerable, docile workers willing to work for low, even substandard wages, fearful of any confrontation with authority, and thus highly unlikely to actively seek unionization. The successful Latino immigrant organizing of the 1990s, mostly concentrated in southern California, played a large role in generating this shift in the conventional wisdom. It also led the AFL-CIO to abruptly abandon its long-standing support for "employer sanctions" in February 2000 and to spearhead an effort to win legalization for undocumented immigrants (Bacon 2001).

Along with the Justice for Janitors campaign and the other cases described in chapter 4, there were additional examples of immigrant organizing in the region during the 1990s, including those among factory and hotel workers (see Zabin 2000; Wells 2000). Foreign-born workers made up a substantial share (although not a majority) of the 74,000 home health care providers that the SEIU organized in Los Angeles in early 1999 in the single largest collective bargaining unit established in the United States since the 1930s (Greenhouse 1999). California farm workers' union activity, after a long period of decline, showed signs of revitalization in the late 1990s too, although in this historically critical sector organizing success proved more elusive than in the past (Greenhouse 1997; Purdum 1999). The imaginative Los Angeles Manufacturing Action Project (LAMAP) helped shape a vision of industrywide and multiunion organizing that would remain influential for years after funding shortfalls and other problems led to the abandonment of the effort in 1997 (Delgado 2000). Even such failed campaigns, despite the fact that they were unable to secure lasting organizational gains, added to the growing evidence of foreign-born workers' capacity for mobilization by the labor movement and of their ongoing interest in securing the benefits of unionism.

Alongside union efforts to recruit immigrants, a variety of community-based organizations (CBOs) emerged in southern California during this period with a focus on economic justice issues. Some of the CBOs had close ties to organized labor, while others were more independent. The living wage movement, led by the Los Angeles Alliance for a New Economy and similar groups around the state, figures especially prominently here, owing to its success in passing ordinances in several jurisdictions raising wage levels for workers employed under government contracts (Luce 2004). A variety of other CBOs also took shape around the state with a focus on advocacy for low-wage workers—most of whom turned out to be foreign-born. Some of these organizations focused explicitly on immigrant workplace rights, especially for domestic workers and day laborers with little or no access to conventional unionism (see Gottlieb et al. 2005, 45–48). Others, like "worker centers"—of which there were twenty-six in California by 2005 (Fine 2006)—focused their appeals on the ethnic identities of the low-wage immigrant workforce and advocated for workers' rights using rhetorical and organizational forms distinctly different from those historically associated with unionism.

Southern California also became the site of an extraordinary process of immigrant political mobilization in the 1990s—a process both rooted in and contributing to the immigrant organizing efforts of unions and CBOs. The catalyst here, ironically, was Proposition 187, a ballot measure proposed by then-governor Pete Wilson in 1994 and approved by the state's voters that would have denied public services—including schooling—to undocumented immigrants and their children had it not been found unconstitutional. The Proposition 187 campaign had a dramatic and entirely unintended impact on voting rates among first- and second-generation immigrants in California (Ramakrishnan and Espenshade 2001, 892–93; Citrin and Highton 2002, 22), as well as on their grassroots mobilization. In Los Angeles the street protests against the initiative were larger than any since the antiwar demonstrations of the Vietnam War era. Although immigrants were not the only protesters, they were in the majority. Even the previously apolitical Mexican hometown associations, whose normal activities revolved around beauty pageants and sporting events, were drawn into the fray (Zabin and Rabadán 1998).

Organized labor in Los Angeles was uniquely positioned to seize this moment of opportunity. In 1994, the same year Proposition 187 was placed on the ballot, the L.A. County Federation of Labor (to insiders, "the Fed") underwent a metamorphosis from an insider ally of the city's Democratic Party establishment to an independent political force with extensive capacity for grassroots mobilization. Among other things, the Fed began to devote extensive resources to helping immigrants eligible for naturalization become citizens (and thus potential voters), as many were eager to do in the fearful atmosphere created by the Proposition 187 campaign. Meanwhile, Miguel Contreras, a former UFW organizer who had been on the staff of the Hotel Employees and Restaurant Employees (HERE) union since 1977, became the Fed's secretary-treasurer. Contreras deepened the Fed's commitment to the Latino community and on that basis built it into the single most important force in L.A. politics.

> Contreras took the helm at the Los Angeles County Federation in the spring of 1996. Since then . . . the Fed has built a political operation the likes of which Los Angeles has not previously seen. Mobilizing thousands of member volunteers, with the most loyal and hardworking invariably provided by two almost entirely immigrant locals—HERE's hotel workers and janitors affiliated with the SEIU—the Fed has plunged itself into 23 hotly contested congressional, legislative and city council races around Los Angeles in the past five years and has won 22 of them. . . . Characteristically, a Fed campaign—which involves mail, phone banks, precinct walking, and work site proselytizing—has two target audiences: union members and new immigrant voters. (Meyerson 2001, 20)

Indeed, the key to the Fed's success was its ability to bring the city's huge new immigrant population into the political process, in what the political journalist Harold Meyerson (2005) has characterized as "the most astonishing and significant civic transformation in recent American history"— a transformation whose key architect was Contreras himself.

The Fed had not only the organizational capacity to mobilize at the grassroots level but also the economic resources to be politically influential in Los Angeles, and eventually statewide. Given the extraordinarily high cost of California political campaigns and the limited resources of the Latino immigrant community, virtually no other entity representing this constituency could aspire to play such a role. Labor's growing political clout led to a seismic shift in Los Angeles's electoral landscape as the new cadre of Latino labor leaders rapidly edged out the old-guard Mexican American political leadership. One pivotal example was the 1994 election of progressive union organizer Antonio Villaraigosa to a State Assembly seat representing northeast Los Angeles. Two years later the Fed helped the Democrats regain control of the State Assembly, conducting field and direct-mail campaigns for three Democratic challengers, all of whom were elected. In 1997 the Fed backed Gilbert Cedillo, then a politically unknown SEIU official, in a special election for an Assembly seat in a heavily Latino downtown L.A. district. Cedillo came from behind to win this contest by a huge margin (Frank and Wong 2004, 160; Gottlieb et al. 2005, 160–61).

In 1998 organized labor statewide campaigned successfully to defeat Proposition 226, which would have prohibited union dues being used for political purposes without annual written authorization from members. This measure was defeated, with Latinos voting against it three to one. In the same election, the Democrats won back the governorship in the person of Gray Davis, and Cruz Bustamante was elected lieutenant governor—the first Latino to win statewide office in the entire twentieth century. A year later Villaraigosa became the speaker of the California State Assembly, a job that would later be held by another Latino with a labor background, Fabian Nuñez, former political director of the L.A. County Fed, who became speaker in 2002. In May 2005, Villaraigosa was elected mayor of Los Angeles.[5]

These were only the most important of labor's many electoral success stories in the 1990s, which became legendary not only in Los Angeles but in other parts of California as well (Tobar 1998; Frank and Wong 2004, 160–62; Meyerson 2001). Not only in the workplace but also in community organizations and electoral politics, the labor movement effectively mobilized the vast and supposedly "unorganizable" Latino immigrant population of southern California. If these successes came as a surprise to many observers at the time, in retrospect a few salient features of the social experience of the immigrant newcomers that facilitated their mobilization stand out in sharp relief.

FACTORS FACILITATING IMMIGRANT "ORGANIZABILITY"

There are at least three reasons why immigrant workers may be easier to organize than their native-born counterparts. First, working-class immigrants tend to have stronger social networks than all but the poorest natives, and typically these networks are deeply embedded in occupational and/or workplace settings, where they can support unionization and political mobilization efforts. Second, class-based collective organizations like labor unions and CBOs may be more compatible with the lived experience, worldviews, and identities of many immigrants (especially Central Americans and Mexicans) than with those of native-born workers. Finally, the shared experience of stigmatization among immigrants, both in the course of migration itself and even after years of settlement, may foster a sense of unity—especially in employment settings where immigrants make up the bulk of the workforce. Separately and in combination, these dimensions of immigrant life experience can foster collective organization, balancing and often outweighing the countervailing factors once thought to make immigrants "unorganizable" (reliance on standards from the home country to evaluate wages and working conditions; sojourner mentalities; and, especially for the undocumented, fear of deportation).

Networks

Of the factors facilitating organizing, immigrant social networks have received the largest share of attention in recent literature. Such networks are relatively unusual among the native-born in the United States today, especially in southern California, where the conspicuous absence of any sense of community in daily life is a long-standing cliché. Among the native-born population, neighbors and coworkers rarely know one another well; transience, fragmentation, and instability are the norm, while enduring ties of mutual interdependence are rare. In sharp contrast, vibrant ethnic social networks and tight-knit communities are thriving among the state's vast population of working-class Mexican and Central American immigrants, reinforced by the Catholic Church and in some cases by CBOs as well. This has long been a resource on which immigrants have drawn in labor disputes and other forms of collective organizing. As noted in one account of a protracted strike in a frozen-food factory in California's Central Valley during the 1980s (in which not a single worker crossed the picket line):

> The frozen food workers all lived and worked in the same community, went to the same churches, played and watched soccer games in the same parks. Large numbers of strikers were actually related to each other, members of the same extended families. . . . Families were able to help one another . . . because they already had close relations and were used to a level of cooperation practically forgotten in metropolitan Anglo culture. (Bardacke 1988, 171)

Even in the far-flung metropolis that is contemporary Los Angeles, Latino immigrants' daily lives are enmeshed in an intricate web of social connections, rooted in extended family and kinship ties as well as in the bonds forged by chain migration. Like their predecessors in earlier eras, today's immigrants rely on social networks to obtain housing, employment, child care, financial assistance in times of crisis, and other means of survival. Although one should not presume that immigrant networks function effectively under all circumstances (see Menjivar 2000), there is ample evidence of their importance, not least in the workplace. As Waldinger and Lichter (2003) have shown in rich detail, L.A. employers in a variety of industries frequently exploit immigrant social networks in recruiting new workers. For example:

> A furniture manufacturer told us how "over the years, reliance on re-ferrals has led us to a largely Hispanic workforce. They are very so-cial. I don't want to sound racist, but I never met a lonely Mexican. They all have extended families." A printer struck the same note, ex-plaining that "a Hispanic household has extended family—friends, neighbors. They always know someone who needs a job." (Wald-inger and Lichter 2003, 110)

The widespread tendency to fill vacancies primarily through referral hir-ing reproduces inside the workplace the dense social networks that char-acterize immigrant communities on the outside. These networks, in turn, can become a foundation for building solidarity among workers. As Waldinger and Lichter observe, this dynamic is especially salient when coworkers are bound by kinship ties—a common effect of referral hiring even if employers have anti-nepotism policies (since such policies are eas-ily subverted). As one employer said, "Too many family members at one location creates problems. . . . If you do something to my brother then we're all gonna walk off, that type of situation." As another stated baldly, "Families lead to unionization" (Waldinger and Lichter 2003, 119).

Indeed, numerous studies have documented the role of immigrant so-cial networks in facilitating the union-building process. "Networks played an important role [in organizing], as workers recruited friends and family members," Delgado (1993, 27) has noted. Similarly, in the L.A. janitors' campaign, when organizers visited workers at home they found clusters of immigrant janitors in the same apartment buildings. In that case, "the fact that the workforce was bound by a series of interlocking networks . . . of ethnicity, residence and occupational concentration made the union's task easier." As one SEIU organizer recalled, "Even though L.A. is famous for no community, we found a community of janitors" (Waldinger et al. 1998, 116–17).

Immigrant networks were also palpable among southern California's drywall workers and by all accounts contributed greatly to the success of their 1992 strike. Many participants and nearly all the key leaders were from the same community of origin—El Maguey, a small village in the

Mexican state of Guanajuato. "That was the key, right there," recalled a drywaller who was involved in the early organizing rounds. "Having that big group from one area. The first jobs he took [us to] were where he knew his friends were at. . . . He went right to the people he knew." Another activist agreed. "We used to have a committee of guys, you know, and they were all from El Maguey," he recalled. "That core group was a very vital, important thing. They were all friends, neighbors, relatives in some way or another." Immigrant networks also helped secure support for the strike from otherwise skeptical coworkers, as one informant noted:

> In a lot of cases there were three or four workers to one, talking about what was really happening, and how those folks staying on the job were really hurting them, hurting their families, and their families' future. That if they didn't do this and do it now, and joining us was part of that battle, that they would ruin their future. . . . It was done with not just one or two people, but by a group of people, and usually by people that that other person knew—in some cases, extended family.

Working-class immigrants typically are more dependent than their native-born counterparts on social networks, if only because they have so few other resources upon which to draw in their daily struggles for survival. This is hardly a new phenomenon: immigrants confronting a new environment, especially those with little economic or cultural capital, have always relied heavily on kin and on ties to other migrants from the same place. This dynamic is by no means peculiar to contemporary southern California, then, but it is especially salient there because social networks are so weak among the region's native-born population. In the context of globalization and in a geographical setting that is arguably one of its key nodal points, it seems that traditional and locally based social bonds continue to play a critical role. Ironically, in this setting networks rooted in those bonds contribute powerfully to working-class mobilization in a classical idiom of labor solidarity often presumed to be obsolete—not in spite of but precisely because of the forces unleashed by globalization.

Immigrant Political Experience and Worldviews

I have already summarized the evidence from survey research suggesting that Latinos generally, and immigrants in particular, have more favorable attitudes toward unions than most other workers do. One reason for this may be that many recent immigrants, especially (though not exclusively) those from Central America, have had positive experiences of unionism and/or other forms of collective organization in their home countries. Indeed, immigrants often arrive in the United States far better acquainted with the cultural idioms of collective organizing, unionism, and class politics than their native-born counterparts. And although no one has yet gathered systematic evidence on this point, it is striking that many of the rank-and-file immigrant union leaders who emerged in the California labor movement in the 1990s were labor or social movement activists in their native lands.[6]

Prominent among the leaders of the L.A. janitors' campaign, for example, were several veterans of the Salvadoran liberation struggle (Acuña 1996, 185), and organizers reported "a high level of class consciousness" among janitors, as well as a willingness to take the risks involved in unionization, both phenomena shaped by experiences back home (Waldinger et al. 1998, 117). Similarly, most of the rank-and-file leaders of a 1990 wildcat strike that sparked unionization at an L.A.-area wheel factory, whose workforce was entirely made up of Mexican and Central American immigrants, had union or left-wing political experience at home. One of these leaders, who became the plant's local union president, had been a dissident unionist in Mexico and had emigrated after being blacklisted by employers there (Zabin 2000, 153–54).

In their research on local unions in northern California, Voss and Sherman (2000, 104) also highlight the role of immigrants' political experience in their home countries in facilitating the process of union revitalization. They cite several cases of organizers who were veterans of progressive social movements in the Philippines and Mexico, as well as examples of union leaders who cut their activist teeth helping organize the UFW. Other researchers have documented the activities of transnational immigrant hometown associations, which also reflect a collective political orientation (Hamilton and Chinchilla 2001, 208–12; Zabin and Ramadán 1998); in some cases these associations have been directly linked to local-level union activity (Fitzgerald 2004).

A similar dynamic was present in earlier waves of immigrant union organizing in the United States. In that respect, today's Central American union leaders bring to mind the radical Jewish unionists who emigrated from Russia and eastern Europe a century ago, many of whom had left-wing views and/or political experience in socialist and union movements at home. Yet the late-twentieth-century version of this phenomenon presents a contrast to the last great wave of union organizing in the 1930s and 1940s, when unionism became a vehicle of assimilation for second-generation European immigrants and ethnic identities were deliberately subordinated to class identity within the political culture of the industrial union movement (Cohen 1990; George Sánchez 1993). The collective action of today's immigrants is often rooted in a national or ethnic identity that remains salient in the context of union organizing campaigns. In the late twentieth century, then, the labor movement was once again a vehicle for collective ethnic advancement, but without the assimilationist thrust common in earlier periods.

Yet, reinforced by rapidly growing class inequalities and formidable obstacles to immigrant social mobility (see Gutiérrez 1998), ethnic (or pan-ethnic) identities can be effectively channeled into a working-class political identity—even among immigrants whose background is not working-class. Thus, Latino immigrants who had professional or other relatively privileged jobs in their native countries but were blocked from securing such positions in the United States may assume leadership roles in unions or otherwise embrace a working-class political orientation. Others, hired as foremen or supervisors, may turn on their employers and help organize their subordinates into unions or other collectivities constructed in the conventional idiom of working-class movements, as the 1992 drywall strike illustrates. Even immigrants who were overtly hostile to left-wing movements at home—the standard example is the Salvadoran janitors who had supported the right-wing military regime at home yet joined in the L.A. Justice for Janitors campaign (see Waldinger et al. 1998, 117)—may become part of ethnically based working-class movements in the United States. In such cases, Latino ethnic identity, forged in the context of a hostile host society, generates collective action in which class fuses with—rather than trumps—ethnicity.

Stigmatization

This last point is closely related to a third factor that often makes immigrants more receptive to unionization efforts than natives, namely, the ordeal of migration itself and the persistent stigmatization that foreign-born persons are forced to endure, even after residing for long periods in the United States. The lived experience of being under siege in a hostile environment, rather than generating passivity and fear, as many commentators once presumed, may instead foster labor solidarity and organization (as well as other forms of oppositional political activity). Under these conditions, if unions or CBOs extend a helping hand to immigrant workers, offering economic and political resources that can ameliorate the unrelentingly difficult conditions of daily life, they are usually welcomed enthusiastically. As David Gutiérrez (1998, 324–25) notes:

> In what is perhaps the supreme irony of the most recent era of migration . . . the very measures that are now being implemented both to stem the flow of migrants and to cow those already in the country into compliance with increasingly stringent welfare, public health, and public education statutes may well prove the spawning grounds for the emergence of serious dissent in the ethnic Mexican and pan-Latino populations. . . . [By] simultaneously demonizing (and criminalizing) Latinos as foreign, nonintegrated "Others" while continuing to ensure that their labor can be exploited at maximum efficiency . . . American policymakers and employers have also unwittingly helped to create a vast new subnational social space that has virtually guaranteed the emergence of alternative—and potentially deeply subversive—diasporic social identities, cultural frames of reference, and modes of political discourse.

In California, and especially southern California, natives' intolerance of the foreign-born and the stigmatization of immigrants that is its direct outgrowth are especially highly developed.[7] The popularity (among natives) of Proposition 187 in 1994 was one manifestation of this. Another ballot initiative, Proposition 209, approved in 1996, had a serious impact on Latinos when it banned affirmative action in all state educational institutions and public agencies. In 1998 California voters approved yet another such measure, Proposition 227, which banned bilingual education in the state's public schools. In reaching out to the immigrant community and explicitly rejecting the popular xenophobia these measures embodied, the labor movement—both unions and CBOs—was greeted with open arms. Particularly in Los Angeles, where the county Fed emerged in the 1990s as a major political force, labor was able to skillfully channel the outrage of immigrants about these measures into progressive electoral politics (Meyerson 2001).

By century's end, it was apparent that when unions did seek to organize immigrant workers, their reception was highly positive. Labor's formidable political accomplishments in southern California, as well as its immigrant unionizing successes in the 1990s, underscored the *potential* for organizing the foreign-born workforce—"Sí, se puede!" (Yes, it can be done!), as the union slogan puts it. But whether or not these early break-throughs would mature into a large-scale phenomenon is another question. Thus far, only a small proportion of the millions of foreign-born workers in Los Angeles, much less in the state or the nation, have been direct beneficiaries of the efforts of unions and labor-oriented CBOs. Most immigrants remain unorganized, working long hours for minimal pay (all too often, less than the minimum wage) under miserable conditions.

IMMIGRANT UNIONIZATION IN TURN-OF-THE-CENTURY LOS ANGELES

By the late 1990s, although a series of successful, high-profile organizing efforts in the region had brought many thousands of immigrants into the labor movement, native-born workers in the L.A. metropolitan area were almost twice as likely to be unionized as their foreign-born counterparts. Only 11 percent of all foreign-born workers employed in the five-county L.A. area over the 1994 to 2001 period were union members, compared to 20 percent of employed native-born workers.[8] The figures were similar for California as a whole (12 percent and 20 percent, respectively). Immigrants may have been "organizable," but relatively few had actually been organized.

As figures 3.1 and 3.2 show, regardless of ethnicity, immigrants remained severely underrepresented in the ranks of L.A. union members during these years. Foreign-born Latinos were 16 percent of all employed workers in the area, but only 10 percent of union members. Similar disparities between employment and unionization levels were also present for Asian and white immigrants; by contrast, native-born whites and African Americans were overrepresented among union members in Los Angeles, relative to their share of employed workers.[9]

These data require careful interpretation, however, given the winner-take-all union representation system and the fact that a relatively small proportion of overall union membership is the product of recent organizing. Although unionized workers are far more likely than their nonunion counterparts to express pro-union attitudes, this is typically a consequence rather than a cause of union affiliation, as Freeman and Rogers (1999, 68–77) have pointed out. Under the peculiar (in comparative terms) U.S. industrial relations system, individual workers rarely have the opportunity to make independent decisions about union affiliation. Instead, unionization usually takes place when entire workplaces (or, in some cases, local or regional labor markets in specific occupations or industries) become organized, either by majority vote or after the union wins recognition directly from the employer. Once established in a given setting, moreover, unionization tends to persist over time: although decertifications may take place and unionized establishments may relocate or close, the decline in union density more often reflects the scarcity or ineffectiveness of efforts to organize new establishments or to penetrate expanding sectors of the economy. In addition, given the extensive turnover that has taken place over the years in workplaces that were unionized long ago and the broader process of deunionization that has occurred over recent decades, pro-union workers may often be found in nonunion settings; conversely, if less frequently, workers with little enthusiasm for organized labor may find themselves employed in union shops.[10]

Moreover, immigrants (like native-born ethnic and racial minorities, as well as women) are not evenly distributed through the workforce but instead tend to be concentrated in particular occupations and industries. Regardless of unionization preferences, the extent to which the foreign-born (or any other specific racial or gender group) are represented in the ranks of union members primarily reflects the degree to which they are employed in workplaces, occupations, or industries that were unionized at some point in the past.[11] This is particularly true of the post-1965 wave of immigrants, most of whom entered the U.S. workforce in an era when new union organizing was at a low ebb and rapid deunionization was eroding historical sectors of union strength.

This point is starkly illustrated by a comparison between the highly organized public sector and the overwhelmingly nonunion private sector. The huge differential in unionization rates between the two sectors is not a function of public-sector workers' more favorable attitude toward unions (although they may in fact be more pro-union) but rather reflects the fact that resistance to unionization tends to be far less intensive when the employer is a federal, state, or local government agency than when it is a private firm. In the 1994 to 2001 period, 54 percent of foreign-born Latinos employed in the public sector in the five-county L.A. area were union members—only slightly less than the 60 percent of native-born whites in the public sector who were unionized at that time (the difference is not statistically significant).[12] However, only 5 percent of the area's foreign-born Latinos worked in the public sector in this period, compared to 17 percent of native-born whites, so that the very high level

FIGURE 3.1   Employed Wage and Salary Workers, by Nativity, Race, and Ethnicity, Los Angeles Metropolitan Area, 1994 to 2001

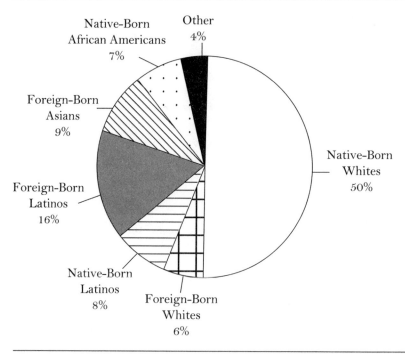

Source: U.S. Current Population Survey, outgoing rotation group earnings files, merged for 1994 to 2001.

of unionization among immigrants in the public sector had almost no impact on their overall unionization rate (11 percent).[13]

More generally, the distinctive patterns of immigrant employment—most importantly, the overrepresentation of foreign-born workers in the most casualized sectors of the labor market, where unionization is rare, and their underrepresentation in the highly unionized public sector—are at the root of their relatively low overall rate of unionization. These differential employment patterns also help explain why the most recent immigrants are less highly unionized than those who have been in the United States longer: newcomers—especially Latinos, the majority of whom have little formal education—are especially likely to be employed in the most casualized (and least unionized) sectors of the labor market. In the 1994 to 2001 period, only 5 percent of foreign-born Latinos in the L.A. metropolitan area who had arrived in the United States after 1990,

FIGURE 3.2 Union Members, by Nativity, Race, and Ethnicity, Los Angeles Metropolitan Area, 1994 to 2001

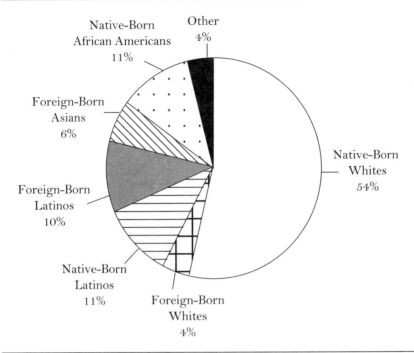

Source: U.S. Current Population Survey, outgoing rotation group earnings files, merged for 1994 to 2001.

and only 7 percent of those who had arrived between 1980 and 1990, were unionized. By contrast, 21 percent of those who had arrived before 1980 were union members. For the last group, the unionization rate was not significantly different from that of the region's native-born workers (20 percent).[14]

In the private sector, where they are almost exclusively employed, 17 percent of foreign-born Latinos were unionized in the L.A. metropolitan area in this period—about the same rate as for native-born African Americans (16 percent) and actually slightly higher than the rate for native-born whites (13 percent); however, these differences are not statistically significant. Thus, despite the successful campaigns among janitors and others that so palpably demonstrated the potential for immigrant unionism, more than four out of five foreign-born Latinos in the private sector remained outside the ranks of organized labor at century's end. And even though the labor movement in California, as well as in its largest metropolis, was in relatively good health in this period (see Milkman and Rooks 2003) and indeed was widely regarded as a leading laboratory of union innovation, bringing the embryonic achievements of this period to scale remains a formidable challenge. Moreover, conditions have worsened significantly since the turn of the century, with recession, a rightward political turn both nationally and in California, and growing xenophobia in the aftermath of the events of September 11, 2001.

The question for the new century is no longer *whether* immigrants can be unionized—clearly they can—but *under what conditions* such efforts are likely to succeed and whether and how they can be replicated on a larger scale. By comparing a set of four case studies of immigrant unionization campaigns from the 1990s—two successes and two failures—the next chapter explores this problem, arguing that success requires simultaneous engagement at two levels: (1) unions must devote substantial resources to developing a strategic analysis of the power structure of the targeted industry or sector, so they can identify and attack key points of employer vulnerability; and equally crucially, (2) unions must actively mobilize the rank-and-file workers who are the potential membership, ideally in conjunction with organizing grassroots and political support in the wider community. At this second level, the relatively high receptivity of recent immigrants to unionism emerges as an important factor, but given the hostile environment with which any union organizing today must contend, it is by no means a guarantee of success.

CHAPTER 4

"SÍ, SE PUEDE": UNION ORGANIZING STRATEGIES AND IMMIGRANT WORKERS

Unions in southern California have launched numerous organizing drives among low-wage Latino immigrant workers in recent years, some of which were spectacularly successful.[1] This chapter compares two of the best-known success stories with two high-profile campaigns that did not achieve their goals, with the aim of developing a deeper understanding of the elements that generate effective union strategies. The two successful cases we examine are: the L.A. Justice for Janitors campaign that began in the late 1980s, achieved an initial victory in 1990, and was consolidated and expanded over the course of the next decade; and the five-month 1992 strike among drywall hangers in the region's residential construction industry that secured union recognition, along with improved pay and benefits, for thousands of previously unorganized immigrant workers. We also consider two unsuccessful cases: the mid-1990s effort to organize garment workers employed at Guess, Inc., which was at first energetically pursued but then abandoned after a few years; and the drive to organize truckers servicing the Los Angeles–Long Beach port, which culminated in a highly effective strike in 1996 but failed to achieve union recognition. On the basis of this four-way comparison among immigrant organizing campaigns that took place over a decade-long period, we assess the conditions that have facilitated, and those that have impeded, efforts to unionize immigrants in the region, focusing particularly on the role of union commitment and strategy.

As previous chapters have documented, in all four of these cases, as in most manual and service occupations in contemporary Los Angeles, the workforce is overwhelmingly made up of foreign-born Latinos. Thus, the presence of an immigrant workforce is a constant, not a variable, in our analysis. All four cases also share (even as they contributed to) the other comparative advantages of being located in southern California—advantages that first became widely apparent in the 1990s as the national labor movement launched efforts to jump-start a major phase of revitalization. As figure 4.1 shows, nationally the long-term erosion of union density continued relentlessly in the period after 1988 (the year the L.A. Justice for Janitors campaign began), falling from 17 percent that year to 13 percent by 2004. Although there were two brief plateaus when it held steady (from 1989 to 1994 and then again from 1997 to 2001), throughout this period there was not a single year in which union density actually rose in the United States as a whole. However, that feat *was* achieved (albeit briefly) in the state of California during the late 1990s, and once again in the opening years of the new century. Nevertheless, over the full sixteen-year period, union density fell from 19 percent to 17 percent in the state. The L.A. metropolitan area fared better: there, density increased slightly in the late 1980s, and did so once again in the opening years of the twenty-first century, with a net loss of only one percentage point in union density over the full period shown in figure 4.1.

In quantitative terms, the four case studies discussed here had little impact on this larger tableau, which was shaped by a variety of influences. Organizing unorganized workers is the main way in which unions themselves can act to increase density, but it is only one of many factors influencing the overall unionization rate. If employment declines in a unionized sector or expands in a nonunion (or weakly unionized) sector, union density will decrease. Given shifting employment trends, combined with normal labor market growth and turnover, unions must recruit large numbers of new members each year just to maintain the existing level of density. Indeed, to increase density by one percentage point nationally over a yearlong period requires organizing an estimated one million new members (Freeman 2004). Considered in this light, the episodic increases in union density shown in figure 4.1 for Los Angeles and for the state of California are all the more impressive. Analyzing the dynamics of recent organizing in the region highlights some of the forces shaping the relative success of the L.A. labor movement as a whole in this period and il-

FIGURE 4.1 Union Density in Los Angeles, California, and the United States, 1988 to 2004

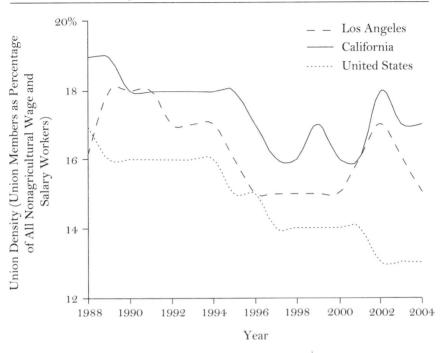

Source: See appendix A.

luminates the conditions under which individual organizing campaigns succeed or fail.

Our first case is the now-legendary Justice for Janitors campaign, which catapulted into the headlines when SEIU Local 399 won a contract from one of Los Angeles's major building cleaning contractors in the summer of 1990. This was the triumphal conclusion of a two-year organizing drive that brought SEIU's janitorial membership in the city to 8,000, up from 1,800 five years earlier—the largest private-sector union victory involving Latino immigrants since the UFW campaigns of the early 1970s. Two years after the janitors' breakthrough, a five-month strike by thousands of Mexican immigrant drywall hangers (workers who install the sheetrock panels that make up the interior walls of modern buildings) halted residential construction throughout southern California. The drywallers' strike settlement led to a union contract that doubled wage rates in Los Angeles and the surrounding counties and brought 2,400 previously nonunion immigrant drywallers into Carpenters' Local 2361—our second case of success.[2]

These dramatic and unexpected victories laid the foundation for a broader move to unionize the region's vast population of foreign-born workers. Yet more than a decade later, as noted in chapter 3, the vast bulk of the immigrant workforce in southern California today remains outside the union fold. For the most part this reflects the underappreciated but critically important fact that relatively few unions have launched *any* major organizing efforts in this period—whether inside or outside of California, whether among immigrants or native-born workers (see Bronfenbrenner and Hickey 2004). Moreover, alongside the scattered immigrant organizing successes that did take place in the L.A. area in the 1990s were some efforts that ended in failure or stalemate. Our third and fourth case studies are drawn from this set of campaigns. One was the organizing drive initiated in the mid-1990s by the ILGWU and then continued by the Union of Needletrades, Industrial, and Textile Employees (UNITE), targeting the designer jeans manufacturer Guess, Inc., originally envisioned as a first step toward organizing the larger L.A. garment industry.[3] The other case involved the thousands of truck drivers who haul freight to and from the Los Angeles–Long Beach waterfront, now the world's third-largest port. They launched a series of grassroots organizing efforts and work stoppages starting in the 1980s, culminating in a massive and highly effective strike in 1996 whose goal was to secure union representation with the Communication Workers of America (CWA). Neither of these energetic and imaginative campaigns achieved its goals, however, and the region's garment workers and port truckers remain nonunion to this day. By dissecting the problems these two efforts encountered and comparing them to the successes of the janitors and drywallers, we expose the factors underlying the disparate outcomes.

Our argument is that internal union difficulties, such as limited strategic capacities and/or compromised union commitment to organizing, were the key factors undermining both the Guess campaign and the 1996 port truckers' strike. As the janitorial and drywall cases show, unionization can be achieved among immigrant workers under conditions broadly similar to those that prevailed in the garment workers' and truckers' cases. What set the successes apart from the failures was not only a solid union commitment to the campaigns—including a willingness to expend significant resources on them—but also comprehensive strategies that combined "bottom-up" grassroots mobilization with "top-down" efforts targeting the power structure of the industries involved. Had they included all these elements, we argue, the Guess and truckers' drives might also have succeeded.

To be sure, there were some formidable additional obstacles that organizers had to confront in the two unsuccessful campaigns. The most obvious of these was the vulnerability to capital flight in the garment industry. Unlike janitorial, construction, or trucking work, none of which are geographically mobile, garment manufacturing can and often is outsourced to cut labor costs and avoid or resist unionization. Indeed, Guess ultimately relocated much of its production to Mexico in the face of the ILGWU-UNITE organizing drive, although we argue that this was as much a result as a cause of the campaign's weakness. Indeed, there were other serious flaws in the effort, including a limited resource commitment on the part of the union and its abandonment of one critical component of the original strategy. These deficiencies, we argue, probably would have derailed the campaign even if Guess had kept all its production in the United States. Moreover, despite the constant threat of capital mobility, there is more apparel employment in Los Angeles today than anywhere else in the country, and more employment in apparel than in any other manufacturing industry in the city; thus, there is no shortage of garment workers for the union to recruit. And as others have documented, the omnipresent threat of capital flight has not prevented workers (both immigrants and natives) from successfully unionizing in manufacturing settings in Los Angeles, and elsewhere, in recent years (for examples, see Delgado 1993; Zabin 2000; Bronfenbrenner and Hickey 2004, 33).

The Los Angeles–Long Beach port truckers also faced some special obstacles in their organizing effort—most importantly the fact that, as "independent contractors," most of them were legally ineligible to participate in union representation elections. Yet this did not prevent the truckers from forming a series of independent labor organizations in the aftermath of deregulation and deunionization in the 1980s and 1990s, nor from launching repeated strikes and other job actions, culminating in the huge 1996 walkout that nearly succeeded in winning union recognition. We argue that the negative outcome of that strike was due primarily to strategic weaknesses within the one union that was willing to represent the truckers, the CWA—which took up the campaign with the best of intentions but was handicapped by its limited knowledge of or experience in this industry—rather than to the independent contractor problem.

This chapter draws inspiration from and in many ways is analogous to Kate Bronfenbrenner's (1997; Bronfenbrenner and Hickey 2004) pioneering research on union strategies, which has done so much to identify the characteristics of organizing campaigns that are most likely to yield success. There are at least two major differences, however, between her work and ours. First, whereas Bronfenbrenner's methodology is quantitative, based on analysis of hundreds of organizing campaigns, ours is qualitative and includes only a few carefully selected cases. Second, Bronfenbrenner analyzes unionization efforts culminating in elections held under the auspices of the National Labor Relations Board, the traditional route to union recognition in the United States, but none of our four cases involved NLRB elections. The characteristics of the industries in which these four union drives were embedded made the electoral option impractical in all of them. Indeed, as the organizers involved fully understood, because building services, residential construction, and garments all rely on extensive subcontracting, a union electoral victory at any one firm would merely lead the affected building owner, housing developer, or clothing manufacturer to shift work to nonunion subcontractors, putting the newly unionized firm out of business and its employees out of work. NLRB-oriented organizing is equally impractical in intermodal trucking, both because of the large number of small firms in the industry and because, as already noted, the owner-operators who now dominate the field are not legally "employees" and thus are not eligible to vote in NLRB elections.

All four of the campaigns discussed here, then, necessarily departed from the traditional NLRB-focused model of unionization and relied instead on alternative organizing approaches. Although widely heralded as innovative in the 1990s context, many of the strategies they used had historical antecedents in the organizing efforts of AFL unions in the early twentieth century (some of which were described in chapter 1). Indeed, it is no accident that the unions involved in all four cases, except for the CWA (which took on the unsuccessful truckers' effort), were former AFL affiliates.[4] The key to the janitors' and drywallers' successes was that the campaigns combined traditional AFL organizing strategies, sometimes labeled "top-down" because they involve union leaders directly pressuring employers, with extensive rank-and-file mobilization—a "bottom-up" strategy historically associated with the CIO's initial ascendancy.

TOP-DOWN AND BOTTOM-UP ORGANIZING STRATEGIES

The top-down and bottom-up approaches feature prominently in recent debates about the future of the deeply troubled U.S. labor movement.

Some commentators passionately argue that union revitalization efforts should concentrate on grassroots, bottom-up organizing efforts in which rank-and-file workers—as opposed to union officials or staff—are the central protagonists. In this view, there is no place for top-down campaigns led by union "bureaucrats"; such efforts are an obstacle to progress, part of the problem rather than part of the solution. Thus, Vanessa Tait (2005, 3) advocates "organizing that values the direct action, flexibility, collaboration, and rank-and-file control common in social justice movements over the bureaucratic and legalistic methods on which traditional unions have often relied." Similarly, Steve Early (2004, 39), one of the most vociferous proponents of this perspective, criticizes the SEIU— by any standard the union that has made the greatest organizing gains in recent years—for its extensive reliance on "outsiders" rather than rank-and-file union members and for its frequent use of trusteeships to impose change on reluctant local affiliates. "From the standpoint of creating real rank-and-file power, SEIU's top-down, technocratic, transformation-by-trusteeship strategy is deeply flawed," Early argues. Along the same lines, Jane Slaughter (in Milkman and Voss 2005, 24–25) criticizes top-down campaigns that involve union leaders exerting pressure on employers instead of relying on workers to do so: "It matters *how* workers get their union. It matters whether you get your union through a backroom deal with the boss or through workers confronting the boss." Slaughter then asks rhetorically, "Will the union structure be dominated by staffers, or will resources be devoted to developing leaders from the rank and file?" These arguments for bottom-up organizing are often made in the name of union democracy; indeed, from this perspective, professional leadership is a threat to workers' control over their own organizations.

Stephen Lerner, director of the SEIU Building Service Division, a key architect of the Justice for Janitors campaign (not only in Los Angeles but also nationally), and author of the main programmatic text (Lerner 2003) that led to the 2005 split in the labor movement, takes a different approach. Basing his arguments explicitly on the experience of the SEIU's recent growth and development, Lerner calls for a research-intensive organizing strategy that targets specific industries. He disagrees explicitly with Early on the role of leadership and rejects out of hand the notion that democracy requires that all leaders be drawn directly from the rank and file. "If 90 percent of all workers in the private sector are outside our unions," Lerner argues, "the notion that the only legitimate leader of the new labor movement we're trying to build is somebody who happens to be out of the rank and file of a particular local is incredibly narrow, it's pseudodemocracy." Lerner also advocates union mergers and consolidations orchestrated from the top, with the goal of developing greater accountability, coordination, and centralization within the labor movement as a whole. He calls for a return to "the approach of taking wages out of competition in individual sectors of the economy" (Milkman and Voss 2005, 19–20).

This fundamental disagreement about the relative merits of bottom-up, rank-and-file–driven organizing approaches and top-down efforts that rely more heavily on strategic planning and professional leadership has a long history. It predates not only the 2005 split but also the crisis of union density that attracted so much attention starting in the 1980s. Its roots lie in the historical iconography of the independent CIO unions' ascent to power through sit-down strikes and other dramatic forms of bottom-up mobilization; this period is typically constructed as the most progressive and democratic moment of U.S. labor history. In fact, as we have seen, the historical record is more complicated—both AFL and CIO unions have relied on a mix of top-down and bottom-up strategies—but there is some truth to the notion that the top-down approach is tied mainly to the history of AFL unionism, and therefore disparaged by many in highly pejorative terms, whereas the bottom-up approach is associated with the early years of the CIO.

What is new is the explicit defense of top-down strategic thinking by the SEIU and other unions—most of them, as we have seen, with historical roots in the old AFL—that emerged as the leading organizing unions in the 1990s. But these unions do not advocate exclusively top-down approaches, in the absence of bottom-up worker mobilization. As we argue, moreover, the former AFL unions have not been successful in cases where they pursued top-down strategies in isolation from rank-and-file mobilization—and bottom-up approaches in isolation have not succeeded either. In the current environment, with a power imbalance between management and labor more extreme than it has been anytime since the birth of the New Deal, unions can be effective only by combining top-down and bottom-up traditions.

Our two cases of success involve unions that now are part of the CTW Federation (SEIU and the Carpenters), both of which have been criticized in some quarters for relying on top-down approaches. But as we emphasize here, one of these campaigns (the drywallers') began as a bottom-up effort, while the other (the janitors') was a top-down effort launched by the SEIU's national leadership. Similarly, our two unsuccessful cases include one campaign (the truckers') that started at the grassroots level and another (the Guess campaign, also led by a CTW union) that emerged out of a strategic plan crafted by professional union leaders. Both the jan-

FIGURE 4.2   Four Organizing Campaigns: Genesis and Outcome

Genesis of Campaign

	Top-Down	Bottom-Up
Successful	Justice for Janitors (SEIU)	Drywallers (Carpenters' union)
Unsuccessful	Guess—garment workers (ILGWU/UNITE)	Port truckers (CWA)

Campaign Outcome (left axis label)

Source: Author's compilation.

itors' (successful) and the garment workers' (unsuccessful) campaigns, then, started as top-down, strategically targeted efforts initiated by union leaders and designed to win union recognition by exerting intense pressure on the powerful individuals and groups controlling each industry. By contrast, the drywallers' and truckers' organizing efforts were initiated from below by rank-and-file workers, among whom, to be sure, were key individuals with strong leadership skills; neither effort, however, was part of a strategic plan developed by professional union leaders. As figure 4.2 shows, there is no association between campaign success and having either a top-down or bottom-up genesis.

Our argument, using these four cases as illustrations, is that the standard juxtaposition between bottom-up and top-down organizing models is a false dichotomy and does a disservice to the wider debate about labor movement revitalization. Successful organizing must be comprehensive in scope, combining and synthesizing bottom-up and top-down approaches rather than emphasizing either one at the expense of the other. What ultimately matters is not whether a union campaign *begins* as a top-down effort to put pressure directly on the decisionmakers in an industry or as a bottom-up, grassroots mobilization of workers on the ground. Rather, success depends on effectively combining the two approaches.

Both the janitors and the drywallers managed to bring these two dimensions together, even though one began as a top-down effort and the other as a bottom-up campaign. Justice for Janitors was indeed launched by established union leaders, many of them "outsiders," and the SEIU had extensive historical experience in top-down organizing. Yet the janitors' campaign would not have succeeded had it not also engaged in intensive grassroots organizing among rank-and-file workers. Similarly, the dry-wallers' campaign was initially the work of rank-and-filers, but they sought and received support from an established union, without which they probably would not have succeeded.

The two unsuccessful campaigns, by contrast, were one-sided efforts. In the Guess case, largely for reasons related to the 1995 union merger that created UNITE, what was originally conceived as a comprehensive campaign devolved into a more limited, top-down effort; here an insufficient resource commitment to grassroots organizing proved fatal. For the port truckers, the converse was true: the campaign's strength was at the level of bottom-up mobilization, while the CWA's coordination efforts at the top foundered, again leading to an unsuccessful outcome. In both cases, problems internal to the unions involved were the critical obstacles to success. Given the intense employer opposition that faces virtually all union organizing today, any lack of resolve or strategic weakness on the union side can easily undermine a campaign. Although it is impossible to know with any certainty what the outcome would have been if the organizers had combined bottom-up and top-down approaches at Guess and in the port truckers' campaign (and surely there must be cases of organizing efforts where the union does everything right but is nonetheless outmaneuvered by powerful employers), our comparison to the janitors' and drywallers' campaigns suggests that determined and skillful organizing that involves both these dimensions, backed up with adequate financial and legal resources, can make or break unionization efforts among immigrant workers.

This seemingly voluntaristic analysis does not entirely lack a structural dimension, however. Indeed, there were particular economic, political, and social factors that made these four occupational groups ripe targets for organizing in the first place, and thus it is hardly accidental that unionization efforts *emerged* in these four cases and not in others. As chapter 2 showed, despite their location in different industries and sectors, all of the occupations involved had been highly unionized in southern California (although garment workers less so than the other three cases) prior to the post-1965 surge in immigration. That they were originally the terrain of AFL-affiliated unions, which have weathered the restructuring of the past few decades more successfully than their CIO-affiliated counterparts, helps explain the fact that they have all become sites of reunionization efforts. In addition, as we saw in chapter 3, the processes of union decline and immigrant incorporation in the labor market during the 1970s and 1980s were remarkably similar across all four cases, and this also helped to spark the subsequent efforts to revive unionism in each. Nonetheless, the four efforts developed distinct trajectories and yielded divergent outcomes. Let us now consider each of them in more detail.

SUCCESSFUL TOP-DOWN ORGANIZING: JUSTICE FOR JANITORS

In the 1980s, then-SEIU president John Sweeney (who would go on to become head of the AFL-CIO in 1995) launched a concerted effort to revitalize his union. He dramatically increased the resources devoted to organizing unorganized workers and recruited scores of new staff members, many of them veterans of the social movements of the 1960s and 1970s. Among other initiatives, Sweeney aimed to rebuild what had once been the SEIU's primary base, building services, an industry in which union density had been severely eroded in many parts of the United States (although not in New York, Chicago, or San Francisco). The result was the national Justice for Janitors campaign, which arrived in Los Angeles in 1988 after some modest successes in smaller cities, most notably Denver. The leadership for this effort, as well as most of the financial resources devoted to it, came from SEIU's national headquarters. Indeed, in Los Angeles as well as in some of the other cities where it was attempted, the campaign proceeded in the face of active resistance from many established local union officials. Not only was it a top-down initiative in that it began with the work of union staff rather than rank-and-file janitors, but it also had its genesis at the very highest levels of the union's internal organizational structure.

Both nationally and in Los Angeles, Justice for Janitors organizers deliberately steered clear of the NLRB representation election process, for several reasons. Not only had that process become increasingly biased in favor of employers generally, but it was structurally problematic in this particular industry. Most contracts with office cleaning firms included thirty-day cancellation clauses, so that if the union won a representation election, the building owner could simply switch to a new, nonunion cleaning contractor and effectively void the result. The architects of the SEIU's Justice for Janitors campaign were also wary of NLRB-focused organizing because of the danger that its highly technical and legalistic aspects would distance the union from rank-and-file workers. "It's an alienating process for workers," one organizer declared of the NLRB approach, and one that "separates the union from the workers."

The L.A. Justice for Janitors drive therefore relied on an alternative organizing strategy that was designed to avoid these problems, namely, the "comprehensive campaign," which one SEIU organizer defined as "a war against the employers [the cleaning contractors] and the building owners, waged on all fronts [without] leaving any stone unturned." In the words of an L.A. janitor, "The strategy was attack, attack, attack." It was also an industrywide organizing strategy, which was an essential element given the building owners' ability to rapidly shift work from one contractor to another. The goal was to exercise union leverage on all the key players in the local labor market so as to effectively take wages out of competition.

One of SEIU's major strengths was a business-oriented understanding of the building service industry. As one organizer put it, "We always try to understand the industry as it understands itself." From its inception, the L.A. campaign "had a full-time research/corporate person. They don't have worker responsibilities—they're information-gatherers and utilizers." Locally gathered information was supplemented by data supplied by researchers at SEIU headquarters in Washington, D.C. As one impressed management informant put it, SEIU had the ability to "ferret out the weaknesses" of the ownership-management structure in any particular situation. This effort depended on access to highly skilled, college-educated organizers and researchers, combined with the technological resources that enabled them to be effective.

This research-intensive approach was important not only for targeting building owners and other key players in the industry but also for educating and activating the rank-and-file membership. "Our economists know how to crunch the numbers . . . the real numbers. Someone will get pissed if they learn that it costs the owner one cent to give them a raise." The effort to thoroughly understand the industry, then, was part of a top-down campaign approach, but over time it also became a tool for empowering workers at the bottom, enabling them to see how and why they had the potential to transform their own workplaces.

Despite its rejection of the NLRB-oriented electoral road to unionism as overly legalistic, the L.A. janitors' campaign did make extensive use of aggressive legal tactics. SEIU Local 399 filed a series of complaints with the NLRB alleging discrimination against union activists and other unfair labor practices (ULPs). Organizers also pursued legal redress through other government agencies in protest of health and safety violations and the like. These efforts were intended to generate economic pressure on the contractors, whose legal costs quickly mounted, and at the same time to position the union as the de facto representative of the workers, even without official recognition from the employers. "We called it 'acting union without a contract,'" an organizer explained. "That was what we tried to do with the workers of the nonunion companies. It didn't require a contract for them to redefine their relationship to their employer and to defend their rights." Filing ULPs also had another important strategic advantage, namely, protecting janitors from being permanently replaced in the event of a strike.[5]

The Justice for Janitors organizers also developed a flair for orchestrating guerrilla-style, "in your face," media-oriented events. For example, in a demonstration at a building profiled in the then-popular television show *L.A. Law*, which was being cleaned by a nonunion firm at the time, the organizers dubbed the structure "the Home of the L.A. Lawless" as they highlighted the employer's violations of janitors' legal rights. On other occasions, SEIU organizers took a group of workers to the country club frequented by the owner of an office cleaning firm, where they "raised a ruckus, chanting and screaming," or performed street theater in front of an upscale restaurant while an industry player dined inside. At the glitzy Century City complex adjacent to Beverly Hills, where the L.A. Justice for Janitors campaign ultimately focused much of its energy, several such publicity stunts were staged to draw attention to the janitors' plight. "The denizens of Century City were not interested in having a bunch of Latino janitors out there in the daytime screaming and yelling. It's fine for us to come in at night and clean their buildings, but they didn't want to look us in the face during the daytime." These tactics were highly effective in publicly embarrassing powerful players in the industry while also making life difficult for building tenants, who were then urged to press the owners to negotiate with the union.

Another critical element of the SEIU strategy involved active outreach to political allies and other organizations in the community.[6] This took several different forms. One stemmed from the fact that the organizing campaign took place in the context of a massive building boom in downtown Los Angeles. As it happened, construction could not begin without approval from the city's Community Redevelopment Authority (CRA), whose board then included the head of the L.A. County Federation of Labor as well as other real or potential union allies. Taking full advantage of this leverage, the SEIU was able to ensure that no downtown office tower built after 1987 opened up without a unionized cleaning crew. The union was able to exert political pressure on developers and owners in other ways as well. "The only people with money to own buildings are banks, insurance companies, and pension funds," an organizer noted with only slight exaggeration, adding that such institutions often were within the orbit of union political networks. The ARCO Center, a huge office tower in downtown Los Angeles that had been built with pension fund money, is one telling example: "The owner didn't call us back," an organizer recalled. "We found out that the pension funds invested in the project came from Ohio PERS [Public Employee Retirement System]. We called the union rep in Ohio, who called the real estate administrator, who then called the development partner, who then called the union."

The SEIU also made excellent use of its ties to local political leaders. In 1990, after the L.A. police violently attacked demonstrating janitors at Century City, the union, with support from the county Federation of Labor, contacted then-mayor Tom Bradley, who immediately telephoned the principal ownership interests at Century City to voice his concern. Still another source of strength tapped into by the janitors' campaign was support from unions representing janitors in other cities. Crucially, the powerful leader of the giant SEIU New York City Local 32B-32J at the time, Gus Bevona, lent a hand after viewing the L.A. police beating the Century City strikers on video. He was uniquely positioned to exert pressure on the main cleaning contractor in Century City, International Service Systems (ISS), which had its headquarters in New York and was also under contract with Local 32B-32J. "Bevona called the president of ISS into his office, and after making him wait for two and a half hours, threatened that if he didn't recognize the L.A. union, all hell would break loose [at ISS's buildings in New York]," an organizer recalled. "The contract with ISS was signed that day."

Many of these tactics relied heavily on the expertise of union staff and were intended, in traditional top-down fashion, to put pressure on the employers. But the success of the L.A. Justice for Janitors campaign also depended on its effectiveness in galvanizing the rank and file into action. Street demonstrations and other shows of strength were central to the larger effort. "At heart and soul, there has to be a mobilized workforce," one organizer declared, adding, "The reason that L.A. is the shining star of the union is that we've had the highest percentage of workers' participation, have the highest worker turnout, and the highest percentage of workers going to jail and getting arrested." The top-down and bottom-up aspects of the campaign were in fact inextricably intertwined. For example, Bevona would not have intervened had it not been for the previous mobilization of strikers on the ground three thousand miles away. Indeed, he had rebuffed an earlier request for assistance from the L.A. organizers, changing his mind only after witnessing the strikers demonstrating in the streets and under attack by police.

The fact that Los Angeles's janitorial workforce was dominated by Latino immigrants facilitated the mobilization process, for reasons discussed in chapter 3. Immigrant janitors' tightly interlocking social networks were central to the bottom-up aspect of the union-building process, and the peculiar conditions of building service work also helped create a sense of occupational community. Mostly working at night, the janitors were thrown together as a group. Many lived in the same neighborhoods or even the same buildings and rode the buses to work together. Among the janitors, moreover, were some seasoned activists from El Salvador and Guatemala who had been involved in left-wing or union activity back home. "Immigrants from Central America have a much more militant history as unionists than we do, and the more militant workers are, the more the union can do," SEIU official (and former UFW vice president) Eliseo Medina noted (Bacon 1995). Reinforcing the leadership of such former activists, the collectively oriented worldviews of the larger immigrant janitor community made them highly receptive to the SEIU's overtures. "If you ask, 'Que piensa de la union?' [what do you think of the union?], they answer, 'La union hace la fuerza' [union is power]," an organizer recalled.

The janitors' campaign, then, married top-down and bottom-up elements. Although it originated as part of a strategic union rebuilding effort conceived by the SEIU's national leadership and relied heavily on research and other staff-intensive means of exerting pressure on the employers, rank-and-file mobilization also played a critical role in its success. Five years after the 1990 victory, however, the bottom-up side of the organization showed some signs of neglect. The L.A. janitors' union attracted widespread criticism at this point thanks to an outbreak of internal factionalism that, at least on the surface, appeared to involve rank-and-file rebellion against the local SEIU officialdom. In the summer of 1995, a local union election unexpectedly displaced incumbent leaders. SEIU Local 399's membership had long included thousands of health care workers as well as the newly recruited janitors, and elements within both groups apparently had grievances against the local union's leadership. That most of the incumbent union officials were "Anglos," whereas those newly elected were mainly Latino and African Americans—they ran on a slate called "the Multiracial Alliance"—complicated the story further. When the dissidents encountered resistance to their move to replace key members of the local union staff, they launched a hunger strike and camped out in front of the local union offices (Nazario 1995; see also Fantasia and Voss 2004, 146–47; Carney 2000, 217–19; Tait 2005, 200–1).

This internal conflict eventually led the SEIU national office to place the local into trusteeship.[7] Indeed, this is a frequently cited example of what Steve Early (2004, 34, 39) roundly criticizes as "transformation by trusteeship"; he reports that a total of 40 of the SEIU's 275 local affiliates have been trusteed since 1996. In Local 399's case, the trustee appointed by the national union was Mike Garcia, himself a former organizer and insurgent who was president of SEIU Local 1877, representing janitors in San Jose, Oakland, and Sacramento (Bacon 1995). During the trusteeship, the L.A. local underwent a restructuring process that separated the health care workers and the janitors: Local 399 retained the health care workers, while the janitors were incorporated into Local 1877.

Meanwhile, the union was negotiating a new five-year agreement for the L.A. janitors. The main union gain in the contract that took effect in 1995 was to narrow pay and benefit differentials between janitors in the core downtown area (as well as Century City) and those in outlying areas (Erickson et al. 2002). Here was a sign that the unionization of the city's immigrant janitors was not some fleeting achievement, despite the internal dissension in the local union and the slump in the local real estate market during the early 1990s.

Indeed, in the years that followed, the L.A. janitors further consolidated their gains and expanded the size of their membership. Whereas the 1995 contract round had produced rather modest pay and benefit improvements, five years later the union made far more impressive advances, including a 25 percent pay raise over a new three-year contract, as well as greatly improved health benefits. This time the contract campaign involved a three-week strike, but the union had prepared its strategy meticulously, and the gamble paid off. Not only did the strike lead to big economic gains for the membership, but the 2000 settlement also brought some five thousand previously nonunion janitors in southern California into the SEIU fold (Erickson et al. 2002).

Like the original Justice for Janitors organizing a decade earlier, the 2000 contract campaign was predicated on an approach that meticulously

combined top-down and bottom-up strategies. It replicated many features of the 1990 effort, with spirited street demonstrations, sophisticated and highly effective public relations work, and a strategic approach
that leveraged the SEIU's ever-growing political clout. The strikers' demand for a one-dollar-per-hour raise struck a chord in the wider community, winning the hearts and minds of Angelenos to the cause of low-
wage immigrant workers in a city of enormous—and conspicuously
displayed—wealth. The strikers garnered support from all over the community, from the Catholic Church officialdom to politicians, who by now
were highly mindful of organized labor's role in local politics and the centrality of the janitors' union to immigrant political mobilization (see
chapter 3). Other unions around the city also rallied in support of the
strikers.

The 2000 walkout itself was preceded by a full year of "internal organizing" (union jargon for mobilizing a union's existing members) designed
to prepare both the union's stewards and the rank-and-file membership
for a possible strike by educating them about the economics of the industry and the issues at stake in the contract fight. Even before the strike began, the union displayed its strength in a mass rally and a public membership vote rejecting the terms of management's last offer. What followed
was a "rolling strike," with janitors marching in their colorful T-shirts,
each day pouring into the streets of a different part of sprawling Los Angeles.

This campaign was not limited to Los Angeles but formed an integral
part of a national SEIU strategy to coordinate the contracts of janitorial
locals across the country, many of whose members worked for the same
national, or in some cases global, building maintenance contractors. The
union had managed to line up contract expiration dates in various key
cities to follow one another in close succession, giving the L.A. strikers
added leverage (Meyerson 2000). Using a similarly coordinated national
strategy, SEIU's janitors in Los Angeles and elsewhere made still further
gains in the 2003 contract round, this time without a strike (Meyerson
2003).

From its beginnings in the late 1980s, then, the Justice for Janitors
campaign succeeded by masterfully combining top-down and bottom-up
strategies. As Harold Meyerson (2000, 24) wrote in assessing the 2000
strike, the outcome was "a tribute to the spirit and tenacity of the janitors
themselves, to the cohesiveness of the L.A. labor movement, and to the
manifest strategic smarts of the international union to which the janitors
belong, the SEIU." He added, somewhat ominously, that this is "about as

good as it gets in the American labor movement today." Indeed, as our other case studies reveal, immigrant organizing efforts were not always this successful, not even in Los Angeles with its various comparative advantages.

AN UNSUCCESSFUL TOP-DOWN CAMPAIGN: THE EFFORT TO ORGANIZE GUESS, INC.

Just a few years after the SEIU leadership had begun to rebuild unionism in its traditional jurisdiction of building services through the Justice for Janitors campaign, a group of organizers on the staff of the ILGWU began to think strategically about how to restore their union's lost strength in the apparel sector. In view of the fact that the garment industry's center of gravity had shifted decisively to Los Angeles, it was fitting that such an effort be focused there. "We figured if we could not crack the L.A. market in some significant way, that our union was going to continue losing power and eventually fade from the scene," one of the architects of this strategy recalled. "It was one of the key things that we had to do . . . to retain the character of the union as a needle trades union." The task, however, was daunting, since by the early 1990s the union had declined so dramatically that it represented a minuscule share of the city's nearly 100,000 garment workers (see table 2.1).

Yet the ILGWU had a talented organizing staff with extensive knowledge of the industry, and now they began to map out a strategic plan to rebuild. In late 1994 the L.A. lead organizer wrote a lengthy memorandum to the ILGWU's national organizing director, proposing that the union target one of the major players in the city's garment industry. The memo argued that the best company for the union to focus on was the upscale designer jeans manufacturer Guess, Inc., then thirteen years old and easily Los Angeles's largest and most profitable apparel firm.[8]

> A tremendous amount of investigative work has been done to analyze the production systems, finances, and trends of the target firms. . . . Guess is the colossus of the L.A. industry, extremely powerful and strong. . . . Guess has the desirable feature of being geographically concentrated, mainly in downtown, of having almost all its production in the U.S., and of having a history of problems in their shops. . . . Guess is selling an overpriced product . . . built on image and advertising. . . . They've also made an issue of having their clothes made in the U.S./L.A. This makes them vulnerable to the

slogan: "Made in the USA—With Sweatshop Labor." . . . Guess is the most important firm in Los Angeles and would establish the union as a force on the west coast. Finally, I believe that a Guess campaign would serve as a catalyst for "community" involvement, capturing the imagination of . . . other unions and community groups. (David Young to Jeff Hermanson, November 14, 1994; copy in authors' possession)

Like Justice for Janitors, then, the Guess campaign was the brainchild of union staffers and part of a larger strategy of union rebuilding and revitalization. But rather than a national union leadership imposing its strategic agenda on reluctant local officials, as in the janitors' case, here it was the ILGWU's L.A. staff, along with its national organizing director, trying to persuade the union's top leadership to support the campaign. In fact, the union's top leaders were lukewarm from the outset, giving the project "a green light with a flashing yellow," as one organizer later recalled. For even in the 1990s, long after the garment industry's center of gravity had shifted decisively to Los Angeles, the ILGWU's most powerful leaders remained deeply rooted in New York City, where the union had managed to retain a significant membership. Those leaders continued to regard Los Angeles as a remote hinterland, one more outpost on the vast nonunion periphery. The Guess organizing strategy, then, emerged from midlevel leaders rather than from those at the peak of the organization.

Locally, the L.A. ILGWU had a good reputation because of its pioneering efforts to organize the immigrant workers who had come to dominate the city's low-wage workforce. As early as the mid-1970s, the union's western organizing director had targeted immigrant workers for recruitment and hired some ten young, progressive Latino organizers for this purpose. They succeeded in winning union representation elections at a variety of small immigrant-employing plants, virtually all of them outside the garment sector: a muffler factory, a furniture shop, a plant that made pillows, and even a firm that fabricated tombstones. This wave of organizing did nothing to reverse the erosion of unionism in the garment industry, which continued apace, but it had other important results. It helped the L.A. ILGWU replace the members it had lost in the garment shops. And as noted in chapter 3, it helped mold a new generation of Latino union organizers, some of whom would devote their lives to the labor movement and to immigrant organizing in particular (although in most cases not to the garment workers' union).

Still, this situation was frustrating for many of the union's L.A. organizers. They were surrounded by the nation's largest concentration of garment workers, the historical base of the ILGWU, and yet they lacked the resources to conduct effective organizing in that sector. Having learned the hard way that a campaign that targets only one garment shop is doomed to failure, cohort after cohort of ILGWU organizers had come to the same conclusion: the only hope of restoring unionism in the L.A. garment industry was to strategically target a distinct subindustry, or a firm making a particular product line, with the goal of taking wages out of competition. The cutthroat competition that prevailed in the industry made keeping the union out, from the employers' perspective, simply a matter of survival. If the union did somehow succeed in organizing an isolated subcontracting shop, the manufacturer would simply shift work elsewhere, forcing the shop to close. Just as in the case of building services, then, NLRB-oriented strategies were an exercise in futility.

This logic pointed to an industrywide regional organizing strategy, but given the national union leadership's lack of enthusiasm, that was not a practical possibility. When the opportunity to develop an organizing strategy for the L.A. garment industry finally presented itself in the 1990s, therefore, the ILGWU organizers settled on the idea of targeting a single company, which turned out to be Guess. "Our feeling was that organizing Guess would be an awfully good alternative to organizing the whole sportswear industry in L.A., and it would give us a base," one of the architects of the campaign later recalled. "It would be a launching pad to do something even bigger than that, which is what our goal was."

Although conceived as a prelude to something even more ambitious, the Guess campaign itself was a daunting undertaking. The firm employed about thirty-five-hundred workers at the time, mostly via its many subcontractors—then numbering around seventy. The organizers well knew that unless they attacked on multiple fronts simultaneously, the company would be able to shift work around easily in response to a strike at any given contractor. "We called it 'the octopus,'" an organizer recalled. "It has all these tentacles. If you grab hold of one, it just sheds that one and kills you with the other ones." The plan was for a limited, strike-based strategy focused on a few key contractors as well as the "inside shop" where Guess housed its sample-making, distribution, and other activities. The goal was to generate ULP strikes (like the janitors had done, thereby avoiding the risk of "permanent replacements" taking strikers' jobs) at these locations and to use them to support workers employed by the rest of the contractors. "We wanted to have an army of five hundred to a thousand workers on strike from all those shops together and use them to picket all the others, and they would be the backbone of the campaign," an organizer explained.

Simultaneous with this effort, which union officials called the "ground war," there were elaborate plans for an "air war," a corporate campaign exposing sweatshop conditions at Guess and its subcontractors. Corporate campaigns essentially rely on in-depth research to identify pressure points in a target firm's network of business relationships and then seek to turn parts of that network against the firm. One organizer explicitly compared the effort to the Vietnam War: "We are the Viet Cong. We are the weaker. We don't have the resources of the employer. But we have the ability to win hearts and minds and make it impossible for us to be defeated. We maybe can't win any particular battle—we can't win all of them, for sure. But we can win the war." This corporate campaign concept dates back to the 1960s, when antiwar activists used it to gain leverage against large corporations involved in supporting the Vietnam War. In the 1970s the same strategy was deployed successfully by ACTWU, the textile workers' union (which merged with the ILGWU to form UNITE in 1995, just when the Guess campaign was getting started), in conjunction with its national boycott of the J. P. Stevens company (Manheim 2001).

The ILGWU's plan from the outset was to intensify pressure on Guess, whose business was highly dependent on its public image, by exposing damaging information about sweatshop conditions in the factories where its products were made. In coordination with a planned consumer boycott as well as a bottom-up organizing effort among workers focused on the ULP strikes, the union hoped to capitalize on the growing public indignation about sweatshops. Along with the campaign's impact on real and potential customers and the general public, the idea was that retailers and others doing business with Guess would be embarrassed by the revelations about working conditions so that pressure on the company to recognize the union would intensify. That Guess was a demonstrably profitable firm that could easily "afford" to pay union wages, and could absorb the costs of its subcontractors in doing so, also figured into the strategy, as did the fact that Guess had been the very first company to enter into a voluntary monitoring agreement with the U.S. Department of Labor after Clinton's election in 1992 to prevent illegal sweatshop practices among its contractors (Bonacich and Appelbaum 2000, 229–30; Esbenshade 2001).

As in the janitors' case, the organizers who planned this campaign conducted extensive research on the power structure of the garment industry in the region, as well as that of Guess in particular. Like their SEIU counterparts, the ILGWU strategists had in mind a comprehensive campaign that would combine bottom-up and top-down elements. As one organizer later explained:

> We tried to systematically look at every aspect of a campaign. All the bottom-up stuff, what are all the vulnerabilities and how can we plan to attack them at the level of boycott, at the level of strike, at the level of their trucking and distribution, and then at the corporate campaign level. Corporate campaigns tend to be something that's done by people like me sitting in an office and often have little or no worker involvement. And people view strikes as the opposite. *Our view was that a corporate campaign can only be enhanced and strengthened by having workers on strike* who are participating in whatever it is you're doing, whether it's taking them to a college campus or participating in a boycott. . . . In other words, *there's no contradiction between running a ground war and an air war. The strongest wars have both.* (emphasis added)

Much like the L.A. Justice for Janitors effort, then, the Guess campaign began as a top-down initiative that was launched by the union rather than emerging from the grass roots and that relied heavily on staff-intensive research. Yet, again like the janitors' case, from the outset rank-and-file mobilization was also meant to be an integral component of the ILGWU campaign. "A consumer boycott is not really effective by itself," one strategist explained. "But when you combine it with a production strike which causes delays in deliveries and, sometimes, quality problems in the merchandise, then it can be very effective." The organizers expended a great deal of effort developing the selective strike strategy and making contacts with interested workers inside the shops. Had they carried out their plan as originally envisaged, the Guess campaign might have closely paralleled that of the janitors. However, a series of unfortunate developments intervened to put the ILGWU's effort on a different, far less auspicious, path.

The most important of these was the merger of the ILGWU and ACTWU, which took place in 1995, just before the Guess campaign was slated to be launched. The internal politics of the merger and the attendant power shifts soon led to a significant scaling back of the original commitment to the Guess effort on the part of the national union leadership as different groups within UNITE scrambled for resources for the projects each wanted to pursue. The original proposal for the Guess campaign had involved a commitment of thirty highly experienced organizers, but in the end, as one key staff member recalled sadly, "we didn't get them. We got fifteen, half of whom were extremely inexperienced." As a result, another organizer stated, "we couldn't get [rank-and-file] committees in more than a few of the major contract shops."

And crucially, UNITE's new leadership in New York believed that the strike strategy as originally envisaged was not viable and should not be pursued. Instead, the organizers were instructed to concentrate their efforts exclusively on the "air war," or the corporate campaign against Guess. It is likely that the ACTWU leaders' long-standing familiarity with corporate campaigns, dating back to the J. P. Stevens boycott in the 1980s, influenced this shift. The new UNITE leadership's decision to cut back on the resources devoted to the Guess campaign also reflected the fact that, as would become obvious a few years later, they regarded the very idea of reorganizing the garment industry in the United States as quixotic. Indeed, by century's end the union would entirely abandon any attempts to reorganize apparel manufacturing, shifting its focus toward industrial laundries, warehouses, and other place-bound operations (Ross 2004, 204).

The Guess campaign nevertheless got off to a promising start in the summer of 1996, when UNITE formally complained to the U.S. Department of Labor that the company's contractors were illegally involved in industrial homework and violating other labor laws as well. The timing was excellent: the complaints were publicized just before the firm was scheduled to launch its initial public stock offering. UNITE picketed at the Waldorf-Astoria in New York, where Guess was holding a reception for potential investors, and distributed a "white paper" alleging various legal violations and sweatshop practices at the company and its contractors.

The white paper reminded its readers that a few years earlier, when Guess had first entered into the U.S. Department of Labor's voluntary monitoring program, it had been required to pay $573,000 in back wages for previous labor violations; moreover, the union claimed, the monitoring had failed to prevent new abuses, so that subminimum pay, homework, and other illegal practices were still routine in Guess's contracting factories. Soon after this, UNITE filed a class action suit on behalf of a group of garment workers in connection with these alleged labor law violations. These efforts generated a great deal of negative national publicity, thanks to Guess's high-profile product line, and at first the "air war" seemed to be going extremely well for the union. The stock offering was postponed, and Guess was suspended from the Department of Labor's "trendsetter" list of garment firms that were voluntarily complying with labor laws. "We had a tremendous impact on them . . . at the level of their image, which is their single biggest vulnerability," one organizer recalled. "They were infuriated and scared."

But then Guess began to fight back. A few months after the campaign was launched, Guess filed the first in what would become a long series of lawsuits against the union. And the company rapidly began shifting work away from contractors where the union had developed some strength, generating layoffs that soon had devastating effects on worker morale. In response to the "air war," meanwhile, Guess launched a public relations countercampaign, which was energetically supported by the L.A. garment industry as a whole. The trade press and employers' organizations understood that if UNITE's campaign was successful, wider organizing efforts in the industry would soon follow.

A bit later, an anti-union committee made up of Guess workers began holding public demonstrations to counter UNITE's campaign, calling for an NLRB election to prove that the workers did not want a union. The employers provided bus transportation to the protest and paid the workers attending (Shaw 1999, 116). UNITE immediately charged that management had illegally manipulated workers into forming the committee—a complaint the NLRB later validated (see Bonacich and Appelbaum 2000, 270–71). This was nevertheless a highly effective anti-union tactic, as it also has been elsewhere (see Penney 2004).

Finally, in January 1997, Guess announced plans to move 40 percent of its production, nearly all of which had been located in the United States until that point, to Mexico. The union filed charges with the NLRB, arguing that the outsourcing was a form of illegal retaliation against the organizing effort. But the company's announcement nevertheless was devastating. "It's basically a death blow," one organizer said. "We have moved the work out of the country, fuck you! You know, you may fight us with some lawsuits for a while, but it's over. Workers know it's over. Society knows it's over. We have the right to produce wherever we want, and if you don't like it, too bad."

The company poured millions of dollars into legal maneuvers, and the union too was forced to devote enormous sums of money to what can only be described as a legal morass. Although UNITE never publicly abandoned the Guess campaign, it gradually withered away even as the union moved further and further away from any attempts to organize the larger L.A. garment industry. The "air war" against Guess did produce a great deal of creative publicity, however, and the union was successful in building alliances in the wider community involving students, religious groups, and others (Shaw 1999, 118–20). The boycott attracted support from celebrities and others who urged consumers not to buy Guess products, and it helped fuel the broader antisweatshop movement (Featherstone 2002). In addition, the lawsuit that UNITE had filed at the outset of the campaign on behalf of workers subjected to illegal sweatshop practices was settled some years later at an estimated cost to Guess of up to $1 million (Cleeland 1999).

The effort to organize Guess was far less successful on the ground, however, largely because of the union's decision not to engage in strike activity and to reduce the number of organizers assigned to the campaign. UNITE's new leaders were unwilling to devote adequate funds to rank-and-file mobilization, in effect undercutting the "ground war." (Although the union ultimately incurred millions of dollars in legal expenses connected to the Guess campaign, this was entirely involuntary.) This is the most striking point of contrast to the Justice for Janitors campaign, to which the national SEIU leadership committed extensive resources, committed as it was to both the bottom-up and the top-down components of the effort.

The Guess campaign's devolution, as it turned out, coincided with a change in the global garment industry's employment patterns. The number of garment workers in Los Angeles County, after having increased for decades, peaked in 1996 and then began to decline.[9] Along with various other globalizing pressures, the 1994 North American Free Trade Agreement (NAFTA) accelerated the shift of jobs to Mexico. More recently, the 2005 expiration of the Multi-Fiber Agreement has accelerated the trend toward outsourcing, especially to China, with the elimination of all import quotas. Although the garment industry still has a huge presence in southern California and is likely to retain a significant amount of employment there, capital mobility presents an increasingly formidable obstacle to organizing efforts.

In the Guess case, however, that obstacle may not have been insurmountable. The campaign strategists recognized the danger from the outset, but they were convinced that the company's widely publicized commitment to sell products "Made in the USA" would obviate the outsourcing scenario. "The company was extremely profitable, and growing," one organizer noted. "You could organize it and keep it here. . . . If you can bring Guess to their knees, where their financial situation is such that they have to make a deal, they can sign a contract that says 75 percent of the work has to be done in the United States and in union shops." Although in the end Guess did export many jobs to Mexico, a more effective union campaign, one with both the top-down and bottom-up elements fully developed, could have led to a different outcome. UNITE's decision to withdraw from the "ground war," in short, was a self-fulfilling prophecy.

SUCCESSFUL BOTTOM-UP ORGANIZING: THE 1992 DRYWALLERS' STRIKE

Whereas both the Justice for Janitors and Guess campaigns began as top-down affairs, the drywallers' highly successful organizing campaign started at the grass roots. The initial phase took shape in October 1991, when Jesus Gomez, an immigrant from El Maguey, a small village in the Mexican state of Guanajuato, complained of being cheated out of some of his pay by a drywall contractor. The regional economy was in a deep recession at the time, and the impact on residential construction had been especially severe. The piecework rates at which drywall hangers were paid had fallen to a new low of about four cents a square foot—which translated into earnings of only about $40 to $75 for a ten-hour day. Premium pay for difficult work had also been eliminated. Gomez, then thirty-three years old, had been hanging drywall since 1975 and vividly remembered the bygone days when the industry was thoroughly unionized and pay rates were double what they had descended to by late 1991. Along with several other experienced drywallers who would soon become leaders of the organizing campaign—most of them also from his hometown of El Maguey—Gomez had been suffering the consequences of the union's decline for a full decade. When his employer paid him $60 less than the already meager amount he was supposed to receive for the third week in a row, Gomez decided it was time to fight back. "If someone is stealing out of your pocket, you have to do something," he explained.

He contacted some Carpenters' union officials, who offered him meeting space in their Orange County union hall. Gomez began visiting job sites and talking up the idea with other drywallers he knew, many of them friends from his hometown. The fact that at least a few hundred men from El Maguey worked in the southern California drywall trade and were bound by close kin and friendship ties was by all accounts a vital source of the solidarity that would prove so effective in the organizing campaign and in the strike it sparked. Although these immigrants from a small village in western Mexico may have lacked the political sophistication and experience of the Salvadorans who helped provide rank-and-file leadership to the janitors' campaign, the drywallers' social networks were probably even stronger. Like the janitors, they also shared an occupational culture, although without the organizational infrastructure that characterized the unionized sector of the construction industry.

Far from radical in their political orientation, some of the rank-and-file leaders of the drywall organizing drive were, or had been, "labor barons"—the immigrant middlemen who recruited and managed work crews for the building contractors. Although in this capacity they had acted as de facto agents of management in earlier years, in the face of the dramatic deterioration of wages and conditions in the late 1980s and early 1990s, some of these middlemen switched their allegiances. "Kind of ironic, isn't it?" one contractor complained. "They brought these labor barons in and started controlling the minds of the Hispanic worker out there and telling them how much more money they could make, how they could get health benefits, this, that, and everything else, if they would get involved." In fact, this shift was not as unprecedented as it may have seemed: the construction industry had always had a fluid class structure, with individuals circulating in and out of positions as small contractors, then returning to the ranks of workers (and to the union) if their business ventures did not pan out (see chapter 1).

In any case, the former labor barons who now turned to labor organizing not only were central figures in the drywall workers' social networks but also had the local knowledge and experience to become highly sophisticated, capable union leaders. "They knew the inside of the industry very well," an attorney who assisted the organizing campaign later recalled. "They could see that the bottom was falling out of the industry and their choice was to either leave it or do something to make it better. A lot of them had been here more than ten years and knew what it was like to live well off this industry."

The organizing got off to a slow start, but after a few months the Saturday morning meetings Gomez and his compatriots convened in the Carpenters' Local 2361 union hall in Orange County were attracting hundreds of workers. As the effort mushroomed, separate committees were formed in each of the six counties involved (Orange, Ventura, San Bernardino, Riverside, Los Angeles, and San Diego). Over a period of about eight months, hundreds of drywallers were recruited into the campaign, and finally they decided to strike on June 1, 1992.

Although the Carpenters did make meeting space available for the organizing effort, the union members and staff—at this point still heavily "Anglo" and relatively conservative—were sharply divided in their views of the drywallers' organizing effort. Some of them saw the potential of the movement, but many others were openly hostile to the Latino workers who now dominated the trade, holding them directly responsible for the deterioration of pay and working conditions that had swept across residential construction in the course of its deunionization during the 1980s. In any case, many building trades workers and unionists were deeply skeptical about the prospects for the organizing drive that Gomez and his compatriots had launched, since they still believed that immigrants were "unorganizable."

The drywallers' organizing effort was launched, then, as a bottom-up campaign that the Carpenters simply would not have attempted on their own. As it turned out, however, the union's initial coolness toward the effort proved fortuitous. The fact that the immigrant drywallers, who called themselves simply "the Movement of Drywall Hangers," were not formally affiliated with any "labor organization" was a huge advantage, for they were not subject to the thirty-day legal limit on picketing for union recognition in construction (after which the law requires that a petition be filed for an NLRB representation election). When the anti-union Building Industry Association filed charges with the NLRB against the Carpenters in response to the strike, the complaints were dismissed for lack of evidence, precisely because the union was not an official sponsor of the strike. The employers were able to win temporary restraining orders against picketers in some cases, but even this proved more difficult than usual, thanks to the strikers' independent status. As management attorneys pointed out later, "Declining representation by a traditional labor organization in the early stages of the strike was an important tactic."

At the outset, the drywallers' walkout was extremely effective, shutting down the entire residential construction industry from Ventura County (just north of Los Angeles) to the Mexican border. There were many allegations of intimidation and violence from the beginning. Although it is difficult to know how extensively such tactics actually were used, they were particularly potent in the context of the immigrant networks within which most drywallers were enmeshed. "The Hispanic community is pretty tight. Most of these people know where everyone lives," one contractor explained. "The guy down the street is a union supporter, you want to go to work, he sees you leave in the morning with your tools, he's going to report you to the union thugs, that you're working. They're going to threaten you." Intimidation aside, immigrant social networks cemented what was by all accounts an extraordinary degree of solidarity among the strikers, with over 90 percent participation.

Solidarity began to falter, however, as the employers moved to defend themselves, winning court injunctions and actively recruiting "replacement workers" from out of state. As the conflict wore on into a second month, the strikers became increasingly desperate financially, and as many as 30 percent of them, by the organizers' own estimates, began drifting back to work. This situation improved, however, when, in response to the crisis, the AFL-CIO regional office set up a "Dry Wallers Strike Fund," soliciting contributions to help strikers pay their rent and other bills, as well as donations of pro-bono legal assistance. This fund ultimately raised over $1 million from over twenty different unions, with the Carpenters contributing easily the largest share. Food and money were also donated by a range of community and church groups, including some from as far away as San Francisco. As the police began to arrest and jail strikers by the hundreds, the AFL-CIO fund also became increasingly critical for bail purposes. Legal assistance was coordinated by the California Immigrant Workers' Association (CIWA), an organization founded in 1989 by the AFL-CIO. The combination of extensive funding for bail payments, on the one side, and sophisticated legal assistance, on the other, proved critical. "The thing that really helped us was being able to bail leaders out of jail and keep 'em on the ground," an organizer explained. "That kept the morale going. As we accelerated the strike and pulled more workers off the job sites, it was the ability of those workers to look out there and constantly see their leaders willing to take the risk, going to jail."

As in the Justice for Janitors and Guess campaigns, the role of the media was also critically important. The strike began only a few months after the L.A. "riots" in the spring of 1992, when the sensitivity of the police to media scrutiny was at its peak. The strike organizers and their supporters in the AFL-CIO and CIWA took full advantage of the timing. "We said, 'It's a Latino Rodney King,'" an organizer recalled. Both for this reason and because of the drama inherent in the strike itself, the drywallers were able to win highly sympathetic media coverage. "There were just great articles talking about the conditions these workers were in," recalled an AFL-CIO staffer. "It was front-page stuff, and it was on television, and here we were in the midst of this hostile, anti-immigrant community, and yet there was such solid public support for these strikers. . . . The media coverage was outstanding."

In late July 1992, after the strike had been going on for about two months, CIWA-funded attorneys filed ULP charges against several builders and contractors with the NLRB, alleging that the temporary restraining orders the employers had obtained to restrict picketing at job sites violated the strikers' legally protected organizing rights. At the same time, in what would prove a far more potent legal offensive, the same attorneys complained to the U.S. Department of Labor that drywall contractors had violated the overtime pay provisions of the 1938 federal Fair Labor Standards Act (FLSA). These complaints, in support of which the attorneys had gathered extensive documentation, were soon followed by dozens of class action lawsuits seeking back pay for the alleged FLSA violations. These suits played a pivotal role in the resolution of the strike, ultimately bringing the contractors to the bargaining table and leading to a settlement in November 1992. Large sums of money were at stake—not only back pay for unpaid overtime over a three-year period but also double punitive damages and attorneys' fees.

The employers' potential liability decidedly tipped the balance in favor of settling the strike, which they had shown little interest in doing until faced with the FLSA lawsuits, filed after a period of several months before and during the walkout when the contractors had intransigently refused to negotiate. "We would have defeated the strike. It was the lawsuits," one drywall executive later recalled. "Once those [suits] were filed, there were some people that had great exposure, and some of those people with great exposure very quickly decided that maybe we should find a way to settle this lawsuit and the strike. It became in their interest to become a union contractor and have all this go away."

Starting in September, the Pacific Rim Drywall Association (PRDA), a trade group made up of nonunion residential drywall contractors that had had no previous involvement in labor issues, began meeting with strike leaders and with representatives of the Carpenters' union, who at this point stepped forward with an offer to represent the strikers and help them obtain a union contract. By November, when the settlement agreement was concluded, the PRDA had grown to embrace an estimated 75 percent of the drywall industry in the five-county L.A. area. In November 1992, the group agreed to recognize the Carpenters as the exclusive bargaining agent for the drywall workers (significantly, without an NLRB representation election). The strikers now became dues-paying members of the Carpenters' union, and the employers signed a two-year contract providing for higher wages and medical benefits in exchange for the union's agreement to withdraw the FLSA suits against the signatory firms.

Although the contract represented a substantial improvement from the viewpoint of the immigrant workers involved, doubling wages relative to their prestrike levels, neither the wages nor the benefits won were comparable to what drywall hangers had enjoyed in the union era. Wages had already risen during the strike, and thus the final contract terms were not perceived as especially onerous by the employers. "It was a good agreement," a drywall contractor said, articulating the employers' typical perspective. "It did have health insurance, but the men had to pay for half of it. And there was no pension, none of the things that you normally associate with a union." Moreover, the contract included an unusual clause providing that if the market share held by union drywall firms in the area fell by 20 percent or more, wage rates would be determined by market conditions. These were employers who well understood the logic of taking wages out of competition.

A significant limitation on the drywallers' victory was the refusal of the drywall employers in San Diego, who had resisted the strike far more vigorously from the outset, to join in the PRDA-brokered settlement. Instead, with financial support from the anti-union Associated Builders and Contractors (ABC), the San Diego firms filed a massive lawsuit against the Carpenters' union under the Racketeer Influenced and Corrupt Organizations (RICO) Act in November 1992, just after the strike was settled to their north, accusing the union of orchestrating the strike and the alleged violence associated with it. The RICO suit was settled out of court two years later, but it cast a dark shadow over union organizing in construction and elsewhere for years to come (Brody 1995).

Nevertheless, by any standard the drywallers' strike was a huge victory for the fledgling immigrant union movement as well as for the efforts that building trades organizers were launching around the country in the late 1980s and early 1990s to rebuild unionism in the construction industry (see Palladino 2005, ch. 9). If those efforts have yet to be fully realized, the drywallers' strike did help persuade previously skeptical unionists that organizing was a worthwhile undertaking. For many of the building trades officials who became involved, the strike was a life-changing experience. "There are people who go through their whole careers as business agents, and they never see anything like this," one Carpenters' union staffer recalled. "It finally brought to view that organizing was possible, that it's not just some B.S. ethereal concept. From then on forward, whenever I bump up into a developer and they find out who I am, it's like, 'Oh, you guys really can blow things up!' I think any craft that had the bucks could try something similar."

After the settlement, the Carpenters' union hired two of the strike leaders as full-time staff members, and the union was able to sustain its new foothold in the regional residential construction industry. It later negotiated a series of contract renewals for the drywallers that maintained the wage rates the strikers had succeeded in obtaining, as well as the union's market share of the drywall trade. However, in contrast to the janitors' case, in which the SEIU was able to build on its initial victory to expand and consolidate its initial gains over the course of the 1990s, the Carpenters have not made further inroads in the residential sector of the construction industry, apart from a 1995 strike by framers that led to a modest increase in the union's membership. A new building boom has kept the union afloat, but workers move in and out of the union (Jordan 2005).

Nationally, however, the Carpenters' union did expand its commitment to organizing the unorganized, under the maverick leadership of Douglas McCarron, who headed the Southern California Council of Carpenters (SCCC) at the time of the drywall strike and became the Carpenters' national president three years later. McCarron had started out as a drywall hanger in southern California's residential construction industry in the 1970s, when the trade was still highly unionized. He quickly rose through the union ranks and became the SCCC head in 1987. Both in that role and then nationally after his ascent to the union presidency, McCarron engineered an ambitious and controversial union restructuring effort. As president, he dedicated half of the union's budget to organizing, while taking steps to merge previously autonomous locals and consolidate power into a few dozen regional councils. He laid off most of the staff at the union's national headquarters while increasing the number of organizers on the union payroll from fifty to seven hundred. He demolished the Washington, D.C., building that had been the Carpenters' headquarters since the 1960s, replacing it with a new structure in which most of the space is rented, generating income to support the union's other activities (Winston 2002; Cleeland 2002; Grabelsky 2004–2005). In 2001 McCarron pulled the Carpenters out of the AFL-CIO, and in 2005 his union became part of the new Change to Win Federation, whose affiliates include the SEIU and five other unions. CTW's program in some respects parallels the Carpenters' own restructuring under McCarron.

The current rapprochement between the SEIU and the Carpenters at the national level presents an interesting counterpoint to the two unions' successes in southern California in the early 1990s. On the surface, the two cases may appear to involve radically different types of organizing.

As we have seen, the Justice for Janitors effort was initiated by SEIU's top national leadership, whereas the drywallers' campaign began as a bottom-up effort, without any official union sponsorship. Led by immigrant middlemen who had once acted as labor contractors and de facto supervisors, the drywallers' campaign had an organizing momentum that was rooted primarily in the resilient immigrant social networks that formed the highly cohesive occupational community of the drywallers themselves. From the union's perspective, "the drywallers were like the hundred-dollar bills that you find in the street—it was handed to you," as one organizer later exclaimed.

Yet once the mobilization effort emerged, the Carpenters' union and the regional AFL-CIO rose to the occasion, providing enormous organizational, financial, and legal resources—including strike benefits as well as funds for bail expenses and legal talent—to support the strike. Without that support, the rank-and-file effort that Gomez and his allies launched would have been doomed to failure. As in the Justice for Janitors case, then, what carried the day for the drywallers was the combination of bottom-up grassroots organizing among the rank and file and the union's top-down contributions of legal expertise, financial resources, and collective bargaining experience. The two campaigns had very different starting points, but they converged over time into surprisingly similar comprehensive efforts.

THE PORT TRUCKERS' 1996 STRIKE: A BOTTOM-UP CAMPAIGN THAT FIZZLED

Our fourth case involves another example of bottom-up organizing, an effort strikingly similar in its origins to the drywallers' campaign, although without a comparably successful conclusion. In the spring of 1996, after a year and a half of organizing, about six thousand Latino truck drivers who hauled container freight from the port of Los Angeles–Long Beach to warehouses, rail terminals, and other local destinations stopped work. Like the drywallers, they were largely self-organized but had turned to an established labor union for assistance. In this case, the union involved was not the one that had historically represented workers in their occupation (the Teamsters) but instead the Communication Workers of America, which took up the truckers' cause energetically despite its lack of previous experience in the transportation sector.

In an earlier era, as chapter 1 recounted, the port truckers had been Teamsters' union members. But in the early 1980s deregulation rapidly transformed their situation, eliminating the union along with conventional forms of employment. Newly recruited, foreign-born "independent contractors" would soon make up the bulk of the workforce. The port truckers now were owner-operators who leased or owned the trucks they drove and were responsible for maintaining the vehicles and buying their own fuel. However, their status as "independent contractors" was questionable from the outset, since most of them relied on the trucking companies for help in buying or leasing their trucks and in obtaining insurance and related details.

The trucking companies benefited from this arrangement, insofar as it transferred risk to the drivers. But the industry's restructuring also reduced the barriers to entry and led to the proliferation of small "mom-and-pop" trucking firms at the port. The resulting cutthroat competition led to a spiral of declining pay rates and deteriorating working conditions. With the shift to owner-operators, moreover, hourly wages were replaced by per-load rates, sparking a dramatic decline in efficiency: once the drivers themselves were forced to absorb the costs of waiting time, neither the shippers nor the trucking companies had any incentive to maintain a centralized dispatching system.

Meanwhile, demand for truckers surged with the rapid expansion of the Los Angeles–Long Beach port—by the 1990s the largest in the United States and the third-largest in the world, where shipping volume surged along with the nation's insatiable appetite for imported goods. The huge growth in ground transportation near the port led to so much traffic congestion that local authorities constructed a direct rail link from the port to the transcontinental train yards near downtown Los Angeles.[10] However, even this huge infrastructural investment was expected to absorb only a fraction of the burgeoning demand for local container transport at the port, while trucking took up the slack. In the decade from 1986 to 1996 alone, trucking employment at the port doubled to about 6,500 drivers, yet this rise in demand did nothing to improve pay and conditions; on the contrary, both continued to deteriorate (Rose and Carlton 1996).

In response to these transformations, the native-born workers who had once dominated port trucking rapidly left the field (see chapter 2). It was not long before the immigrants who took their place began to organize themselves collectively. The process began in the late 1980s— greatly aided, ironically, by the long periods of time that the drivers were forced to spend waiting for their loads at the port. These waiting times, for which the owner-operators were not compensated, were also one of the main issues that galvanized the truckers' protest actions. A two-and-a-half-week strike in the summer of 1988 launched by the independent Waterfront/Rail Truckers Union, for example, focused primarily on the issue of excessive waiting time (Woodyard 1988). The port truckers walked out once again in November 1993, in a more loosely organized protest action sparked by diesel fuel price hikes and new environmental regulations (Jesus Sanchez 1993). Another grassroots group, the Latin American Truckers' Association, emerged in the aftermath of this strike.

Such fleeting episodes of solidarity failed to produce any lasting organization, however. On several occasions, the independent truckers made overtures to the Teamsters, as well as other unions, but they were repeatedly rebuffed. The Teamsters had made some attempts to reorganize the port truckers in the early 1980s, but after these efforts failed they apparently lost interest, a failure of leadership that the union would later come to regret. Nevertheless, the drivers' periodic independent work stoppages demonstrated their potential disruptive power: collectively, they were capable of bringing the region's entire transportation network to a standstill. No one understood this better than the truckers themselves, and thus they continued to pursue the elusive goal of unionization over the years. Finally, in the mid-1990s, they found a labor union that was interested in assisting their organizing and representing them. This was CWA Local 9400, whose membership was primarily made up of telephone workers; it had begun recruiting in a variety of other occupations, however, to compensate for declining membership in its traditional jurisdiction, as many other unions also were doing at the time. When a rank-and-file trucker active in the independent organizing at the port approached a personal contact on the CWA staff in 1994, the union proved receptive.

With rudimentary support from the CWA, the rank-and-file truckers—some of whom had been leaders of the earlier strikes—now began organizing steadily, in a process much like the early stages of the drywallers' campaign. "It was an absolutely disciplined group of people with a tremendous desire to get a union," one CWA official later recalled. "We didn't have to organize them, they already were organized." Similarly, as the Local 9400 organizing director told a newspaper reporter, "this isn't traditional union organizing by any measure. This is building a movement with the people" (Silverstein and Leeds 1996).

Starting with about a dozen workers, the weekly meetings gradually attracted more and more drivers. "We had about forty at one meeting, and the people were starting to understand what was happening. Then

the following week we got sixty," one activist recalled. "And the week after that we got a hundred. Then we weren't fitting in there [the room]
anymore." Eventually, after a series of moves to larger and larger meeting spaces and the development of a systematic recruitment drive by
rank-and-file "mobilizers," first hundreds and later thousands of truckers
were in regular attendance. By the spring of 1996, the meetings had got-
ten so large that the CWA rented a college football stadium for one of the
meetings, and it was filled to capacity with some five thousand truckers.
"It just grew," a CWA official recalled. "They wanted a union. I had been
organizing for thirty years, and I'd never seen this kind of turnout."

Although, unlike the drywallers, the immigrant truckers were not
drawn from a single hometown, or even from a single country (they included Mexicans, Central and South Americans, and a few drivers from
other parts of the world), more dispersed immigrant networks did aid in
the organizing process. In this case, however, a more important facilitating factor was the ongoing opportunity for interaction that truckers had
while they waited for containers in the physically isolated space of the
port terminals. Organizers made excellent use of the long hours that
truckers were compelled to spend idly waiting for their loads in long
lines. "They couldn't go anyplace," one CWA staffer recalled. "We had a
captive audience." As they waited and as they worked, moreover, the
truckers continually had before them the spectacle of durable unionism
inside the shipping terminal gates, where the International Longshore
and Warehouse Union (ILWU) had long represented the well-paid cargo
handlers.

The first phase of the CWA effort focused on the political and legislative avenues through which the drivers' legal status as "independent contractors" might be challenged, since in many respects they more closely
resembled employees. Success on this front would have removed one key
obstacle to unionization, making the truckers legally eligible to participate in NLRB elections. As it was, the union feared that the truckers
might even be vulnerable to sanction under antitrust law if they organized as independent contractors—an angle the employers later pursued.
But the CWA made little headway on the legal front. "We were getting
nowhere," a staffer recalled, "so we decided we were going to start bringing some of this to public attention."

With help from the union, the truckers proceeded to organize a series
of demonstrations to publicize their plight and seek support from the
wider community. In October 1995, they drove in a giant convoy of
trucks from the port all the way to downtown Los Angeles, where they

extracted a supportive resolution from the L.A. City Council. In January 1996, a similar convoy descended on downtown Long Beach, with UFW leaders and AFL-CIO officials on hand to lend support. Although the union did not win the city council's support initially, the following month it did pass a motion supporting the drivers. These demonstrations of strength attracted some publicity for the truckers' demands, which included the establishment of a centralized truckload dispatching system, pay for the time spent waiting for loads, and changing the legal status of the drivers to that of direct employees of the trucking companies (Mongelluzzo 1996b).

However, neither the trucking firms nor the far more powerful shipping companies in the port showed any interest in addressing the drivers' concerns. The CWA now turned to a two-pronged strategy. First, the union demanded recognition from the dozen or so trucking companies operating at the port that still had traditional employment structures. Although these firms employed only a few hundred drivers, they were the one segment of the industry where the independent contractor issue was absent. "We used a normal top-down approach [to those employers]," a CWA official later recalled, but in most cases, "we got no response." The real breakthrough was the other half of the strategy, which involved the much larger number of drivers who were (technically if not substantively) independent contractors. The CWA encouraged these workers to become part of an enterprise developed by Donald Allen, a former insurance agent who approached the CWA in early 1996. Allen had proposed establishing a new firm, the Transport Maritime Association (TMA), which would hire the truckers as conventional employees and then recognize CWA Local 9400 as their union. The notion was that TMA could corner the market by hiring the thousands of drivers who had become part of the CWA campaign—by all accounts the vast bulk of the port trucking workforce—and then lease these drivers' services to the existing trucking companies, thus short-circuiting the independent contractor problem. Allen promised not only to buy the drivers' vehicles but also to pay them $25 per hour, including pay for their waiting time (several times their net earnings at the time), and to provide health insurance and other benefits (Rose and Carlton 1996; Mongelluzzo 1996a).

Lured by the promise of a substantial increase in pay and a generous fringe benefit package, and with active encouragement from both rank-and-file organizers and CWA officials, some five thousand truckers signed up to sell their trucks to TMA and become its employees. Although as independent contractors they could not legally strike, they were entirely free to decline offers of work from other trucking companies and then to accept Allen's offer of employment. On April 29, 1996, several thousand of them did precisely that, becoming TMA employees and then immediately voting to join the CWA. This move was scheduled to coincide with a May Day strike by the relatively small group of drivers who were not independent contractors; for this group, the strike demand was union recognition from the small number of firms that still had traditional employment arrangements.

The coordinated, double-pronged work stoppage was a formidable show of strength for the truckers, the culmination of almost two years of careful planning. It brought the port to a virtual standstill in early May, reducing container ground transport operations by 80 percent (Mongelluzzo 1996c). The shipping companies, visibly alarmed by the specter of unionization, responded initially by threatening to reroute ships to other West Coast ports. The trucking companies, meanwhile, maintained a solid anti-union front, refusing to do business on TMA's terms and instead hiring "replacement" drivers at premium pay rates (with the shipping firms in many cases absorbing the extra costs). The Pacific Maritime Association, the shippers' trade organization, also intervened, winning court injunctions barring mass picketing in front of the terminal gates (Mongelluzzo 1996d; Brennan 1996).

Faced with intransigence on all sides, yet confident because he had signed up the bulk of the drivers, Allen indicated that he would operate as a conventional trucking company rather than as a leasing operation if the trucking firms continued to refuse his services. However, this soon proved problematic as the shippers made clear that they were strongly opposed to the unionization effort and would support the trucking firms' de facto boycott of TMA. As the standoff continued, questions began to arise as to whether Allen had adequate financial resources to support the TMA scheme, an angle that the CWA had not investigated in any detail (Rose and Carlton 1996). When the TMA was slow to come up with money to buy the drivers' trucks, as it had promised to do, some of them began drifting back to work. "The people aren't stupid," one trucker recalled bitterly. "Once they see that they don't buy your trucks, they said, 'That didn't work. TMA doesn't have the money.'"

Still, about nine hundred truckers stuck with the campaign for the next four months. There was extensive community support for this group, who were now CWA members but with no access to employment or income. Local church and community groups organized food banks and the like, and the CWA set up a "member assistance fund" to help those threatened with foreclosure on their homes and other financial problems. Several local unions endorsed the organizing effort, and some donated money. But as the weeks went by, TMA collapsed in the face of a steady boycott of its services, and the truckers' long-standing hopes for unionization were thwarted once again (Leeds 1996).

The highly innovative strategy developed by TMA and CWA to address the legal issues surrounding the independent contractor status of the drivers galvanized the most effective port truckers' organizing effort since the industry's deregulation and restructuring in the early 1980s. However, the 1996 campaign was unable to overcome a number of obstacles. One major problem was that Allen evidently lacked sufficient capital to sustain TMA, especially in the face of the united and unbending opposition of the shippers and the trucking firms. The CWA officials, to their later regret, had never closely investigated Allen's financial situation. They did attempt to research the maritime shipping and trucking sector in the course of the campaign, but the CWA's capacity to do this proved inadequate. "It was a whole new field for us," one of them later recalled, adding that the national union's research staff was also unfamiliar with this sector of the economy. Thus, in striking contrast to the extensive research effort behind the janitors' and Guess campaigns, the CWA went into this campaign with limited knowledge of the trucking industry and its power structure. Moreover, neither Allen's TMA nor the union was prepared for the intense opposition to the unionization effort of both the trucking firms and the powerful shippers, although in retrospect that should have been anticipated.

Other, more conjunctural difficulties also played a role in the defeat of the truckers' 1996 organizing effort. The two high-level local CWA officials who took charge of the campaign were non-Spanish-speaking "Anglos." Although they hired some rank-and-file activists onto the union staff, the two officials continued to preside over the weekly truckers' meetings throughout the many months of organizing leading up to the strike and boycott. Since most of the truckers were monolingual Spanish speakers, the leaders relied on translators to run the meetings. When one of the two CWA officials suffered a stroke a few days after the walkout began, the result was widespread disorientation and disarray.

As in the Guess case, the truckers' organizing effort was undermined by internal union difficulties. The main problem was CWA's lack of previous experience in and understanding of the port trucking industry. Whereas with the Guess campaign what had proved fatal was a reluctance to engage in rank-and-file mobilization and to devote financial resources to that side of the effort, in the port truckers' case the union made a strong financial commitment and a self-organized immigrant workforce was keenly motivated. But the port truckers lacked adequate guidance and expertise on the part of the union leadership to confront the multibillion-dollar shipping industry, which was deeply committed to resisting the port truckers' unionization.

The CWA nationally had undergone an impressive process of revitalization in the 1990s (see Katz, Batt, and Keefe 2003), and Local 9400 had the best of intentions in undertaking this campaign. Yet the union ultimately proved unable to develop the detailed understanding of the power structure of the organizing target that is an increasingly vital ingredient in successful union campaigns today. It had no previous history of involvement in the trucking industry, in contrast to the other three cases discussed in this chapter, all of which involved unions organizing within their traditional jurisdictions. The CWA lacked the high-powered research capacity that the SEIU brought to the janitors' campaign, nor did it have the kind of legal leverage that proved so pivotal in the drywallers' strike. For all these reasons, the union was not able to bring the port trucking campaign to a successful conclusion. Instead, the rank-and-file enthusiasm gradually dissolved into disillusion and defeat. "We'll have a union in the year 3000," one trucker who had been involved in the 1988, 1993, and 1996 strikes told us.

After the 1996 debacle, advocacy efforts on behalf of the port truckers continued. For example, a major class action suit filed in 1997 challenged the drivers' legal classification as independent contractors. However, the court ultimately decided this case in favor of the trucking companies, which were represented by one of the nation's most prominent management-side labor and employment law firms (Business Wire, Inc. 2000; Cleeland 2000a). The drivers' interest in unionization remained active, however, since all the grievances that had sparked the mid-1990s campaign continued to rankle. Sporadic efforts at self-organization continued over the late 1990s, and then in early 2000 the Teamsters' union announced plans for a national port truckers' organizing drive in which they envisioned a reprise of the CWA strategy, once again involving the establishment of new firms that would hire the drivers as employees (Greenhouse 2000). However, this has yet to develop into a serious undertaking.

THE INGREDIENTS OF ORGANIZING SUCCESS

Latino immigrants are ripe for organizing, but success is unlikely without a strong resource commitment and aggressive leadership from existing unions. The unionization of southern California janitors and dry-wallers in the 1990s was predicated on the availability of extensive financial resources—not only to support organizing staff but also to cover legal expenses and public relations efforts. Despite frequent exhortations over the past decade from the national AFL-CIO leadership and others urging labor to devote more funds to organizing the unorganized, only a few unions have actually done so (Bronfenbrenner and Hickey 2004). All four of the campaigns discussed in this chapter were based on a major resource commitment from the unions involved, at least initially, although in the Guess case UNITE scaled back its commitment at a critical stage.

Yet as Marshall Ganz (2000) has shown, and as the port truckers' case illustrates especially vividly, the deployment of union resources by itself is not sufficient to guarantee success, which also depends on the capacity of union leaders to utilize the available resources in a strategically viable manner. To do so requires, among other things, a thorough understanding of the power structure and economic dynamics of the industry targeted for unionization. Given the extensive resources that employers typically deploy to defend themselves against unionization efforts, this is an increasingly essential ingredient in organizing success. It is the top-down component of a comprehensive unionization strategy that must include a bottom-up dimension as well.

Indeed, in the two cases considered here that lacked one of these ingredients, success proved extremely elusive. In the Guess case, UNITE's sophisticated anti-sweatshop "air war" was solidly rooted in a strategic analysis of the apparel industry, but the union's reluctance to commit resources to bottom-up organizing undermined the campaign's effectiveness. By contrast, in the case of the port truckers, an enormously effective rank-and-file mobilization effort was not complemented by adequate strategic expertise or knowledge of the industry on the part of the union leadership; here too the missing ingredient made the difference between success and failure. Given the hostile environment that unions face in the United States today, anything less than a comprehensive strategy on the union side is unlikely to overcome employer opposition. It matters little whether the top-down or bottom-up component of the organizing effort is deployed first (the janitors and drywallers were exact opposites in this respect, as we have seen), so long as both eventually emerge and are coordinated and sustained over the course of the campaign.

Although they can be contrasted in regard to the sequencing of their top-down and bottom-up components, the two successful campaigns described in this chapter shared many common elements. Both involved industrywide organizing: the janitors organized the entire office building market in downtown Los Angeles and Century City, while the drywallers organized virtually all of the workers in their trade throughout the southern California region's residential construction industry. Both campaigns devised creative strategies to overcome the many obstacles to unionization in industries where subcontracting made NLRB elections impractical and developed alternative means to gain leverage over the targeted employers. In both cases, union recognition was directly linked to contract negotiation, and thus the long delays that so often plague even the most successful NLRB-oriented campaigns were avoided.

Both the janitors' and drywallers' organizing efforts were also deeply embedded in the broader community (see Safford and Locke 2001). The unions built alliances with a variety of stakeholders and actively sought support in the wider society, using media-savvy tactics that not only helped intensify pressure on the employers but also proved effective in neutralizing the impact of the police activity that was deployed against both strikes. In both campaigns too, immigrant networks played a critical role in rank-and-file mobilization. The janitors' and drywallers' drives not only galvanized large numbers of workers but also led to the recruitment and training of new union leaders from the immigrant community.

These examples offer a glimpse of the potential for successful union organizing among the nation's vast low-wage immigrant workforce, even under the difficult conditions of the current period. Yet these exemplary campaigns were at best modest in size—each brought a few thousand workers into the union fold in a metropolitan area where the workforce numbers in the millions. The challenge of reproducing such successes on a larger scale, whether in Los Angeles or in the nation as a whole, remains formidable—even for the former AFL unions (such as the SEIU and the Carpenters) that are relatively well positioned to undertake such a project. Let us now turn to consider their future prospects.

EPILOGUE AND CONCLUSION

The dynamism of the southern California labor movement in the late twentieth century was the product of a combustible mix of ingredients—a vast immigrant working class strongly predisposed toward collective action; an imaginative and committed cadre of union leaders buoyed by the comparative advantages that flowed from the region's exceptional labor history; and just enough geographical distance from organized labor's old guard to open up a political space for organizational innovation. Nowhere in the United States is there more palpable evidence of the potential for today's working-class immigrants to reenact the drama of union upsurge that brought earlier generations of newcomers to the United States into the economic mainstream in the 1930s and 1940s. Paradoxically, the late development of Los Angeles in the early twentieth century—in both its trajectory of industrial growth and the evolution of labor unionism in the region—produced its antithesis at the century's end, when the region emerged as a rare bright spot in an otherwise gloomy labor scene in the United States.

But is Los Angeles a model for labor in the rest of the country or an anomaly? Is the recent emergence of immigrant unionization there a forerunner of changes that will spread more widely, or is it an exceptional product of the peculiar political economy of the region? Although the obstacles are formidable, there is nonetheless potential for the embryonic labor movement revitalization now evident in southern California to burst forth onto the national stage as the maverick unionists who pioneered such efforts as the L.A. Justice for Janitors campaign pursue the elusive goal of reproducing their successes on more spacious ground.

In seeking to explain the recent trajectory of the L.A. labor movement, I have presented evidence in support of three key claims. One of them involves the region's exceptional labor history, discussed in detail in chapter 1. The critical factor here is the long-standing predominance in the regional labor movement of former AFL affiliates generally, and of the SEIU in particular. This gave L.A. unionists an edge in both facilitating the wave of immigrant organizing that emerged in the 1990s and pursuing the broader process of union revitalization. Labor market transformation came sooner and was more extreme in the region than elsewhere (my second claim), but at the same time the historical legacy of the local labor movement left the unions favorably positioned to challenge the new regime of casualized, deregulated, and, all too often, sweatshop-like employment. Ironically, Los Angeles's historical marginality to the national labor movement and the relative weakness of old-guard unionists in the region also proved advantageous, opening up a political space with unusual freedom to experiment.

A second claim about Los Angeles's recent emergence as a center of labor movement revitalization involves the role of the region's employers. As chapter 2 showed, they took the lead in the national (and ultimately global) process of labor market restructuring and workforce casualization that has characterized the late twentieth century. Managerial efforts to weaken unions in the 1970s and 1980s found especially fertile ground in southern California, in part because the economy and population of the region expanded so rapidly in this period. Growth provided a safety valve, neutralizing one major potential obstacle to change: namely, labor opposition. Although some native-born, high-wage unionized workers would leave the region entirely (especially former aerospace industry workers whose jobs evaporated in the aftermath of the cold war), others were able to move laterally into still-desirable positions in the local labor market when their old employment niches suffered precipitous deterioration in wages, benefits, and working conditions as a result of deunionization. With their membership thus cushioned against the impact of labor market restructuring, the unions involved mounted little or no resistance to it. And employers simply turned to the vast supply of recently arrived immigrants to fill the resulting vacancies—blissfully oblivious to the possibility that these new workers would themselves soon strive to restore unionism.

My third claim is predicated on southern California's status as the premier destination for recent immigrants from Mexico and Central America, including vast numbers of undocumented persons. No other region of the nation has experienced such an intensive and homogeneous immigrant working-class influx. Contrary to expectations, the newcomers not only turned out to have a keen desire for economic advancement but also proved ready and able to mobilize collectively, once offered opportunities to do so. As chapter 3 argued, thanks to worldviews rooted in their life experiences prior to arriving in the United States, the burgeoning ranks of Latino immigrants—undocumented and documented alike—have been far more receptive to unionization than most native-born workers. The record of immigrants' active engagement in the L.A. labor movement—much of it initiated from below, as illustrated by the drywallers' and port truckers' campaigns, described in chapter 4—has long since liquidated the presumption that they are "unorganizable." Such engagement has not been restricted to the southern California region, but nowhere else has it been so vibrant or fully developed.

All three of these claims highlight the comparative advantages enjoyed by the southern California labor movement in the 1990s. Indeed, Los Angeles's unions held their own in this period of relentless national labor movement decline, and in some sectors they even managed to recapture some of the ground that organized labor had lost in the 1970s and 1980s. That is no small achievement. Still, as chapter 4 noted, even in the regional context the scale of organizing success has been modest, measured in thousands of workers, not millions. But labor's recent advances in southern California do suggest the potential for a larger-scale labor resurgence.

All three of the conditions that I have identified as fostering labor movement growth in the L.A. region during the 1990s have since become increasingly widespread throughout the nation. Latino immigrants, once highly concentrated in southern California, are now far more geographically dispersed and can be found in nearly every corner of the United States. The employer-driven processes of deunionization and workforce casualization, likewise, have become increasingly ubiquitous. And crucially, the center of gravity of the U.S. labor movement as a whole has now decisively shifted toward the former AFL unions. This development, whose positive effects in southern California in the 1990s were themselves a spur to change on the national level, also had deep structural roots in the broader political economic transformations that swept the United States as a whole during the 1970s and 1980s. Deindustrialization devastated the economic base of the industrial unions formerly affiliated with the CIO, which simultaneously found themselves disoriented by the devolution of the New Deal–era labor relations machinery (the NLRB and other government regulatory agencies), alongside which they had matured organizationally and on which they had come to rely so heavily.

Once home to organized labor's most progressive leaders, in recent decades the former CIO affiliates have found themselves mired in defensive struggles as basic manufacturing has rapidly disappeared from the nation's economic landscape and New Deal institutions like the NLRB have been effectively decapitated. Although many former AFL unions have also been struggling to survive within the emerging neoliberal order, on the whole they have weathered the storm far better than their CIO counterparts. One major advantage is that most AFL unions have an occupational focus, not an industrial one, and are rooted in sectors of the economy, such as services and construction, that are largely insulated from the effects of globalization and capital mobility. And because these unions came of age well before the establishment of the NLRB, they have access to a broader strategic repertoire than their CIO counterparts.

If there is any hope, then, for a major upsurge of labor movement activity of the sort that took place in the United States during the 1930s and 1940s, it is likely to come from these former AFL unions. Among them, by far the most promising organizational model is that of the giant SEIU, which today claims 1.8 million members. The Justice for Janitors campaign is but one of many successful SEIU organizing initiatives; the union has also made huge inroads in organizing health care workers and in the public sector. This impressive expansion is a national phenomenon but has played out on an especially grand scale in Los Angeles, where the SEIU is the labor movement's undisputed powerhouse. It accounted for over 15 percent of all union members in the L.A. metropolitan area in 2001–2002, nearly double its national share of union membership (Milkman and Rooks 2003, 11, 29). The SEIU has also contributed mightily to the political power of the L.A. County Federation of Labor, dwarfing any other union.

Nationally, moreover, SEIU membership has tripled over the past quarter-century, in a period when overall union density has declined precipitously. Although some of this growth was the result of mergers and accretion, the SEIU also has a long history as an organizing union, as we have seen. Starting in 2003, the SEIU led a dissident group of unions that sought to transform the structure of the AFL-CIO; the failure of that bid for reform sparked a major schism within the labor movement, culminating in the mid-2005 disaffiliation of four large unions from the federation and the formation of the new Change to Win (CTW) Federation shortly afterward.

It is no accident that nearly all of the unions now under the CTW umbrella are former AFL affiliates—besides the SEIU they include the Teamsters, the Laborers, the Carpenters, and UNITE HERE.[1] That these unions—once seen as bastions of conservatism and corruption—have emerged in the vanguard of current labor revitalization efforts is a powerful testimony to the renewed relevance of the AFL's historical legacy. With the recent restoration of pre–New Deal conditions for labor—thanks to deindustrialization, deregulation, and deunionization itself—one can easily imagine a future U.S. labor movement whose shape closely resembles that of its pre-1930s counterpart. In the early twentieth century, after all, union density was in the single digits, just as it is today in the private sector. Likewise, organized labor then was largely restricted to a few key urban centers—again, much like today. But this is the pessimistic outlook for a new labor movement in which the former AFL unions are once again the dominant force.

The SEIU and the new CTW Federation have a far different scenario in mind. They are attempting to update the legacy of AFL-style unionism for the twenty-first century, with the aim of restoring density to mid-twentieth-century levels while at the same time adapting their organizational structures and strategies to the shifts in the political economy that have occurred since then. They have completely renounced the AFL's historical legacy of overt hostility to women, African Americans, and immigrants, and today they boast highly diverse memberships and, increasingly, leaderships as well. The CTW is the first U.S. labor federation ever to be headed by a woman (SEIU's Anna Burger), and its second top officer is an African American (Edgar Romney of UNITE HERE). The September 2005 founding convention of CTW explicitly showcased a series of immigrant organizing efforts led by its affiliated unions, among them the Houston Justice for Janitors campaign, which, like the L.A. effort fifteen years earlier, won recognition for building janitors in a right-to-work southern state that is legendary for its hostility to organized labor (Greenhouse 2005).

The CTW unions are advocates of extensive structural changes in the labor movement as a whole. Their contention is that as global corporations have increasingly replaced locally based employers, the decentralization and local union autonomy that was characteristic of many AFL unions in the past has outlived its usefulness. Indeed, prior to the 2005 split, the SEIU and its allies called on the AFL-CIO to adopt a more centralized labor movement structure with a strengthened central body that would have the power to enforce its policies with the affiliates and make them accountable. The proposed change was modeled on the SEIU's own recent internal restructuring effort, the "New Strength Unity" program adopted at the union's 2000 convention. This was a five-year plan to merge and consolidate local unions on a regional and industrial basis in order to increase leverage in collective bargaining. Just as this program involved merging local unions into larger entities that mirror the highly centralized employers for whom SEIU members work, so the CTW unions called for restructuring the AFL-CIO as a whole by merging the smaller unions together and eliminating inter-union competition by assigning fixed jurisdictions to each organization. Jurisdictional boundaries are a long-standing labor movement tradition, but in recent decades they have virtually collapsed, giving rise to de facto general workers' unions that sometimes compete with one another to recruit the most "organizable" workers. Insofar as multiple unions represent workers in the same industry or sector, employers can pit one group against the other, while unions squander valuable resources fighting one another rather than the employers (Lerner 2003).

The SEIU and its allies also called on the AFL-CIO to devote a far greater portion of its resources to new organizing, arguing that increasing union density and taking wages out of competition in strategically targeted sectors of the economy is imperative for the labor movement's very survival. Although the CTW program does not explicitly engage this point, it is difficult to imagine a massive new drive to recruit currently unorganized workers into labor's ranks that does not rely heavily on recruiting "outsiders" onto union staffs, as the SEIU and other former AFL unions have frequently done in the past. Any large-scale new organizing drive would also draw extensively from the broad strategic repertoire, largely outside the NLRB framework, that unions like SEIU, UNITE HERE, and the building trades have developed in recent years, drawing on AFL organizational legacies that stretch back to the pre–New Deal era. Among other things, that repertoire involves comprehensive campaigns combining top-down and bottom-up approaches, as illustrated in chapter 4.

Perhaps the most important feature of the current labor reform effort is its daring, intrepid character. The new CTW Federation characterizes itself as a "mean, lean organizing machine" and has pledged to devote the vast bulk of its considerable resources to recruiting new members. Considered objectively, investing extensively in union organizing may seem foolhardy or simply irrational. For as everyone agrees, unions that are organizing today must confront formidable obstacles. Employer power has been strengthened by corporate globalization and the growing ability to outsource jobs, while inside the United States employers are more staunchly committed than ever to "union prevention" and uniformly intransigent in their opposition to any labor organizing efforts that dare to challenge their hegemony. At the federal level, the United States has the most anti-union political regime in nearly a century, and the same is true in a growing number of states. After decades of devolution, moreover, the structure of labor law severely restricts the room for maneuver open to unions engaged in new organizing, and the few protections that do remain in the letter of the law are enforced so poorly that employers routinely honor them in the breach rather than the observance.

Yet none of these conditions have dissuaded the SEIU and other organizing unions from their energetic efforts to rebuild unionism. Their view—and one that their success in places like Los Angeles would seem to bear out—is that "the impossible can be achieved," as Richard Bensinger, the AFL-CIO's organizing director in the early years of the Sweeney regime, put it in an essay entitled "When We Try More, We Win More" (Bensinger 1998, 41). He made the case then—echoed a decade later by CTW—for pouring union financial and intellectual resources into organizing the unorganized in strategic campaigns to take wages out of competition in specific corporations, geographical regions, industries, and sectors.

The ascent of John Sweeney to the AFL-CIO presidency in 1995 was fueled by widespread hopes for exactly this sort of organizing program. What the decade since then has revealed is that neither Sweeney nor any other AFL-CIO leader was able to impose such a program on unions that are not independently committed to it, thanks to the decentralized structure of the AFL-CIO itself, which is unable to enforce its policies on the affiliated unions. The federation has had four different organizing directors in the last decade (Bensinger was the first), all of whom have been talented and committed; none of them, however, has been able to overcome this problem or to reverse the relentless national decline in private-sector union density. That frustration is precisely what led to the 2005 split.

Martin Luther King once wrote that "progress never rolls in on the wheels of inevitability" (quoted in Bensinger 1998, 41). Similarly, as the sociologist Alvin Gouldner (1980, 105) has noted, "Structural analysis . . . is commonly taken by surprise when change erupts." There can be no guarantee that the ambitious efforts of the new union reform movement will prove successful on a national scale, but the recent achievements of unions in southern California—and for that matter, successful labor struggles throughout history, all of which faced difficult odds—are a testimony to this perspective. "Sí, se puede!"

APPENDIX A

TABLE A.1   Labor Union Membership in Los Angeles and Union Density in
Los Angeles, California, and the United States, 1933 to 2004

Date	Union Members in Los Angeles	Union Density (Union Members as Percentage of All Nonagricultural Wage and Salary Workers)		
		Los Angeles	California	United States
1933 to 1939[a]				
May 1933	20,000 or less	NA	NA	11%
December 1933	30,000	NA	NA	11
December 1934	40,000	NA	NA	12
December 1935	45,000	NA	NA	13
December 1938	100,000	NA	NA	28
December 1939	170,000	17%	23%	29
1943 to 1949[b]				
June 1943	259,299	23	39	31
June 1944	298,332	27	41	34
June 1945	252,396	25	45	36
June 1946	258,883	23	39	35
June 1947	362,894	32	45	34
May 1948	343,947	29	41	32
May 1949	431,100	38	50	33
1951 to 1987[c]				
July 1951	538,300	33	41	33
July 1952	569,900	34	40	33
July 1953	594,200	32	40	34
July 1954	688,300	37	41	35
July 1955	722,500	37	39	33
July 1956	754,300	36	39	33
July 1957	763,500	35	38	33
July 1958	751,800	35	38	33
July 1959	756,800	33	36	32
July 1960	760,400	32	36	31
July 1961	753,300	32	35	30
July 1962	769,000	31	33	30
July 1963	783,600	30	33	29
July 1964	802,900	33	32	29
July 1965	745,900	30	32	28
July 1966	774,000	30	31	28

TABLE A.1   (*Continued*)

Date	Union Members in Los Angeles	Union Density (Union Members as Percentage of All Nonagricultural Wage and Salary Workers)		
		Los Angeles	California	United States
July 1967	800,700	30%	31%	28%
July 1968	799,900	29	31	28
July 1969	812,600	28	30	27
July 1970	822,800	28	31	27
July 1971	832,700	30	31	27
July 1973	849,700	28	28	26
July 1975	808,300	27	27	26
July 1977	815,500	25	25	25
July 1979	873,200	24	23	24
July 1981	823,400	23	22	22
July 1983	766,600	22	21	20
July 1985	782,100	20	20	18
July 1987	788,900	20	19	17
1988 to 2004[d]				
1988	958,200	16	19	17
1989	1,050,600	18	19	16
1990	1,068,800	18	18	16
1991	1,038,500	18	18	16
1992	1,027,300	17	18	16
1993	1,005,700	17	18	16
1994	979,400	17	18	16
1995	1,085,300	16	18	15
1996	911,700	15	17	15
1997	912,700	15	16	14
1998	973,600	15	16	14
1999	980,200	15	17	14
2000	989,000	15	16	14
2001	1,056,600	16	16	14
2002	1,178,800	17	18	13
2003	1,084,900	16	17	13
2004	1,019,200	15	17	13

Notes and sources:

[a] For Los Angeles: Perry and Perry (1963, 245, 266, 275, 317, 490, 495, 497, 537); for California in 1939 (no month specified): Troy (1957, 18). Troy reports a lower 1939 figure for the United States as a whole (21.5 percent) than that shown here, which is the annual average reported in U.S. Department of Labor (1980, 412).

[b] For Los Angeles and California: computed from California Employment Development Department (CEP, 1943 to 1949); California Department of Industrial Relations (ULIC, 1943 to 1949). 1943 to 1946 union membership figures in column 1 (from ULIC) are for "Los Angeles Metropolitan Area," and 1947 to 1949 figures are for Los Angeles County. For 1943 to 1946, the ULIC defines the Los Angeles metropolitan area as "Los Angeles County plus contiguous portions of Orange and San Bernardino Counties." To approximate equivalence for the numerator and denominator used to compute the figures in column 2 for 1943 to 1946, the denominator used here is the California Employment Development Department data for total employment in Los Angeles and Orange Counties (but not San Bernardino County), matched by month. For the United States 1943 to 1949 (annual averages): U.S. Department of Labor (1980, 412).

[c] For Los Angeles and California: computed from California Department of Industrial Relations (ULIC, 1951 to 1987), California Department of Industrial Relations (CLSB, 1951 to 1970), and California Employment Development Department (CLMB, 1971 to 1987). Union membership figures for 1951 to 1964 are for Los Angeles and Orange Counties; figures for 1965 to 1987 are for Los Angeles County. For 1951 to 1964, these figures do not include members of union locals with statewide or regional jurisdictions, but starting in 1965 these were apportioned to each region and are included in the figures. Note that the denominator used to compute the density figures is based on a different data series (CLSB and CLMB) than that used for the second panel of the table (CEP), and that the CEP used a different enumeration methodology than its successors and is thus not strictly comparable to the latter. The apparent drop-off in union density between 1949 and 1951 for both Los Angeles and California is an artifact of this change in denominator data source and so should be interpreted with extreme caution. Data from 1950 are omitted entirely since the Los Angeles and California enumerations were conducted differently from those for other years. For the United States 1951 to 1978 (annual averages): U.S. Department of Labor (1980, 412). This data series ended in 1978. The union density data shown for the United States for 1979 to 1987 are for all wage and salary workers (both agricultural and nonagricultural) and are from Hirsch and Macpherson (2005, 11).

[d] Hirsch and Macpherson (various years). These data are drawn from the U.S. CPS and are not strictly comparable to the data series shown for earlier years. The figures are for union members only (they do not include nonmembers covered by union contracts) and include all wage and salary workers (both agricultural and nonagricultural). The figures listed in column 1 are for the Los Angeles–Anaheim–Riverside consolidated metropolitan statistical area.

APPENDIX B

ADJUSTING FOR CHANGES IN THE U.S. DECENNIAL CENSUS INDUSTRY AND OCCUPATION CLASSIFICATIONS, 1970 TO 2000

The U.S. Census Bureau's industry and occupation classification scheme changed significantly between 1970 and 1980, and again between 1990 and 2000; minor changes were made between 1980 and 1990 as well. It is necessary to adjust for these changes to reliably track historical trends over this period (as represented in table 2.3 and figure 2.2). To do so, the U.S. Census Bureau's industry and occupation crosswalks for 1970 to 1980, 1980 to 1990, and 1990 to 2000 (U.S. Census Bureau 1989, 1994, 2003) were used to adjust all estimates for the occupations and industries shown in table 2.3 (and in table B.1 for the United States as a whole) to be consistent with the 2000 census industry and occupation codes.[1]

A step-wise procedure was used to adjust the 1970 to 1990 industry and occupation data to their 2000 equivalents. Each step involved using one or more of the three crosswalks to translate between the industry and occupation categories of adjacent census years. For example, translating the 1990 estimates to reflect the census 2000 classification system requires only one step, using the 1990 to 2000 crosswalk. By contrast, translating the 1970 estimates requires three steps: (1) using the 1970 to 1980 crosswalk to translate the 1970 codes into the 1980 categories; (2)

using the 1980 to 1990 crosswalk to translate the 1980 codes into the 1990 categories; and (3) using the 1990 to 2000 crosswalk to translate the 1990 codes into the 2000 categories. Translating the 1980 estimates requires two steps, moving first from 1980 to 1990 and then from 1990 to 2000.

Changes in the occupation and industry classification schemes can affect both the estimates for the numbers of workers in each occupational group (the "population estimates" shown in tables 2.3 and B.1) and the estimates for the demographic composition of each. To adjust for this, the tables present weighted averages of the descriptive statistics for each occupation, where the weights represent the contribution of occupations to their respective 2000 occupation/industry category. For example, five 1990 occupations would have been classified as truckers had the 2000 occupational classification system been used in 1990: (1) supervisors and proprietors, sales occupations; (2) sales representatives, mining, manufacturing, and wholesale; (3) news vendors; (4) truck drivers; and (5) driver-sales workers. Very small portions of all but category 4 would have been classified as "truckers" in the 2000 system. To estimate the demographic characteristics for truckers in 1990 under the 2000 classification system, we estimate a weighted average of the demographic characteristics for each of these five occupations, where the weights are the proportion of the total estimate contributed by the respective occupation.

Some of the occupations shown are more affected by changes in the coding scheme than others. For drywallers, the occupational classification is largely consistent from 1970 to 2000; the codes from 1980 through 2000 are fully comparable (U.S. Census Bureau 1994, 2003), and the change in classification from 1970 to 1980 is small (U.S. Census Bureau 1989). For garment workers, the codes also have been relatively stable, with over 90 percent of garment workers classified within a single industry code since 1970. By contrast, janitors and truckers have been more drastically affected by changes in the occupational classification system over time. Despite this, our adjusted and "unadjusted" results (not shown here but available from the author on request) are very similar for all four occupations.[2]

Table B.1 summarizes the adjusted data for the United States, using the same procedures employed to construct table 2.3. These data are also the basis for the U.S. data shown in figure 2.2.

TABLE B.1   Employment in Selected Occupations in the United States, by Race, Ethnicity, and Nativity, 1970 to 2000

Occupation	1970	1980	1990	2000
Drywallers				
Native-born white	85.4%	79.8%	71.2%	54.6%
Foreign-born white	4.2	3.4	2.3	1.6
Native-born black	4.1	4.2	4.7	4.1
Native-born Hispanic	3.6	5.8	5.5	5.9
Foreign-born Hispanic	**1.6**	**4.7**	**13.2**	**29.6**
Other	1.0	2.3	3.1	4.1
Population estimate	36,689	63,987	98,146	129,768
Truckers				
Native-born white	80.9%	81.0%	77.3%	71.5%
Foreign-born white	1.6	1.6	1.8	2.1
Native-born black	10.5	10.4	10.3	10.4
Native-born Hispanic	4.1	4.0	4.5	5.3
Foreign-born Hispanic	**1.6**	**1.6**	**3.9**	**6.4**
Other	1.3	1.3	2.2	4.1
Population estimate	1,553,141	2,084,790	2,490,670	2,953,143
Garment workers				
Native-born white	68.6%	61.7%	56.0%	39.9%
Foreign-born white	10.0	6.4	4.2	3.7
Native-born black	8.4	11.8	12.9	9.5
Native-born Hispanic	5.3	5.3	4.2	5.0
Foreign-born Hispanic	**5.5**	**9.6**	**13.9**	**23.6**
Foreign-born Asian	1.3	3.8	7.2	14.7
Other	0.9	1.4	1.7	3.6
Population estimate	930,966	1,103,760	811,593	406,445
Janitors				
Native-born white	62.4%	64.9%	57.3%	50.0%
Foreign-born white	6.3	4.0	3.1	3.3
Native-born black	22.8	19.0	17.8	14.8
Native-born Hispanic	4.5	4.8	5.7	6.7
Foreign-born Hispanic	**2.4**	**4.6**	**11.8**	**18.4**
Other	1.5	2.8	4.4	6.9
Population estimate	679,015	1,006,748	1,074,976	1,214,513

Sources: U.S. Census Bureau, integrated public use microdata series (IPUMS), version 3.0. For 1970: 1 percent form 1 state sample, 1 percent form 1 metro sample, 1 percent form 1 neighborhood sample; for 1980: 5 percent state sample; for 1990: 5 percent state sample; for 2000: 5 percent census sample. All estimates are calculated using person-level weights. In all cases except trucking, the data are for wage and salary workers in the labor force only (trucking includes the self-employed) for the five-county Los Angeles metropolitan area (Los Angeles, Orange, Ventura, Riverside, and San Bernardino Counties), except for 1980, which also includes Imperial County. Because of significant changes in the industry and occupational classification systems in 1980 and 2000, all estimates have been adjusted to reflect the most recent (2000) U.S. census classification system.
Note: The categories "white" and "black" include only non-Hispanics.

NOTES

INTRODUCTION

1. The janitors' campaign, discussed in more detail in chapter 4, has been documented extensively; see, for example, Waldinger et al. (1998), Fisk, Mitchell, and Erickson (2000), and Erickson et al. (2002).
2. See www.seiu.org/who/fast_facts/. As discussed later in the chapter, some of SEIU's membership growth over this period was the result of increased employment in already unionized units or of mergers with preexisting unions, rather than new organizing of previously unorganized workers. Unfortunately, precise figures are not available as to how much of the union's growth can be attributed to these various factors.
3. For one example of the comparison of Los Angeles to the Third World, see Rieff (1992); on the recent growth of economic inequality in the region, see Milkman and Dwyer (2002).
4. The United Brotherhood of Carpenters and Joiners of America is the oldest of these unions, founded in 1881. UNITE HERE is the product of a long series of union mergers; one component, the Hotel Employees and Restaurant Employees (HERE), dates to 1891, while the Union of Needletrades, Industrial, and Textile Employees (UNITE) is composed of two unions that merged in 1995, the International Ladies' Garment Workers' Union (ILGWU), founded in 1900, and the Amalgamated Clothing and Textile Workers' Union (ACTWU), which dates from 1914. The International Brotherhood of Teamsters was founded in 1903; the Laborers' International Union of North America, founded in 1903 as the International Hod Carriers' and Building Laborers' Union of America, adopted its present name in 1965. The SEIU is among the youngest of these organizations, founded in 1921 as the Building Service Employees International Union (BSEIU) (Craft and Peck 1998, 24, 326, 478, 510, 583, 850, 979). The case of the UFCW is more complex, since it is the product of a long series of union mergers. Two of its largest components, the Amalgamated Meat

201

Cutters and Butcher Workmen, founded in 1896, and the Retail Clerks, founded in 1890, are among the oldest AFL unions. But the UFCW also includes the formerly CIO-affiliated Packinghouse Workers of America (founded as the Packinghouse Workers Organizing Committee in 1937). Two other unions, the Barbers and Beauticians, an AFL affiliate founded in 1886, and the Footwear and Leather Workers, whose origins date back even before the AFL's establishment, are also part of today's UFCW. See http://www.ufcw.org/about_ufcw/where_we_come_from/industries/index.cfm.

5. Wages are "taken out of competition" if unions organize enough employers in a given labor market to establish a common wage standard, or if government regulations set limits on the extent to which employers can reduce wages (for example, through minimum-wage laws). Under such conditions, wage levels are stabilized and firms compete on the basis of innovation, productivity, or quality.

6. As Eileen Appelbaum and her colleagues (2000) show, there are exceptions to this trend: "high-performance" workplaces where employers invest extensively in worker training and other productivity-enhancing practices.

7. Dan Clawson (2003, 140–44) estimates that two-thirds of all U.S. jobs are insulated from globalization pressures.

8. Las Vegas, even more peripherally located, was another site of extensive and highly successful union organizing in the 1990s; see Fantasia and Voss (2004, 150–59).

9. Although the CTW unions are nearly all rooted in the old AFL, the converse is not true. Many former AFL unions have been highly critical of CTW, such as the more elite building trades unions as well as the International Association of Machinists (IAM), all former AFL affiliates.

10. U.S. unions, many of which have or once had members in Canada, generally refer to themselves as "International" unions, and in common parlance most refer to their top-level leadership—as opposed to their local unions and regional bodies—as "the International."

11. In the 1980s and 1990s some commentators (myself included; see Milkman 1993) identified feminism as a key source contributing to labor movement revitalization. It has indeed had some influence on the process, as Clawson (2003) notes, but the main focus of recent organizing has been on low-wage workers, many of them foreign-born, whereas gender equality has been at best a secondary concern.

12. This was not the case, however, in the CIO's formative period, when many left-wing intellectuals worked as organizers; the policy only emerged as the CIO unions developed into permanent institutions! In the mid-1940s, C. Wright Mills (1948, 72, 98) found that, on average, CIO union leaders had far more formal education than their AFL counterparts and that it was

more common for CIO than AFL leaders to have entered the labor movement as hired organizers.

13. Here Arthur Stinchombe's (1965) classic argument that the characteristics developed in the period of an organization's initial formation tend to persist over time is once again confirmed.

CHAPTER 1

1. Significantly, however, the ILGWU nearly declined to join the CIO when it split from the AFL two years later (now renamed the Congress of Industrial Organizations). The ILGWU's support for the *Committee* on Industrial Organization in 1935 also was by a close vote and involved serious reservations. In 1940 these reservations won out, and the ILGWU withdrew from the CIO and reaffiliated with the AFL (Morris 1958, 216, 268–69).

2. In trucking, as in many sectors that the AFL unions organized, cutthroat competition among employers was widespread. By contrast, the CIO's industrial organizing focused primarily on highly concentrated, oligopolistic industries like auto and steel manufacturing, where wage competition was not at issue.

3. This figure is for immigrants born in Mexico who lived in the city of Los Angeles in 1930. The U.S. Census Bureau classified Mexicans as "white" until 1930, when they were reclassified as a separate race, defined rather awkwardly as "persons who were born in Mexico and are not definitely white, Negro, Indian, Chinese or Japanese" (Ngai 2004, 54). Many scholars believe this resulted in a significant undercount (Gratton and Gutmann 2000, 145). In 1940 most Mexican Americans were again enumerated as "white" (see note 14). Today it is widely recognized that Latinos—or "Hispanics," as they often are labeled—can be of any race. Here I conform to contemporary usage while recognizing its socially constructed and at times problematic character.

4. San Francisco's 1910 population was 417,000, compared to 504,000 in Los Angeles County and 319,000 in the city of Los Angeles (Fogelson 1967, 78). McWilliams does not specify whether the union density figures he cites refer to the city or to Los Angeles County.

5. Again, a striking comparison can be made to New York City, which also had a large port, a huge construction industry, and extensive employment in entertainment-related enterprises. Although manufacturing was more developed in New York than in Los Angeles in this period, it mostly involved small-scale nondurable goods production (as would be the case in Los Angeles half a century later), rather than the mass production that was the base of the CIO. As the historian Joshua Freeman (2000, xiv) notes of midcentury New York, "small firms and craft or conglomerate unions . . .

most often affiliated with the American Federation of Labor (AFL) dominated."

6. Troy (1957, 4–5) reports that 79 percent of California union members in 1939 were AFL-affiliated, compared to 59 percent nationally. The remaining 9 percent of the state's union members, and 13 percent of those in the United States, were in unaffiliated or independent unions.

7. Precise figures on the ethnic composition of the workforce are not available. The U.S. 1930 census counted 1,911 Mexican women among the 12,500 females employed in the clothing industry throughout the state of California but did not produce separate figures for Mexicans in Los Angeles, where contemporary reports suggest that the majority of urban female Mexican workers were concentrated primarily in the dress industry (U.S. Department of Commerce 1933, vol. 5, 86; vol. 4, 176). Pesotta (1944, 19) estimated that "about 75 per cent [of Los Angeles dress workers] were Mexican women and girls" in 1933; Marie Louise Wuesthoff (1938, 81), whose analysis was based on interviews with ILGWU officials a few years after the strike, gives a figure of 50 percent. Paul Taylor (1928/1980, 113) notes that in the Los Angeles factories he visited in the late 1920s, "the proportion of Mexican women to all women employees was greatest in the clothing and needle trades," but he does not venture a numerical estimate.

8. Mexican women made up 75 percent of the ILGWU's membership in Los Angeles after the 1933 strike, but only six of the nineteen officials on the executive board of the dressmakers' local union (Vargas 2005, 88). At the higher levels of the union bureaucracy, their underrepresentation was even more extreme.

9. Twenty years later, in 1957, Beck was interrogated in the U.S. Senate's McClellan Committee hearings and then suspended from his position as AFL-CIO vice president; eventually he was convicted of larceny and tax evasion and sentenced to five years in federal prison (Russell 2001, 187–88).

10. An important exception was the Communist-led UAW aircraft industry organizing campaign, but this culminated in disaster when bayonet-wielding U.S. Army troops crushed the massive June 1941 North American Aviation strike (Lichtenstein 1982, 56–63).

11. The other 7 percent of Los Angeles's union members, and the remaining 10 percent nationally, were in independent unions.

12. A somewhat similar and equally complicated effort had led to the organization of Japanese American fruit-stand workers, first into an independent union and then, on the eve of World War II and the Japanese American internment, into the AFL-affiliated Retail Clerks' union; see Modell 1977, 140–53.

13. The Asian American population was smaller, about 2 percent of total employment in the L.A. region in 1950, compared to about 5 percent each for

African Americans and Mexican Americans (Laslett 1996, 65). A variety of European immigrants were also present in the region, though in much smaller numbers than in other large U.S. cities, as noted earlier.

14. In 1930 Mexicans were enumerated separately, and although data at the city level were not published, they can be extrapolated from the occupational distribution for the state, combined with the enumeration for "other races" at the city level (see note 3). By 1940, however, the Census Bureau had shifted its approach to the Mexican American population: "Persons of Mexican birth or ancestry who were not definitely Indian or of other non-white race were returned as white in 1940. Such persons were designated Mexican in 1930 (but not in prior censuses) and were included in the general class of 'Other races'" (U.S. Department of Commerce 1943, vol. 3, 1).

15. In the entire state of California, there were 611 Mexican janitors in 1930, out of a total of 20,075 janitors statewide. Even if all of them were among the 854 Los Angeles janitors of "other races," they would be less than 1 percent of the 6,345 janitors in the city. There were 1,877 Mexican "chauffeurs and truck and tractor drivers" in the state in 1930, or 3 percent of a total of 58,681 workers in that occupation statewide; another 701 were Chinese, Japanese, or Filipino. In Los Angeles, 6.7 percent of truck drivers were enumerated as "other races" in 1930. If we assume that a small number of these were Asian, an estimate of 6 percent Mexican results. The figures in the text for construction occupations were derived in similar fashion from U.S. Department of Commerce (1933, vol. 5, 86–99, vol. 4, 193–96, 200–2).

16. This brings to mind Selig Perlman's classic 1928 treatise (written prior to the emergence of the CIO) in which he argued that "conservative union leaders in this country [the United States] have, on the whole, always been more aggressive against the employers, and have striven more relentlessly for a full job control than have their radical rivals" (Perlman 1928, 131).

CHAPTER 2

1. This was also the case in the United States as a whole over these years; see Goldfield (1987, 10).

2. The figures in appendix A and figures 1.2 and 2.1 actually understate this decline because they do not disaggregate private- and public-sector union membership. Public-sector union density in fact expanded rapidly during this period, while in the private sector density fell sharply.

3. There is a substantial literature on the factors contributing to union decline in the United States during the last few decades of the twentieth century. One important finding is that a major component of the overall decline involves employment shifting away from sectors where unions were once strong (Farber and Western 2001). My focus here, however, is on the

decline of unionism *within* precisely those sectors. Similarly, the lack of "demand" for unions among nonunion workers (emphasized in Farber and Krueger 1993) is largely irrelevant to the component of union decline involving what were previously highly unionized industries. For present purposes, then, the emphasis on managerial anti-unionism in the work of Freeman and Medoff (1984), Freeman (1988), and Goldfield (1987) is more relevant, as is the evidence of limited new organizing efforts by unions in this period (Freeman and Medoff 1984; Farber and Western 2002).

4. This dynamic closely parallels the process of occupational feminization that took place in roughly the same period, as documented by Barbara Reskin and Patricia Roos and their colleagues (1990). As they show, men abandoned various occupations in which rewards and working conditions had declined, leading employers to turn to women workers to fill the resulting vacancies. The main difference between the two cases is that whereas deunionization was the main force driving the deterioration of pay and conditions in the blue-collar jobs from which L.A. native-born workers exited, it was largely irrelevant to the deterioration of the (mostly white-collar and professional) occupations analyzed by Reskin and Roos.

5. The discrepancy is due to the fact that substantial numbers of building trades union members were unemployed, working in other industries, in the military, on strike, or the like. See California Department of Industrial Relations (ULIC, 1956, 10, n. 2).

6. Disaggregated figures are not available, but the 1955 data collected by the California Department of Industrial Relations (ULIC, 1956; CLSB, 1956) found 68,900 union members in "transportation and warehousing," a category that also included bus drivers, pilots, and other transportation workers. With 75,700 wage and salary workers in this sector in 1955, clearly union density was high throughout it.

7. The fact that 1975 was a recession year, when unemployment was at a peak level, means that the actual density drop was even sharper than these data indicate: the 1975 denominator (the number of wage and salary workers) was at an unusually low point in this cyclically sensitive industry, whereas retention of union membership by many unemployed building trades workers kept the numerator high.

8. The last year for which these data are available is 1992; in 1995 the ILGWU merged with the Amalgamated Clothing and Textile Workers' Union (ACTWU) to form the Union of Needletrades, Industrial, and Textile Employees (UNITE).

9. Unfortunately, systematic longitudinal data tracking the specific employment trajectories of native-born workers who left these jobs are not available.

10. Borjas (1999, 64–78) points out the complexity of distinguishing cause and effect in analyzing the relationship between immigration and wages, since

native-born workers can "vote with their feet" in response to an influx of immigration. This is one possible interpretation of the out-migration of native-born workers from California to other states in the 1980s, which in Borjas's view enlarged the labor supply in the receiving regions and thus depressed wages there as well. Borjas neither examines the relationship of immigration to deunionization, however, nor considers the possibility that deunionization was an intervening variable precipitating both increased demand for immigrant labor and the observed decline in wages for relatively low-skilled jobs.

11.   Note that these figures include immigrants of all racial and ethnic groups. The makeup of New York's immigrant population is far less homogeneous than that of Los Angeles. In 1990 foreign-born Latinos made up 33 percent of New York's building service workers, whereas in Los Angeles the figure was 56 percent (as shown in table 2.3). The New York figures were computed from the U.S. census public use microdata series (PUMS) using the same methods employed in constructing table 2.3 (see appendix B for details). The data are for the New York metropolitan area, which includes the five boroughs of New York City as well as Putnam, Rockland, and Westchester counties.

12.   Again, these figures include immigrants of all racial and ethnic groups, and the caveats in note 11 apply.

13.   Allen's (1994) figures are from his analysis of Current Population Survey (CPS) data. The CPS did not collect information on nativity until 1994. The U.S. census data for one segment of the construction workforce—namely, drywallers—do indicate some decline in the native-born white proportion of this occupation nationally, although the decline was relatively modest before 1980 (see appendix B and figure 2.2).

14.   Although it is not apparent in the data in appendix B, there is some evidence in CPS data of a modest increase in African American employment in trucking after deregulation (Heywood and Peoples 1994). A recent case study of truckers in the Louisiana oilpatch found a pattern with striking parallels to what occurred among L.A. port truckers in the 1980s. In this case, intrastate trucking remained regulated until 1994, when the state of Louisiana passed deregulatory legislation. Prior to that time, "white, male social networks . . . prevented outsiders, as well as blacks and women, from successfully entering the trucking industry" in the Louisiana oilpatch. After 1996, however, deregulation led to a dramatic decline in truckers' incomes in the area, and now "women, blacks, and outsiders enter[ed] the industry with much greater ease than in earlier periods. . . . *Many of the Cajun men who traditionally comprised the trucking workforce abandoned the industry, and the space created by their departure allowed new groups to enter the labor pool*" (Gardner 2002, 396, emphasis added).

15.   Massey and his colleagues do not consider the effects of factors other than

IRCA in the proliferation of subcontracting and employment casualization (what they call "informalization"), but they do present evidence that the trend toward these practices *preceded* IRCA; cash payments to workers, for example, rose in the early 1980s (Massey, Durand, and Malone 2002, 123). In my view, IRCA was not the main cause of employment casualization, contrary to what Massey and his colleagues suggest, but it surely gave employers of immigrants additional incentives to continue down the low road on which they had already embarked.

CHAPTER 3

1. Shortly after the law was passed, however, the ILGWU—which, as we have seen, already had more experience than most other unions in organizing the new immigrants—broke ranks and took a stand against employer sanctions, arguing that in the absence of systematic enforcement efforts, employers were simply using the new law as an anti-union tool when confronted by organizing campaigns (Haus 2002, 79).

2. The only exception to this shown in table 3.1 is the case of garment workers, among whom native-born white males were rarely found at all and, when present, were employed in the most desirable (and extremely well-paid) jobs. Catanzarite (2004) has also found that, when other factors are held constant, unionization reduces these wage penalties.

3. The WRPS, a nationwide representative sample of 2,408 adults, is described in detail in Freeman and Rogers (1999). The question for which results are reported here was asked of all respondents who were neither managers nor current union members: "If an election were held today to decide whether employees like you should be represented by a union, would you vote for the union or against the union?" The data for the ethnic and racial groups discussed here are unpublished, but they are available at http://www.nber.org/~freeman/wrps.html. (The WRPS did not collect data on nativity.) The figure in the text for "African Americans" includes both respondents who identified themselves as "black" and those who identified themselves as "African American" and differs slightly from those reported for "blacks" in Freeman and Rogers (1999, 71). All of these results are statistically significant ($p < .001$ for African Americans; $p < .01$ for Latinos; $p < .05$ for Asians).

4. This finding is from the 2001–2002 California Workforce Survey (CWS), a statewide survey of 1,404 respondents that included a question identical to the one in the WRPS. However, the results of the two surveys are not strictly comparable. The WRPS asked the question of almost all workers except high-level managers who were not current union members; by contrast, the CWS asked it only of nonsupervisory respondents who were not current union members, excluding a much broader group of middle-level

managers. The CWS results are statistically significant (p < .01 for the race-ethnicity variable and p < .05 for the citizen status variable).

5. The untimely death of Miguel Contreras preceded this election by eleven days. The Fed officially backed the incumbent (James Hahn) in this race, although the fact that four years earlier labor had so enthusiastically supported Villaraigosa's unsuccessful bid for the mayoralty not only helped produce his 2005 victory but also meant that few labor activists were inclined to actively campaign for Hahn (see Meyerson 2005).

6. Leon Fink (2003) and Jennifer Gordon (2005) make the same point about the organizers they encountered in North Carolina and Long Island, New York, respectively.

7. Compare Los Angeles, for example, to New York City, the other leading immigrant gateway city, where there is far more tolerance among natives as well as a political and institutional culture that is far more open to newcomers' participation on the local and grassroots levels (Mollenkopf 1999).

8. These figures are based on analysis of a multi-year pooled dataset constructed from the U.S. CPS March supplements for 1994 to 2001 for all employed wage and salary workers age eighteen to sixty-four in the five-county area (Los Angeles, Orange, Ventura, San Bernardino, and Riverside counties). The CPS did not ask respondents about their place of birth until 1994. Because the CPS sample of union members for any single year for this region is relatively small, the pooled data are far more reliable. All results were calculated using the CPS unrevised sampling weights. Thanks to Christine Schwartz for assembling the merged dataset and for her assistance in analyzing it. These data are the basis for all figures on unionization in the L.A. area cited in this section. All the intergroup comparisons noted are statistically significant unless otherwise indicated.

9. All references to "whites" in the text refer to non-Hispanic whites.

10. As Gregory DeFreitas (1993, 286) points out, "Excess demand by workers for unionized positions is less the exception than the rule . . . in an era of sharply declining union organizing drives."

11. This is not always acknowledged in the economics literature. Edward Funkhouser (1993), for example, in an otherwise highly informative analysis of 1983 data on immigrant and native unionization "propensities," imputes "individual union preferences" as part of his explanation for observed unionization rates.

12. The figure for native-born African Americans is 60 percent. The differences in public-sector unionization rates between foreign-born Latinos and native-born whites, and between foreign-born Latinos and native-born African Americans, are not statistically significant at the p < .05 level, using t-tests.

13. The fact that the public sector is much more highly unionized in Los Angeles, and in California as a whole, is also the key factor behind the wide gap

in unionization rates between immigrants and natives there. That gap is narrower in the United States as a whole, where 12 percent of immigrants were union members in the 1994 to 2001 period, compared to 15 percent of native-born workers.

14. The difference between the group arriving between 1980 and 1990 and the group arriving after 1990 is not statistically significant at the p < .05 level (using t-tests), nor is the difference between the native-born unionization rate and that for immigrants arriving before 1980. Funkhouser (1993, 251) reports a similar cohort effect in his analysis of national data for 1983, but he also notes that immigrant and native males with similar labor market experience had similar unionization rates. See also Waldinger and Der-Martirosian (2000, 68–69).

CHAPTER 4

1. This chapter, coauthored with Kent Wong, is an expanded and updated version of Milkman and Wong (2001). "Sí, se puede" means "Yes, it can be done."

2. More detailed accounts of these campaigns with extensive bibliographical citations can be found in Waldinger et al. (1998) and in Milkman and Wong (2000a).

3. UNITE was formed in 1995 by a merger between the ILGWU and the Amalgamated Clothing and Textile Workers (ACTWU). In 2004 UNITE merged with the Hotel Employees and Restaurant Employees union (HERE) to become UNITE HERE.

4. The CWA is an intermediate case; its predecessor organization, the National Federation of Telephone Workers, a federation of autonomous local unions that shared many structural characteristics with AFL unions, was independent of both the AFL and the CIO until 1947, when it adopted its present name and affiliated with the CIO (see www.cwa-union.org/about/historical-timeline.html). As discussed in chapter 1, the port truckers had once been organized by the AFL-affiliated Teamsters, although this union was not involved in the campaign of the mid-1990s.

5. U.S. labor law allows employers to "permanently replace" economic strikers who are demanding higher wages or benefits, but not workers who are striking over ULPs.

6. In their research on labor revitalization in the building trades in Boston and Portland, Sean Safford and Richard Locke (2001) make a persuasive case for the importance of leveraging such social and institutional ties, which they conceptualize as a type of union "social embeddedness."

7. A trusteeship is a mechanism that enables a national (or International) union to temporarily assume control of the affairs of a local union that is experiencing administrative problems.

8. For background on the firm, see Bonacich and Appelbaum (2000, 51–52,

212–14). Our account of the Guess campaign draws on interviews with organizers as well as press coverage in the *Los Angeles Times* and *Women's Wear Daily*. See also the account in Ross (2004, 200–5).

9. For data on garment employment in Los Angeles County in the 1990s, see http://www.calmis.ca.gov/file/indhist/la$haw.xls.

10. This was the Alameda Corridor, which opened in 2002. For details, see www.acta.org/.

EPILOGUE AND CONCLUSION

1. The United Food and Commercial Workers, which is the product of multiple mergers, includes both AFL and CIO components, and the seventh CTW union, the United Farm Workers, was established after the 1955 merger of the AFL and CIO.

APPENDIX B

1. For drywallers, the 2000 occupation code is 633 ("Drywall installers, ceiling tile installers, and tapers"). For truckers, the 2000 occupation code is 913 ("Driver/sales workers and truck drivers"). For garment workers, the 2000 industry codes are 168 and 169 ("Cut and sew apparel manufacturing" and "Apparel and accessories and other apparel manufacturing," respectively). For janitors, the 2000 occupation codes are 420 and 422 ("First-line supervisors/managers of housekeeping and janitorial workers" and "Janitors and building cleaners," respectively).

2. The "unadjusted" results are those that have not been adjusted to the 2000 classification system, but are based on nominally comparable occupation and industry categories. These categories are defined as follows. For drywallers the occupation codes are 633 in 2000 ("Drywall installers, ceiling tile installers, and tapers"), 573 in 1990 and 1980 ("Drywall installers"), and 615 in 1970 ("Drywall installers and lathers"). For truckers the occupation codes are 913 in 2000 ("Driver/sales workers and truck drivers"), 804 in 1990 ("Truck drivers"), 805 in 1980 ("Truck drivers, heavy"), and 715 in 1970 ("Trucker drivers"). For garment workers the industry codes are 168 and 169 in 2000 ("Cut and sew apparel manufacturing" and "Apparel accessories and other apparel manufacturing," respectively), 151 in 1980 and 1990 ("Apparel and accessories, except knit"), and 319 in 1970 ("Apparel and accessories"). For janitors the occupation codes are 420 and 422 in 2000 ("First-line supervisors/managers of housekeeping and janitorial workers" and "Janitors and building cleaners," respectively), 448 and 453 in 1990 and 1980 ("Supervisors, cleaning and building service workers" and "Janitors and cleaners," respectively) and 903 in 1970 ("Janitors and sextons").

REFERENCES

Acuña, Rodolfo. 1996. *Anything but Mexican: Chicanos in Contemporary Los Angeles.* New York: Verso.

Allen, Steven G. 1994. "Developments in Collective Bargaining in Construction in the 1980s and 1990s." In *Contemporary Collective Bargaining in the Private Sector,* edited by Paula B. Voos. Madison: Industrial Relations Research Association.

Appelbaum, Eileen, Thomas Bailey, Peter Berg, and Arne L. Kalleberg. 2000. *Manufacturing Advantage: Why High-Performance Systems Pay Off.* Ithaca, N.Y.: Cornell University Press.

Appelbaum, Eileen, and Rosemary Batt. 1994. *The New American Workplace: Transforming Work Systems in the United States.* Ithaca, N.Y.: Cornell University Press.

Arroyo, Luis L. 1981. "Mexican Workers and American Unions: The Los Angeles AFL, 1890–1933." Chicano Political Economy Collective Working Paper Series 107. Berkeley: University of California.

Bacon, David. 1995. "Immigrant Workers Fight to Run Local 399" (September 16). Available online at: dbacon.igc.org/Imgrants/01Loc399.html.

———. 2001. "Labor Fights for Immigrants." *The Nation,* May 21, 15–22.

Baisden, Richard. 1958. "Labor Unions in Los Angeles Politics." Ph.D. diss., University of Chicago.

Bardacke, Frank. 1988. "Watsonville: A Mexican Community on Strike." In *Reshaping the U.S. Left: Popular Struggles in the 1980s,* edited by Mike Davis and Michael Sprinker. New York: Verso.

Barrett, James. 1987. *Work and Community in the Jungle: Chicago's Packinghouse Workers, 1894–1922.* Urbana: University of Illinois Press.

Beadling, Tom, Pat Cooper, Grace Palladino, and Peter Pieragostini. 1992. *A Need for Valor: The Roots of the Service Employees International Union, 1902–1992.* Washington, D.C.: Service Employees International Union.

Belzer, Michael H. 1994. "The Motor Carrier Industry: Truckers and Teamsters Under Siege." In *Contemporary Collective Bargaining in the Private Sec-*

tor, edited by Paula B. Voos. Madison: Industrial Relations Research Association.

———. 2000. *Sweatshops on Wheels: Winners and Losers in Trucking Deregulation.* New York: Oxford University Press.

Bensinger, Richard. 1998. "When We Try More, We Win More: Organizing the New Workforce." In *Not Your Father's Union Movement*, edited by Jo-Ann Mort. New York: Verso.

Berkman, Leslie. 1986. "Construction Unions Try to Stem Job Losses." *Los Angeles Times*, March 16.

Bernstein, Harry. 1989. "While Building Owners' Profits Soar, Janitors Get Poorer." *Los Angeles Times*, August 15.

Bernstein, Irving. 1957. "The Politics of the West Coast Teamsters and Truckers." *Proceedings of the Industrial Relations Research Association* 10: 12–31.

———. 1959. "Trade Union Characteristics, Membership, and Influence." *Monthly Labor Review* 82(May): 530–35.

Bertram, Gordon W. 1966. *Consolidated Bargaining in California Construction.* Los Angeles: University of California, Institute of Industrial Relations.

Block, Fred. 1990. *Postindustrial Possibilities: A Critique of Economic Discourse.* Berkeley: University of California Press.

Bluestone, Barry, and Bennett Harrison. 1982. *The Deindustrialization of America.* New York: Basic Books.

Bonacich, Edna, and Richard P. Appelbaum. 2000. *Behind the Label: Inequality in the Los Angeles Apparel Industry.* Berkeley: University of California Press.

Borjas, George J. 1999. *Heaven's Door: Immigration Policy and the American Economy.* Princeton, N.J.: Princeton University Press.

Bourdon, Clinton C., and Raymond E. Levitt. 1980. *Union and Open-Shop Construction.* Lexington, Mass.: Lexington Books.

Brennan, Terry. 1996. "L.A.–Long Beach Trucking Standoff Continues." *Traffic World*, May 13, 21.

Briggs, Vernon M. 2001. *Immigration and American Unionism.* Ithaca, N.Y.: Cornell University Press.

Brody, David. 1960. *Steelworkers in America: The Nonunion Era.* New York: Harper & Row.

———. 1964. *The Butcher Workmen: A Study of Unionization.* Cambridge, Mass.: Harvard University Press.

———. 1967/2005. *Labor Embattled: History, Power, Rights.* Urbana: University of Illinois Press.

———. 1993. *In Labor's Cause: Main Themes on the History of the American Worker.* New York: Oxford University Press.

———. 1995. "Criminalizing the Rights of Labor." *Dissent* (Summer): 363–67.

Bronfenbrenner, Kate. 1997. "The Role of Union Strategies in NLRB Certification Elections." *Industrial and Labor Relations Review* 50: 195–211.

Bronfenbrenner, Kate, and Robert Hickey. 2004. "Changing to Organize: A National Assessment of Union Strategies." In *Rebuilding Labor: Organizing and Organizers in the New Union Movement,* edited by Ruth Milkman and Kim Voss. Ithaca, N.Y.: Cornell University Press.

Building Service Contractors' Association International. 1995. *1994 Financial and Operating Ratios Survey.* Fairfax, Va.: BSCAI.

Building Service Employees' International Union. Various years. *Proceedings.* New York: BSEIU.

————. Various years. *Report to Locals.* New York: BSEIU.

————. 1955. *"Going Up!" The Story of Local 32B.* New York: BSEIU.

Bullock, Paul, with Cara Anderson, Jack Blackburn, Edna Bonacich, and Richard Steele. 1982. *Building California: The Story of the Carpenters' Union.* Los Angeles: UCLA Center for Labor Research and Education.

Burawoy, Michael. 1985. *The Politics of Production: Factory Regimes Under Capitalism and Socialism.* New York: Verso.

Business Wire, Inc. 2000. "Three-Judge Panel Unanimously Affirms Independent Contractor Status of Harbor Truck Drivers" (January 19). Available online at: www.lexisnexis.com/universe.

California Department of Industrial Relations. Division of Labor Statistics and Research. Various years. *Union Labor in California* (cited as ULIC). San Francisco: DIR.

————. Various years. *California Labor Statistics Bulletin: Area Supplement* (cited as CLSB). San Francisco: DIR.

California Employment Development Department. Employment Data and Research Division. Various years. *California Labor Market Bulletin: Statistical Supplement* (cited as CLMB). Sacramento: EDD.

————. Various years. *California Employment and Payrolls* (cited as CEP). Sacramento: EDD.

Cappelli, Peter. 1999. *The New Deal at Work: Managing the Market-Driven Workforce.* Boston: Harvard Business School Press.

Carlson, Oliver. 1938. "Los Angeles Grows Up." *The Nation,* January 8, 43–44.

Carney, Andrea. 2000. "I Declined to Join the Staff." In *The New Rank and File,* edited by Staughton Lynd and Alice Lynd. Ithaca, N.Y.: Cornell University Press.

Catanzarite, Lisa. 2002. "The Dynamics of Segregation and Earnings in Brown-Collar Occupations." *Work and Occupations* 29(3): 300–42.

————. 2004. "Immigration, Union Density, and Brown-Collar Wage Penalties." *The State of California Labor* 4: 107–30.

Christie, Robert A. 1956. *Empire in Wood: A History of the Carpenters' Union.* Cornell University Studies in Industrial and Labor Relations 7. Ithaca, N.Y.: Cornell University.

Citron, Jack, and Benjamin Highton. 2002. *How Race, Ethnicity, and Immigration Shape the California Electorate.* San Francisco: Public Policy Institute of California.

Clark, Paul F., and Lois S. Gray. 2004. "The Evolution of Administrative Practices in American Unions: Results of a Longitudinal Study." Unpublished paper.

Clawson, Dan. 2003. *The Next Upsurge: Labor and the New Social Movements*. Ithaca, N.Y.: Cornell University Press.

Cleeland, Nancy. 1999. "Guess to Pay Up to $1 Million to End Suit." *Los Angeles Times*, July 21.

———. 2000a. "Harbor Drivers Independent, Panel Says." *Los Angeles Times*, January 19.

———. 2000b. "Heartache on Aisle 3: Sweatshop for Janitors." *Los Angeles Times*, July 2.

———. 2002. "Organize or Die: As Chief of the Powerful United Brotherhood of Carpenters and Joiners, Douglas McCarron Has Made Plenty of Friends and Enemies." *Los Angeles Times*, March 10.

Cobble, Dorothy Sue. 1991a. *Dishing It Out: Waitresses and Their Unions in the Twentieth Century*. Urbana: University of Illinois Press.

———. 1991b. "Organizing the Postindustrial Work Force: Lessons from the History of Waitress Unionism." *Industrial and Labor Relations Review* 44: 419–36.

———. 1997. "Lost Ways of Organizing: Reviving the AFL's Direct Affiliate Strategy." *Industrial Relations* 36: 278–301.

Cobble, Dorothy Sue, and Leah F. Vosko. 2000. "Historical Perspectives on Representing Nonstandard Workers." In *Nonstandard Work: The Nature and Challenges of Changing Employment Arrangements*, edited by Françoise Carré, Marianne A. Ferber, Lonnie Golden, and Stephen A. Herzenberg. Champaign, Ill.: Industrial Relations Research Association.

Cohen, Lizabeth. 1990. *Making a New Deal: Industrial Workers in Chicago, 1919–1939*. New York: Cambridge University Press.

Conference Board. 1997. "Implementing the New Employment Compact." *HR Executive Review* 4(4): 3–18.

Coons, Arthur C., and Arjay R. Miller. 1942. "An Economic and Industrial Survey of the Los Angeles and San Diego Areas (Summary)." Mimeo. Sacramento: California State Planning Board.

Cowie, Jefferson. 1999. *Capital Moves: RCA's Seventy-Year Quest for Cheap Labor*. New York: New Press.

Craft, Donna, and Terrance W. Peck, eds. 1998. *Profiles of American Labor Unions*. Detroit: Gale Research.

Cranford, Cynthia. 2001. "Labor, Gender, and the Politics of Citizenship: Organizing Justice for Janitors in Los Angeles." Ph.D. diss., University of Southern California at Los Angeles.

Cross, Ira. 1935. *A History of the Labor Movement in California*. Berkeley: University of California Press.

Dark, Taylor E. 1999. "Debating Decline: The 1995 Race for the AFL-CIO Presidency." *Labor History* 40(3): 323–43.

———. 2001. *The Unions and the Democrats: An Enduring Alliance.* 2nd ed. Ithaca, N.Y.: Cornell University Press.

Davis, Mike. 1997. "Sunshine and the Open Shop: Ford and Darwin in 1920s Los Angeles." *Antipode* 29: 356–82.

———. 2000. *Magical Urbanism: Latinos Reinvent the U.S. Big City.* New York: Verso.

DeFreitas, Gregory. 1993. "Unionization Among Racial and Ethnic Minorities." *Industrial and Labor Relations Review* 46: 284–301.

Delgado, Hector L. 1993. *New Immigrants, Old Unions: Organizing Undocumented Workers in Los Angeles.* Philadelphia: Temple University Press.

———. 2000. "The Los Angeles Manufacturing Action Project: An Opportunity Squandered?" In *Organizing Immigrants: The Challenge for Unions in Contemporary California*, edited by Ruth Milkman. Ithaca, N.Y.: Cornell University Press.

Del Olmo, Frank. 1998. "'Giant' Is Awake and Is a Force: Latino Voters' Pivotal Role in the Election Puts All Politicians on Notice." *Los Angeles Times*, June 7.

Early, Steve. 2004. "Reutherism Redux: What Happens When Poor Workers' Unions Wear the Color Purple." *Against the Current* 19(4): 31–39.

Eliaser, Ralph. 1998. Oral history interview by Louis Jones. Detroit: Wayne State University Archives of Labor History and Urban Affairs.

Engineering News-Record. 1981. "Union Construction in Trouble" (special report). November 5, 26.

Erickson, Christopher L., Catherine L. Fisk, Ruth Milkman, Daniel J. B. Mitchell, and Kent Wong. 2002. "Justice for Janitors in Los Angeles: Lessons from Three Rounds of Negotiations." *British Journal of Industrial Relations* 40(3): 543–67.

Esbenshade, Jill. 2001. "The Social Accountability Contract: Private Monitoring from Los Angeles to the Global Apparel Industry." *Labor Studies Journal* 26(1): 98–120.

Fantasia, Rick, and Kim Voss. 2004. *Hard Work: Remaking the American Labor Movement.* Berkeley: University of California Press.

Farber, Henry S., and Alan B. Krueger. 1993. "Union Membership in the United States: The Decline Continues." In *Employee Representation: Alternatives and Future Directions*, edited by Bruce E. Kaufman and Morris M. Kleiner. Madison: Industrial Relations Research Association.

Farber, Henry S., and Bruce Western. 2001. "Accounting for the Decline of Unions in the Private Sector, 1973–1998." *Journal of Labor Research* 22: 459–85.

———. 2002. "Ronald Reagan and the Politics of Declining Union Organization." *British Journal of Industrial Relations* 40: 385–401.

Fausset, Richard. 2001. "Employer Pays Janitor Part of Wages Owed." *Los Angeles Times,* June 13.

Featherstone, Liza. 2002. *Students Against Sweatshops: The Making of a Movement.* New York: Verso.

Fine, Janice. 2006. *Worker Centers: Organizing Communities at the Edge of the Dream.* Ithaca, N.Y.: Cornell University Press.

Fink, Gary M., ed. 1977. *Labor Unions.* Westport, Conn.: Greenwood Press.

Fink, Leon. 2003. *The Maya of Morgantown: Work and Community in the Nuevo New South.* Chapel Hill: University of North Carolina Press.

Firestone, David. 1999. "Victory for Union at Plant in South Is Labor Milestone." *New York Times,* June 25.

Fisk, Catherine L., Daniel J. B. Mitchell, and Christopher L. Erickson. 2000. "Union Representation of Immigrant Janitors in Southern California: Economic and Legal Challenges." In *Organizing Immigrants: The Challenge for Unions in Contemporary California,* edited by Ruth Milkman. Ithaca, N.Y.: Cornell University Press.

Fitzgerald, David. 2004. "Beyond 'Transnationalism': Mexican Hometown Politics at an American Labor Union." *Ethnic and Racial Studies* 27(2): 228–47.

Flanagan, Robert J. 2005. "Has Management Strangled U.S. Unions?" *Journal of Labor Research* 26(Winter): 33–63.

Fogelson, Robert M. 1967. *The Fragmented Metropolis: Los Angeles, 1850–1930.* Cambridge, Mass.: Harvard University Press.

Frank, Larry, and Kent Wong. 2004. "Dynamic Political Mobilization: The Los Angeles County Federation of Labor." *Working USA: The Journal of Labor and Society* 8: 155–81.

Fraser, Steven. 1983. "Dress Rehearsal for the New Deal: Shop-Floor Insurgents, Political Elites, and Industrial Democracy in the Amalgamated Clothing Workers." In *Working-Class America: Essays on Labor, Community, and American Society,* edited by Michael H. Frisch and Daniel J. Walkowitz. Urbana: University of Illinois Press.

———. 1991. *Labor Will Rule: Sidney Hillman and the Rise of American Labor.* New York: Free Press.

Freeman, Joshua B. 2000. *Working-Class New York: Life and Labor Since World War II.* New York: New Press.

Freeman, Richard B. 1988. "Contraction and Expansion: The Divergence of Private-Sector and Public-Sector Unionism in the United States." *Journal of Economic Perspectives* 2: 63–88.

———. 2004. "Searching Outside the Box." In *The Future of Labor Unions: Organized Labor in the Twenty-first Century,* edited by Julius G. Getman and Ray Marshall. Austin: University of Texas, Ray Marshall Center for the Study of Human Resources.

Freeman, Richard B., and James L. Medoff. 1984. *What Do Unions Do?* New York: Basic Books.

Freeman, Richard B., and Joel Rogers. 1999. *What Workers Want*. Ithaca, N.Y.: Cornell University Press.

Frey, William H. 2002. "Census 2000 Reveals New Native-Born and Foreign-Born Shifts Across U.S." Research report 02-520. Ann Arbor: University of Michigan, Institute of Social Research, Population Studies Center.

Friedlander, Peter. 1975. *The Emergence of a UAW Local, 1936–1939*. Pittsburgh: University of Pittsburgh Press.

Funkhouser, Edward. 1993. "Do Immigrants Have Lower Union Propensities Than Natives?" *Industrial Relations* 32(Spring): 249–61.

Galenson, Walter. 1983. *The United Brotherhood of Carpenters: The First Hundred Years*. Cambridge, Mass.: Harvard University Press.

Ganz, Marshall. 2000. "Resources and Resourcefulness: Strategic Capacity in the Unionization of California Agriculture, 1959–1966." *American Journal of Sociology* 104: 1003–62.

———. 2004. "Why David Sometimes Wins: Strategic Capacity in Social Movements." In *Rethinking Social Movements: Structure, Meaning, and Emotion*, edited by Jeff Goodwin and James M. Jasper. New York: Rowman & Littlefield.

Ganz, Marshall, Kim Voss, Teresa Sharpe, Carl Somers, and George Strauss. 2004. "Against the Tide: Projects and Pathways of the New Generation of Union Leaders, 1984–2001." In *Rebuilding Labor: Organizing and Organizers in the New Union Movement*, edited by Ruth Milkman and Kim Voss. Ithaca, N.Y.: Cornell University Press.

Gardetta, Dave. 1993. "Clocking Time with Janitors Organizer Rocio Saenz." *L.A. Weekly*, August 5.

Gardner, Andrew M. 2002. "The Long Haul from Deregulation: Truck Drivers and Social Capital in the Louisiana Oilpatch." *Human Organization* 61: 390–98.

Garnel, Donald. 1972. *The Rise of Teamster Power in the West*. Berkeley: University of California Press.

Gillingham, J. B. 1956. *The Teamsters Union on the West Coast*. Berkeley: University of California, Institute of Industrial Relations.

Glenn, Susan A. 1990. *Daughters of the Shtetl: Life and Labor in the Immigrant Generation*. Ithaca, N.Y.: Cornell University Press.

Goldfield, Michael. 1987. *The Decline of Organized Labor in the United States*. Chicago: University of Chicago Press.

Goldin, Claudia, and Robert A. Margo. 1992. "The Great Compression: The Wage Structure in the United States at Midcentury." *Quarterly Journal of Economics* 107: 1–34.

Gordon, Colin. 1994. *New Deals: Business, Labor, and Politics in America, 1920–1935*. New York: Cambridge University Press.

———. 1999. "The Lost City of Solidarity: Metropolitan Unionism in Historical Perspective." *Politics and Society* 27: 561–85.

Gordon, Jennifer. 2005. *Suburban Sweatshops: The Fight for Immigrant Rights*. Cambridge, Mass.: Harvard University Press.

Gordon, Margaret S. 1954. *Employment Expansion and Population Growth: The California Experience, 1900–1950.* Berkeley: University of California Press.

Gosselin, Peter. 2004. "If America Is Richer, Why Are Its Families So Much Less Secure?" *Los Angeles Times*, October 10.

Gottlieb, Robert, Mark Vallianatos, Regina M. Freer, and Peter Dreier. 2005. *The Next Los Angeles: The Struggle for a Livable City.* Berkeley: University of California Press.

Gouldner, Alvin W. 1980. *The Two Marxisms: Contradictions and Anomalies in the Development of Theory.* New York: Seabury Press.

Grabelsky, Jeff. 2004–2005. "Building and Construction Trades Unions: Are They Built to Win?" *Social Policy* 36(2): 35–39.

Gratton, Brian, and Myron P. Gutmann. 2000. "Hispanics in the United States, 1850–1990: Estimates of Population Size and National Origin." *Historical Methods* 33: 137–53.

Gray, Lois W. 1981. "Unions Implementing Managerial Techniques." *Monthly Labor Review* 104(June): 3–13.

Greene, Julie. 1998. *Pure and Simple Politics: The American Federation of Labor and Political Activism, 1881–1917.* New York: Cambridge University Press.

Greenhouse, Steven. 1997. "Chavez's Son-in-Law Tries to Rebuild Legacy." *New York Times*, June 30.

———. 1999. "In Biggest Drive Since 1937, Union Gains a Victory." *New York Times*, February 26.

———. 2000. "On the California Waterfront, Mostly Tough Times for Port Truckers." *New York Times*, April 15.

——— 2004. "Though United in Politics, Unions Face Internal Turmoil." *New York Times*, August 1.

——— 2005. "Union Claims Texas Victory with Janitors." *New York Times*, November 28.

Greenstone, J. David. 1969. *Labor in American Politics.* New York: Alfred A. Knopf.

Greer, Scott. 1959. *Last Man In: Racial Access to Union Power.* Glencoe, Ill.: Free Press.

Gutiérrez, David G. 1995. *Walls and Mirrors: Mexican Americans, Mexican Immigrants, and the Politics of Ethnicity.* Berkeley: University of California Press.

———. 1998. "Ethnic Mexicans and the Transformation of 'American' Social Space: Reflections on Recent History." In *Crossings: Mexican Immigration in Interdisciplinary Perspective*, edited by Marcelo M. Suárez-Orozco. Cambridge, Mass.: Harvard University, David Rockefeller Center for Latin American Studies.

Haber, William. 1930. *Industrial Relations in the Building Industry.* Cambridge, Mass.: Harvard University Press.

Haggerty, Cornelius J. 1976. "Labor, Los Angeles, and the Legislature." Oral history interview conducted by Amelia R. Fry, November 1969. Berkeley:

University of California, Bancroft Library, Regional Oral History Office, Earl Warren Oral History Project.

Hamilton, Nora, and Norma S. Chinchilla. 2001. *Seeking Community in a Global City: Guatemalans and Salvadorans in Los Angeles.* Philadelphia: Temple University Press.

Harris, Howell John. 1982. *The Right to Manage: Industrial Relations Policies of American Business in the 1940s.* Madison: University of Wisconsin Press.

Haus, Leah A. 2002. *Unions, Immigration, and Internationalization: New Challenges and Changing Coalitions in the United States and France.* New York: Palgrave Macmillan.

Heckscher, Charles. 1988. *The New Unionism: Employee Involvement in the Changing Corporation.* New York: Basic Books.

Heywood, John S., and James H. Peoples. 1994. "Deregulation and the Prevalence of Black Truck Drivers." *Journal of Law and Economics* 37: 133–55.

Hirsch, Barry T., and David A. Macpherson. Various years. *Union Membership and Earnings Data Book: Compilations from the Current Population Survey.* Washington: Bureau of National Affairs.

Hirschhorn, Larry. 1984. *Beyond Mechanization: Work and Technology in a Post-Industrial Age.* Cambridge, Mass.: MIT Press.

Hise, Greg. 2001. "'Nature's Workshop': Industry and Urban Expansion in Southern California, 1900–1950." *Journal of Historical Geography* 27: 74–92.

Hourwich, Issac A. 1912. *Immigration and Labor: The Economic Aspects of European Immigration to the United States.* New York: Putnam.

Hurd, Richard. 2004. "The Failure of Organizing, the New Unity Partnership, and the Future of the Labor Movement." *Working USA* 8(September): 5–25.

International Ladies' Garment Workers' Union. Various years. *Financial and Statistical Report* (cited as FSR). New York: ILGWU.

———. Various years. *Report of the General Executive Board* (cited as GEB). New York: ILGWU.

Jacoby, Sanford. 1997. *Modern Manors: Welfare Capitalism Since the New Deal.* Princeton, N.J.: Princeton University Press.

James, Ralph C., and Estelle Dinerstein James. 1965. *Hoffa and the Teamsters: A Study of Union Power.* New York: D. Van Nostrand.

Jentz, John B. 1997. "Citizenship, Self-Respect, and Political Power: Chicago's Flat Janitors Trailblaze the Service Employees International Union, 1912–1921." *Labor's Heritage* 9: 4–23.

———. 2000. "Unions, Cartels, and the Political Economy of American Cities: The Chicago Flat Janitors' Union in the Progressive Era and 1920s." *Studies in American Political Development* 14: 51–71.

Johnston, Paul. 1994. *Success While Others Fail: Social Movement Unionism and the Public Workplace.* Ithaca, N.Y.: ILR Press.

Jordan, Miriam. 2005. "Carpenters' Union Courts Immigrants to Increase Clout." *Wall Street Journal*, December 15.

Katz, Harry C., Rosemary Batt, and Jeffrey H. Keefe. 2003. "The Strategic Initiatives of the CWA: Organizing, Politics, and Collective Bargaining." *Industrial and Labor Relations Review* 56: 573–89.

Kazin, Michael. 1986. "The Great Exception Revisited: Organized Labor and Politics in San Francisco and Los Angeles, 1870–1940." *Pacific Historical Review* 55: 371–402.

———. 1987. *Barons of Labor: The San Francisco Building Trades and Union Power in the Progressive Era.* Urbana: University of Illinois Press.

Kennedy, Van Dusen. 1955. *Nonfactory Unionism and Labor Relations.* Berkeley: University of California, Institute of Industrial Relations.

———. 1959. "Association Bargaining." *Monthly Labor Review* 82(May): 539–42.

Kimeldorf, Howard. 1988. *Reds or Rackets? The Making of Radical and Conservative Unions on the Waterfront.* Berkeley: University of California Press.

Kochan, Thomas A., Harry C. Katz, and Robert B. McKersie. 1986. *The Transformation of American Industrial Relations.* New York: Basic Books.

Krugman, Paul. 2002. "For Richer." *New York Times Magazine,* October 20, 62.

Laslett, John H. M. 1996. "Historical Perspectives: Immigration and the Rise of a Distinctive Urban Region, 1900–1970." In *Ethnic Los Angeles,* edited by Roger Waldinger and Mehdi Bozorgmehr. New York: Russell Sage Foundation.

Laslett, John, and Mary Tyler. 1989. *The ILGWU in Los Angeles, 1907–1988.* Inglewood, Calif.: Ten Star Press.

Leeds, Jeff. 1996. "For Truckers, Long Haul Is a Costly One." *Los Angeles Times,* May 30.

Lerner, Stephen. 2003. "An Immodest Proposal: A New Architecture for the House of Labor." *New Labor Forum* 12(2): 9–30.

Lester, Richard A. 1958. *As Unions Mature: An Analysis of the Evolution of American Unionism.* Princeton, N.J.: Princeton University Press.

Levine, Louis. 1924. *The Women's Garment Workers: A History of the International Ladies' Garment Workers' Union.* New York: B. W. Huebsch.

Levinson, Harold M. 1980. "Trucking." In *Collective Bargaining: Contemporary American Experience,* edited by Gerald G. Somers. Madison: Industrial Relations Research Association.

Levitan, Mark. 1998. "Opportunity at Work: The New York City Garment Industry." Mimeo. New York: Community Service Society of New York.

Levy, Frank. 1999. *The New Dollars and Dreams: American Incomes and Economic Change.* New York: Russell Sage Foundation.

Lichtenstein, Nelson. 1982. *Labor's War at Home: The CIO in World War II.* New York: Cambridge University Press.

———. 2002. *State of the Union: A Century of American Labor.* Princeton, N.J.: Princeton University Press.

Liebes, Richard. 1998. Oral history interview by Louis Jones. Detroit: Wayne State University, Archives of Labor History and Urban Affairs.

Linder, Marc. 2000. *Wars of Attrition: Vietnam, the Business Roundtable, and the Decline of Construction Unions.* Iowa City: Fanpihua Press.

Lopez, Steven Henry. 2004. *Reorganizing the Rust Belt: An Inside Story of the American Labor Movement.* Berkeley: University of California Press.

Luce, Stephanie. 2004. *Fighting for a Living Wage.* Ithaca, N.Y.: Cornell University Press.

Manheim, Jarol B. 2001. *The Death of a Thousand Cuts: Corporate Campaigns and the Attack on the Corporation.* Mahwah, N.J.: Lawrence Erlbaum Associates.

Maram, Sheldon L. 1980. "Hispanic Workers in the Garment and Restaurant Industries in Los Angeles County." Working paper 12. San Diego: University of California, Program in U.S.–Mexican Studies.

Martin, Philip L. 1996. *Promises to Keep: Collective Bargaining in California Agriculture.* Ames: Iowa State University Press.

Massey, Douglas S., Jorge Durand, and Nolan J. Malone. 2002. *Beyond Smoke and Mirrors: Mexican Immigration in an Era of Economic Integration.* New York: Russell Sage Foundation.

McDermott, Michael. N.d. "Local 399: The Blighted Crown Jewel." Unpublished paper in author's possession.

McWilliams, Carey. 1946/1973. *Southern California: An Island on the Land.* Salt Lake City: Gibbs M. Smith.

———. 1949/1999. *California: The Great Exception.* Berkeley: University of California Press.

Menjivar, Cecilia. 2000. *Fragmented Ties: Salvadoran Immigrant Networks in America.* Berkeley: University of California Press.

Merton, Robert K. 1959. "Notes on Problem-Finding in Sociology." In *Sociology Today: Problems and Prospects*, edited by Robert K. Merton, Leonard Broom, and Leonard S. Cottrell Jr. New York: Basic Books.

Meyerson, Harold. 2000. "A Clean Sweep." *The American Prospect* 11(15): 24–29.

———. 2001. "California's Progressive Mosaic." *The American Prospect* 12(11): 17–23.

———. 2003. "Janitorial Justice." *The American Prospect Online* (June 26). Available online at: www.prospect.org.

———. 2005. "The Architect: Miguel Contreras, 1952–2005." *L.A. Weekly*, May 13–18.

Michels, Robert. 1915/1962. *Political Parties: A Sociological Study of the Oligarchical Tendencies in Modern Democracy.* New York: Free Press.

Milkman, Ruth. 1993. "Union Responses to Workforce Feminization in the United States." In *The Challenge of Restructuring: North American Labor Movements Respond*, edited by Jane Jenson and Rianne Mahon. Philadelphia: Temple University Press.

Milkman, Ruth, and Rachel Dwyer. 2002. "Growing Apart: The 'New Economy' and Job Polarization in California, 1992–2000." *The State of California Labor* 2: 3–35.

Milkman, Ruth, and Daisy Rooks. 2003. "California Union Membership: A Turn-of-the-Century Portrait." *The State of California Labor* 3: 3–37.

Milkman, Ruth, and Kim Voss. 2005. "New Unity for Labor?" *Labor: Studies in Working-Class History of the Americas* 2(1): 15–25.

Milkman, Ruth, and Kent Wong. 2000a. "Organizing the Wicked City: The 1992 Southern California Drywall Strike." In *Organizing Immigrants: The Challenge for Unions in Contemporary California,* edited by Ruth Milkman. Ithaca, N.Y.: Cornell University Press.

———. 2000b. *Voices from the Front Lines: Organizing Immigrant Workers in Los Angeles.* Los Angeles: UCLA Center for Labor Research and Education.

———. 2001. "Organizing Immigrant Workers: Case Studies from Southern California." In *Rekindling the Movement: Labor's Quest for Relevance in the Twenty-first Century,* edited by Lowell Turner, Harry C. Katz, and Richard W. Hurd. Ithaca, N.Y.: Cornell University Press.

Mills, C. Wright. 1948. *The New Men of Power: America's Labor Leaders.* New York: Harcourt, Brace.

Mills, Daniel Quinn. 1972. *Industrial Relations and Manpower in Construction.* Cambridge, Mass.: MIT Press.

Mines, Richard, and Jeffrey Avina. 1992. "Immigrants and Labor Standards: The Case of California Janitors." In *U.S.-Mexico Relations: Labor Market Interdependence,* edited by Jorge A. Bustamante, Clark Reynolds, and Raul Hinojosa-Ojeda. Stanford, Calif.: Stanford University Press.

Mink, Gwendolyn. 1986. *Old Labor and New Immigrants in American Political Development: Union, Party, and State, 1875–1920.* Ithaca, N.Y.: Cornell University Press.

Modell, John. 1977. *The Economics and Politics of Racial Accommodation: The Japanese of Los Angeles, 1900–1942.* Urbana: University of Illinois Press.

Mollenkopf, John Hull. 1999. "Urban Political Conflicts and Alliances: New York and Los Angeles Compared." In *The Handbook of International Migration: The American Experience,* edited by Charles Hirshmann, Philip Kasinitz, and Josh DeWind. New York: Russell Sage Foundation.

Mongelluzzo, Bill. 1994. "L.A. Attorney Alleges Blacklisting of Drivers." *Journal of Commerce,* January 3.

———. 1996a. "New Driver Leasing Firm Steals Spotlight at Los Angeles–Long Beach." *Journal of Commerce,* February 26.

———. 1996b. "Independent Truck Drivers Push Demands in California." *Journal of Commerce,* Feb. 9.

———. 1996c. "Unionization Spreads up California Coast." *Journal of Commerce,* May 1.

———. 1996d. "Stakes Grow in L.A.–Long Beach Trucker Unionization Standoff." *Journal of Commerce,* May 9.

Monroy, Douglas. 1999. *Rebirth: Mexican Los Angeles from the Great Migration to the Great Depression.* Berkeley: University of California Press.

Montgomery, David. 1986. "Nationalism, American Patriotism, and Class Consciousness Among Immigrant Workers in the United States in the Epoch of World War I." In *"Struggle a Hard Battle": Essays on Working-Class Immigrants,* edited by Dirk Hoerder. De Kalb: Northern Illinois University Press.

———. 1987. *The Fall of the House of Labor.* New York: Cambridge University Press.

Moody, Kim. 1997. *Workers in a Lean World: Unions in the International Economy.* New York: Verso.

Moore, Thomas Gale. 1986. "Rail and Trucking Deregulation." In *Regulatory Reform: What Actually Happened,* edited by Leonard W. Weiss and Michael W. Klass. Boston: Little, Brown.

Morris, James O. 1958. *Conflict Within the AFL: A Study of Craft Versus Industrial Unionism, 1901–1938.* Ithaca, N.Y.: Cornell University Press.

Nazario, Sonia. 1995. "Hunger Strike Marks Union's Split." *Los Angeles Times,* August 8.

Ngai, Mae M. 2004. *Impossible Subjects: Illegal Aliens and the Making of Modern America.* Princeton, N.J.: Princeton University Press.

Nicolaides, Becky M. 2002. *My Blue Heaven: Life and Politics in the Working-Class Suburbs of Los Angeles, 1920–1965.* Chicago: University of Chicago Press.

Nutter, Steve. 1997. "The Structure and Growth of the Los Angeles Garment Industry." In *No Sweat: Fashion, Free Trade, and the Rights of Garment Workers,* edited by Andrew Ross. New York: Verso.

Offe, Claus, and Helmut Wiesenthal. 1980. "Two Logics of Collective Action: Theoretical Notes on Social Class and Organizational Form." *Political Power and Social Theory* 1: 67–115.

Orange County Human Relations Commission. 1989. "Zero Dollars per Hour: A Report on Labor Exploitation in Orange County." Mimeo. Santa Ana, Calif.: Orange County Human Relations Commission.

Osterman, Paul. 1994. "How Common Is Workplace Transformation and How Can We Explain Who Does It?" *Industrial and Labor Relations Review* 47(January): 173–88.

Palladino, Grace. 2005. *Skilled Hands, Strong Spirits: A Century of Building Trades History.* Ithaca, N.Y.: Cornell University Press.

Penney, Robert A. 2004. "Workers Against Unions: Union Organizing and Anti-Union Countermobilizations." In *Rebuilding Labor: Organizing and Organizers in the New Union Movement,* edited by Ruth Milkman and Kim Voss. Ithaca, N.Y.: Cornell University Press.

Perlman, Selig. 1928. *A Theory of the Labor Movement.* New York: Macmillan.

Perry, Charles R. 1986. *Deregulation and the Decline of the Unionized Trucking Industry.* Philadelphia: Wharton School, Industrial Research Unit.

Perry, Louis B., and Richard S. Perry. 1963. *A History of the Los Angeles Labor Movement, 1911–1941.* Berkeley: University of California Press.

Pesotta, Rose. 1944. *Bread upon the Waters.* New York: Dodd, Mead.

Piore, Michael J. 1979. *Birds of Passage: Migrant Labor and Industrial Societies.* New York: Cambridge University Press.

———. 1994. "Unions: A Reorientation to Survive." In *Labor Economics and Industrial Relations: Markets and Institutions,* edited by Clark Kerr and Paul D. Staudohar. Cambridge, Mass.: Harvard University Press.

———. 1997. "The Economics of the Sweatshop." In *No Sweat: Fashion, Free Trade, and the Rights of Garment Workers,* edited by Andrew Ross. New York: Verso.

Piore, Michael J., and Charles F. Sabel. 1984. *The Second Industrial Divide: Possibilities for Prosperity.* New York: Basic Books.

Portes, Alejandro, and Rubén G. Rumbaut. 1990. *Immigrant America: A Portrait.* Berkeley: University of California Press.

Purdum, Todd S. 1999. "A Setback for United Farm Workers." *New York Times,* May 27.

Ramakrishnan, S. Karthick, and Thomas J. Espenshade. 2001. "Immigrant Incorporation and Political Participation in the United States." *International Migration Review* 35(3): 870–909.

Ransom, David. 1980. *"So Much to Be Done": George Hardy's Life in Organized Labor.* Washington, D.C.: Service Employees' International Union.

Reskin, Barbara F., Patricia A. Roos et al. 1990. *Job Queues, Gender Queues: Explaining Women's Inroads into Male Occupations.* Philadelphia: Temple University Press.

Rieff, David. 1992. *Los Angeles: Capital of the Third World.* New York: Simon & Schuster.

Rose, Frederick, and Jim Carlton. 1996. "Businessman Is Making Waves at Harbor." *Orange County Register,* May 8.

Rose, Nancy L. 1987. "Labor Rent Sharing and Regulation: Evidence from the Trucking Industry." *Journal of Political Economy* 95: 1146–78.

Ross, Robert J. S. 2004. *Slaves to Fashion: Poverty and Abuse in the New Sweatshops.* Ann Arbor: University of Michigan Press.

Russell, Thaddeus. 2001. *Out of the Jungle: Jimmy Hoffa and the Remaking of the American Working Class.* New York: Alfred A. Knopf.

Safford, Sean C., and Richard M. Locke. 2001. "Unions on the Rebound: Social Embeddedness and the Transformation of Building Trades Locals." Working paper 4175-01. Cambridge, Mass.: MIT Sloan School of Management.

Sánchez, George J. 1993. *Becoming Mexican American: Ethnicity, Culture, and Identity in Chicano Los Angeles, 1900–1945.* New York: Oxford University Press.

Sanchez, Jesus. 1993. "Truckers Disrupt Port Traffic to Protest Higher Fuel Costs." *Los Angeles Times,* November 12.

SEIU Archives. Executive Office Microfilm Collection (cited as SEIU Executive Office Collection), Wayne State University.

———. Research Department Historical Files Collection (cited as SEIU Research Department Historical Files Collection), Wayne State University. Box 14, folder "Local 399: General."

―――――. George Hardy Collection (cited as SEIU George Hardy Collection), Wayne State University.

Sennett, Richard. 1998. *The Corrosion of Character: The Personal Consequences of Work in the New Capitalism.* New York: W. W. Norton.

Service Employees' International Union. Local 399. 1995. "A Penny for Justice: Janitors and L.A.'s Commercial Real Estate Market." Mimeo. Los Angeles: SEIU, Local 399.

Shaw, Randy. 1999. *Reclaiming America: Nike, Clean Air, and the New National Activism.* Berkeley: University of California Press.

Silver, Beverly. 2003. *Forces of Labor: Workers' Movements and Globalization Since 1870.* New York: Cambridge University Press.

Silverstein, Stuart. 1994. "Survey of Garment Industry Finds Rampant Labor Abuse." *Los Angeles Times,* April 15.

Silverstein, Stuart, and Jeff Leeds. 1996. "Independent Truckers, Union Form a Convoy." *Los Angeles Times,* May 11.

Soldatenko, Maria Angelina. 1992. "The Everyday Lives of Latina Garment Workers in Los Angeles." Ph.D. diss., University of California at Los Angeles, Department of Sociology.

Sorokin, Pitirim A., Guy C. Hanna, Celia Israel, Lewis L. McKibben, Mildred Parten, Marion B. Rothem, Mami Tanquist, Elmer N. Eddy. 1927. "Leaders of Labor and Radical Movements in the United States and Foreign Countries." *American Journal of Sociology* 33(3): 382–411.

Stimson, Grace Heilman. 1955. *Rise of the Labor Movement in Los Angeles.* Berkeley: University of California Press.

Stinchcombe, Arthur L. 1959. "Bureaucratic and Craft Administration of Production: A Comparative Study." *Administrative Science Quarterly* 4(2): 168–87.

―――――. 1965. "Social Structure and Organizations." In *Handbook of Organizations,* edited by James G. March. Chicago: Rand McNally.

Su, Julie. 1997. "El Monte Thai Garment Workers: Slave Sweatshops." In *No Sweat: Fashion, Free Trade, and the Rights of Garment Workers,* edited by Andrew Ross. New York: Verso.

Taft, Philip. 1968. *Labor Politics American Style: The California State Federation of Labor.* Cambridge, Mass.: Harvard University Press.

Tait, Vanessa. 2005. *Poor Workers' Unions: Rebuilding Labor from Below.* Boston: South End Press.

Taylor, Paul S. 1928/1980. "Mexican Women in Los Angeles in 1928." *Aztlan* 11(1): 99–131.

Tipton, Gene B. 1953. "The Labor Movement in the Los Angeles Area During the Nineteen-Forties." Ph.D. diss., University of California at Los Angeles.

Tobar, Hector. 1998. "In Contests Big and Small, Latinos Take Historic Leap." *Los Angeles Times,* November 5.

Tomlins, Christopher. 1979. "AFL Unions in the 1930s: Their Performance in Historical Perspective." *Journal of American History* 65: 1021–42.

Troy, Leo. 1957. "Distribution of Union Membership Among the States: 1939 and 1953." Occasional paper 56. New York: National Bureau of Economic Research.

Tsukashima, Ronald Tadao. 1998. "Notes on Emerging Collective Action: Ethnic-Trade Guilds Among Japanese Americans in the Gardening Industry." *International Migration Review* 32: 374–400.

U.S. Census Bureau. 1989. "The Relationship Between the 1970 and 1980 Industry and Occupation Classification Systems." Technical Paper 59. Washington: U.S. Census Bureau.

———. 1994. "Changes to the 1980 Industrial and Occupational Classification Systems for the 1990 Census of Population." Unpublished paper. Washington: U.S. Census Bureau.

———. 2003. "The Relationship Between the 1990 Census and Census 2000 Industry and Occupation Classification Systems." Technical Paper 65. Washington: U.S. Census Bureau.

U.S. Department of Commerce. 1933. *Fifteenth Census of the United States: 1930, Population.* Washington: U.S. Government Printing Office.

———. 1943. *Sixteenth Census of the United States: 1940, Population.* Washington: U.S. Government Printing Office.

———. 1953. *Census of Population: 1950.* Washington: U.S. Government Printing Office.

U.S. Department of Labor. Bureau of Labor Statistics. 1980. *Handbook of Labor Statistics.* Bulletin 2070. Washington: U.S. Government Printing Office.

U.S. Senate. Subcommittee of the Committee on Education and Labor. 1940. "Open-Shop Activities," part 64, "Supplementary Exhibits." In *Violations of Free Speech and Rights of Labor.* 76th Cong., 3rd sess., part 57. Washington: U.S. Government Printing Office.

Vargas, Zaragosa. 2005. *Labor Rights Are Civil Rights: Mexican American Workers in Twentieth-Century America.* Princeton, N.J.: Princeton University Press.

Verhovek, Sam Howe. 1999. "The New Language of American Labor." *New York Times,* June 26.

Voos, Paula B. 1984. "Trends in Union Organizing Expenditures, 1953–1977." *Industrial and Labor Relations Review* 39(1): 52–63.

Voss, Kim, and Rachel Sherman. 2000. "Breaking the Iron Law of Oligarchy: Union Revitalization in the American Labor Movement." *American Journal of Sociology* 106: 303–49.

Waldinger, Roger. 1986. *Through the Eye of the Needle: Immigrants and Enterprise in New York's Garment Trades.* New York: New York University Press.

Waldinger, Roger, and Claudia Der-Martirosian. 2000. "Immigrant Workers and American Labor: Challenge . . . or Disaster?" In *Organizing Immigrants:*

The Challenge for Unions in Contemporary California, edited by Ruth Milkman. Ithaca, N.Y.: Cornell University Press.

Waldinger, Roger, Chris Erickson, Ruth Milkman, Daniel J. B. Mitchell, Abel Valenzuela, Kent Wong, and Maurice Zeitlin. 1998. "Helots No More: A Case Study of the Justice for Janitors Campaign in Los Angeles." In *Organizing to Win: New Research on Union Strategies*, edited by Kate Bronfenbrenner, Sheldon Friedman, Richard W. Hurd, Rudolph A. Oswald, and Ronald L. Seeber. Ithaca, N.Y.: Cornell University Press.

Waldinger, Roger, and Michael Lichter. 2003. *How the Other Half Works: Immigration and the Social Organization of Labor*. Berkeley: University of California Press.

Weir, Margaret. 2002. "Income Polarization and California's Social Contract." *The State of California Labor* 2: 97–131.

Wells, Miriam J. 2000. "Immigration and Unionization in the San Francisco Hotel Industry." In *Organizing Immigrants: The Challenge for Unions in Contemporary California*, edited by Ruth Milkman. Ithaca, N.Y.: Cornell University Press.

Wilensky, Harold L. 1956. *Intellectuals in Labor Unions: Organizational Pressures on Professional Roles*. Glencoe, Ill.: Free Press.

Winston, Sherie. 2002. "Carpenters Take Center Stage." *Engineering News-Record* 248(10): 10.

Woodyard, Chris. 1988. "Truckers Told to Avoid Violence in Port Strike." *Los Angeles Times*, July 22.

Wuesthoff, Marie Louise. 1938. "An Inquiry into the Activities of the International Ladies' Garment Workers' Union in Los Angeles." M.A. thesis, University of Southern California, Los Angeles.

Ybarra, Michael J. 1988. "Janitors Claim Cleaning Companies Mistreat Them." *Los Angeles Times*, December 30.

Zabin, Carol. 2000. "Organizing Latino Workers in the Los Angeles Manufacturing Sector: The Case of American Racing Equipment." In *Organizing Immigrants: The Challenge for Unions in Contemporary California*, edited by Ruth Milkman. Ithaca, N.Y.: Cornell University Press.

Zabin, Carol, and Luis Escala Rabadán. 1998. "Mexican Hometown Associations and Mexican Political Empowerment in Los Angeles." Aspen Foundation, Nonprofit Sector Research Fund. Working paper (Winter). Available online at: laborcenter.berkeley.edu/publications/mexhome.pdf.

Zuboff, Shoshana. 1988. *In the Age of the Smart Machine: The Future of Work and Power*. New York: Basic Books.

INDEX

Boldface numbers refer to figures and tables.